(*I.C.L. London*)

(1) MAGNETIC TAPE UNIT (2) CENTRAL PROCESSOR (3) PUNCHED CARD READER (4) MAGNETIC DISC STORE (5) AUTOMATIC CARD PUNCH (6) LINE PRINTER (7) CONSOLE

A COMPUTER INSTALLATION

COMPUTER SCIENCE

P. HARVEY

B.Sc., C.Eng., M.I.E.E., A.F.I.M.A.

Senior Lecturer
Department of Electrical Engineering and Computer Science
Lincoln College of Technology

LONDON

NORMAN PRICE (PUBLISHERS) LTD

NORMAN PRICE (PUBLISHERS) LTD
17 TOTTENHAM COURT ROAD, LONDON, W.1

Printed in Great Britain by
A. Brown & Sons Ltd., *Hull.*

PREFACE

THIS book covers the 'Computer Science' required for the City & Guilds Course 49 Computers 'A' (and parts of Computers 'B'); 'A' Level Computer Science; and 'Computers' as an endorsement subject to Engineering courses. It will also serve as a general introduction to computers for anyone interested in the subject. There is no special emphasis on Data Processing and 'A' Level students who choose this option are advised to read this book in conjunction with others on commerce and programming.

The book is concerned with 'principles' and is not a review of the latest sophisticated techniques. It is appreciated, for example, that integrated circuits are used in many modern computers. Anyone reading this book, however, will find it easy to adapt the principles described to any make or generation of computer.

With reference to programming (Chapter 9), it is becoming clear that computer 'education' is best achieved by the study of machine code programming. In this way the basic operation of the computer can be appreciated. The teaching of high-level languages is, at best, computer 'training' in which the machine may remain a mysterious 'black box' to the student.

An attempt has been made to include information not readily available in many existing books at this level; the historical section has been compiled from original sources wherever possible and the more difficult subjects of machine division and conversion have not been glossed over as one so often finds. The importance of analogues in computing must not be underestimated and a general survey of several different types has been given.

Problems and examples have been included, although in some cases, particularly in binary–decimal conversion, the reader can easily make up his own for further practice.

The terminology and symbols are in accordance with the current standards BS 3939:1969, and the ECMA Standard for flow charts.

I wish to thank the many people with whom this book has been discussed, particularly Dr. J. Fines (for advice on the historical material), and to I.C.L. London, Reyrolle Parsons Automation Ltd and the Science Museum for permission to use their excellent photographs. My thanks are also due to my wife for reading the manuscript and working through the problems and examples.

P. HARVEY

Reepham,
Lincolnshire.
1971.

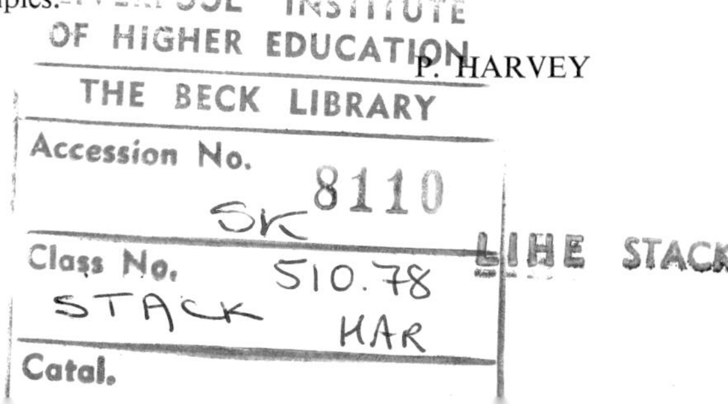

CONTENTS

1

WHAT IS A COMPUTER?

In recent years the word 'computer' has come to have a very specialized meaning. Human beings, slide-rules, cash registers and calculating machines are computers in the general sense of the word, but are not included in the class of electronic machines implied by the current use of the word 'computer'. The difference between a slide-rule and an electronic computer is obvious, but the difference between an electronic calculating machine and a computer is not. The difference here is so subtle that many desk calculators have been advertised as computers because they have some features in common with the larger electronic machines. Before we can define what is now meant by a computer we must examine the processes involved in automatic computation.

In all computers the numerical quantities must be represented by some physical means, *e.g.* mechanical displacements or electrical signals. Numbers may be represented in a desk calculator by the position of a numbered wheel and in a digital computer by electrical pulses.

An important distinction is made between the two following principles:

(a) If the number is represented by the **magnitude** of a mechanical movement or voltage pulse, it is called an ANALOGUE system.

(b) If the number is represented by the **number** of movements or voltage pulses, it is called a DIGITAL system.

Analogue computers are based on the principle of **measuring**; digital computers are based on the principle of **counting.**

Consider the case of a single electrical pulse of amplitude 3 volts, Fig. 1.1.

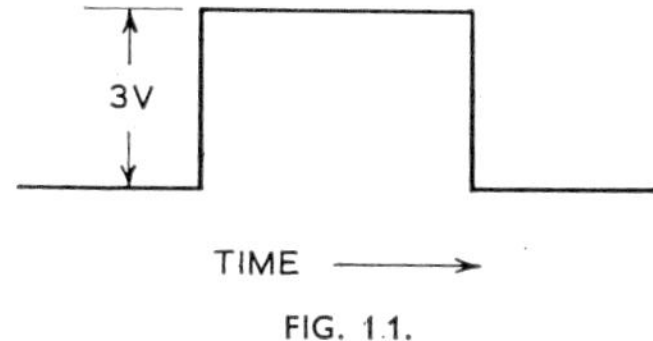

FIG. 1.1.

This could represent the quantity '3' on an analogue computer, or '1' (because there is only one pulse) on a digital computer. In the latter case the magnitude of the pulse is not related to the number it represents.

Analogue and digital systems of measuring and counting are familiar to us in everyday life, Fig. 1.2.

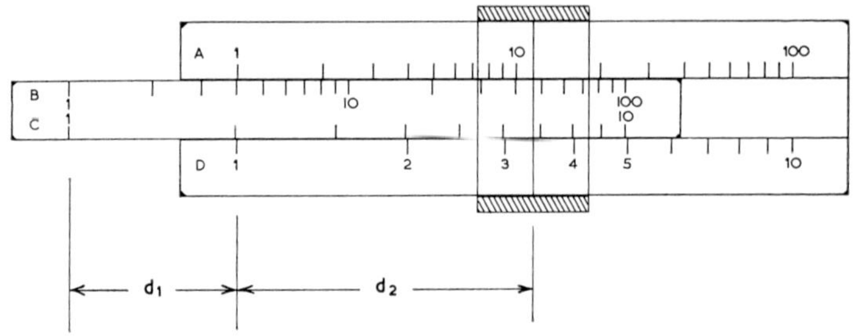

ANALOGUE PRINCIPLE

Distance is analogous to numbers. Accuracy depends upon manufacture and the skill of the operator.

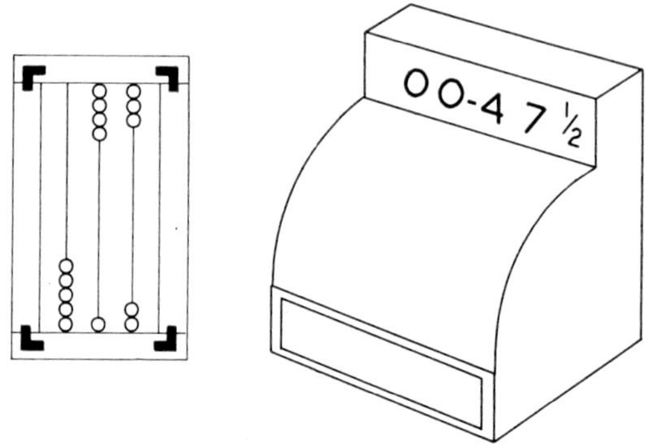

DIGITAL PRINCIPLE

Numerical quantities represented by the 'count' of separate objects. Accuracy is determined by the number of significant figures available.

FIG. 1.2.

(1) ANALOGUES

Speedometer: shaft rotation is analogous to speed.
Spring-Balance: spring deflection is analogous to weight.
Clock: shaft rotation is analogous to time.
Slide-rule: distance is analogous to numerical quantity.

(2) DIGITAL

Cash Register
Abacus
Desk Calculator
Turnstile.

Problem 1. In a clock the shaft rotation is the analogue of time, but is obtained by **counting** pendulum swings. Is it based on analogue or digital principles?

(Answer is on page 174)

Modern analogue computers use shaft rotation and voltage to represent numerical quantities, whereas digital computers use holes punched in paper and voltage pulses. The simple desk calculator is a digital instrument using shaft rotation.

A Comparison between Analogue and Digital Computers

ANALOGUE COMPUTERS are used for solving equations in science and technology, particularly differential equations. The answers are obtained as a voltage or shaft rotation and may be displayed on a voltmeter, an oscilloscope or drawn on an automatic graph plotter. The accuracy that can be obtained is limited to about 0·1% in favourable circumstances, and is more likely to be 1% if the problem is complicated. However, this is usually better than the known input data and is acceptable in many cases.

If the problem to be solved represents the behaviour of a mechanical, electrical or other physical system, the analogue computer may be thought of as a 'model' of the system being investigated. The terms 'simulator' and 'predictor' were formerly used for some special-purpose computers. The computer model is set up to obey the same mathematical equations as the real system and the effects of variations in design data and operating controls may be observed just as they would occur in the physical situation.

For example, the behaviour of a jet aircraft, ship or rocket may be simulated by the computer and its performance assessed without going to the expense of building the vehicle. The best design figures are obtained from the computer at low cost, and the final products built without expensive prototypes. Small analogue computers may be built into a complex control system and adjusted to give the best operating performance. A cheap non-variable electronic unit having the same characteristics may then be inserted in place of the computer.

Further discussion of analogue computers will be left until Chapter 10.

DIGITAL COMPUTERS are basically large adding machines, and as such are capable of great accuracy. Results can be obtained from 7 to 12 significant figures in general use, and to a much greater accuracy with special programming. The penalty to be paid for insisting on a high degree of accuracy is the computing time. In some cases the answers can be produced to any degree of accuracy if one is prepared to wait long enough. π has been calculated to 10,000 decimal places in 33 hours using a Pegasus computer.* To give a more recent example, a solution of the equation

$$x^2 - 8x - 10 = 0$$

has been found to 200 decimal places in 10 seconds on an Atlas computer.†

Two more basic features of the digital computer are (a) its high speed of working; and (b) its large capacity for storing information. This makes the machine particularly suited to 'data processing' in such fields as stock control, accounting and statistical analysis.

* Felton, *Proc. Oxford Math. Conf.*, April 1957.

† Churchhouse and Muir, *J. Inst. Maths Applics* (1969), Vol. 5, pp 318-328.

It can be seen that the analogue and digital computers are 'complementary' rather than 'competitive', although in recent years many problems formerly solved on analogue computers have been transferred to digital machines. The advantages of both types of machine can be obtained by combining the analogue and digital techniques in one computer, known as a **hybrid** computer. These computers are rather expensive and are reserved for special applications.

The Essentials of a Digital Computer

In order to perform even the simplest useful calculation we require the following facilities:

(a) A place to hold numbers in use (*working space*)
(b) A store to keep numbers not in use (*memory*)
(c) An arithmetic unit (*adder or subtractor*)
(d) An input and output unit (*reader and writer*)
(e) A controller.

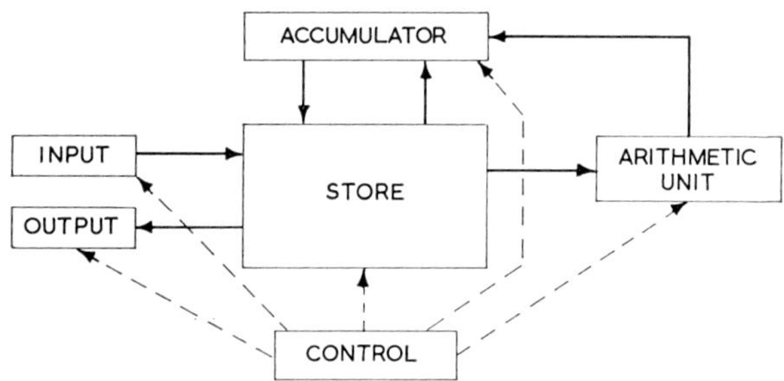

FIG. 1.3. THE ESSENTIALS OF A COMPUTER

In preparing the computer for use the first step is to feed information into the store. This information must contain numerical **data** and the programmer's **instructions.** The data and instructions are stored in the form of digits called **bits.** A string of digits holding one instruction or one number is called a **word.** The word length is the number of digits allocated to form a word and varies from one machine to another, typical values being in the range 8 to 64 digits.

When the instructions and data have been put into the store, the computation can be started by selecting the first instruction. Data is taken from the store to the accumulator (the working space) and to the arithmetic unit in accordance with the instruction, and the result of the operation is placed back into the store. The next instruction is automatically selected by the controller and the machine proceeds to perform a sequence of arithmetical operations. At the end of the program the answer is sent to the output unit which may either print the answer or punch it on to cards or tape.

Input

Information is inserted into a computer by means of punched cards or paper tape. The data and instructions are represented by holes punched in paper and are read by electrical contacts passing over the card as it is fed into the machine; or by a photoelectric cell which detects light passing through the holes in the paper.

The normal punched card has 80 columns (Fig. 1.4), each column having 12 positions in which holes may be punched, known as index positions. The figure shows the usual coding for the numbers 0 to 9 and the alphabet. Note that 2 holes are required in any column to represent an alphabetical character.

The layout of the card columns may be changed to suit the user's information by 'plugging' the wires from the hole-sensing circuit to any desired part of the input circuit. The stationery and card design should be specified by the systems analyst who must ensure that only relevant information is fed into the computer and that only the required information is printed out.

As an example of card layout, consider the simple problem of updating a bank account. The information required on each card may be:

(i) Customers name
(ii) Account number
(iii) Amount
(iv) Deposit or withdrawal
(v) Information to the computer to indicate the type of card being fed in (Designation).

A typical layout is shown in Fig. 1.5.

If the whole card is not used, as in this case, the blank columns are known as the 'filler space' and the used columns as the 'field'.

Problem 2. If a hole in column 56 indicates a 'deposit', decode the card shown in Fig. 1.5 in accordance with the code in Fig. 1.4.

(Answer is on page 174)

One transaction per card is possible by this method, and as up to 600 cards per minute can be fed into a computer at the present stage of development, this would be a practical system for a fairly large bank branch or similar organization.

Paper tape (Fig. 1.6) is quicker to run into the machine but is less versatile. The removal of errors is easier in a stack of cards than in a long length of paper tape, but the handling and storing of tape is easier than for cards. Cards may be sorted external to the computer and hence without using computer time, whereas the information on tape has to be sorted by the computer.

The paper tape is driven by a toothed wheel engaging in the feed holes and the information is read from the tape into the computer store by techniques similar to those described for punched cards.

Magnetic tape may be used for large quantities of data that are repeatedly to be fed into the computer and updated or modified frequently. This works on a principle similar to that of a tape recorder, the data being stored as sequences of digits by magnetizing the oxide surface of the tape. A reel of magnetic tape is then used to represent a 'ledger' or 'file'. Safeguards must be incorporated to prevent the accidental erasure of the tape, and it must be capable of being printed out or 'listed' by the computer for visual inspection or audit.

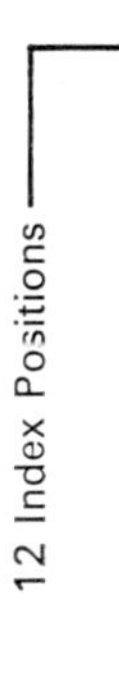

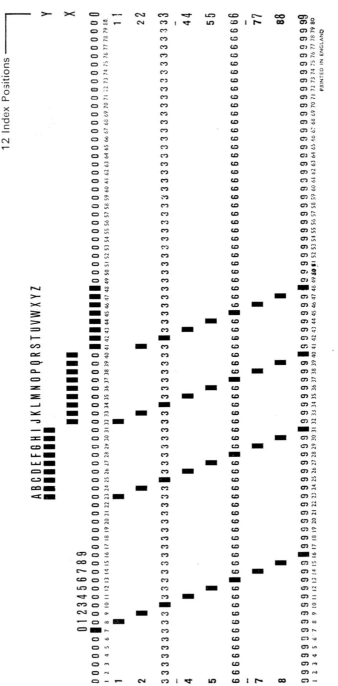

FIG. 1.4. THE PUNCHED CARD CODE

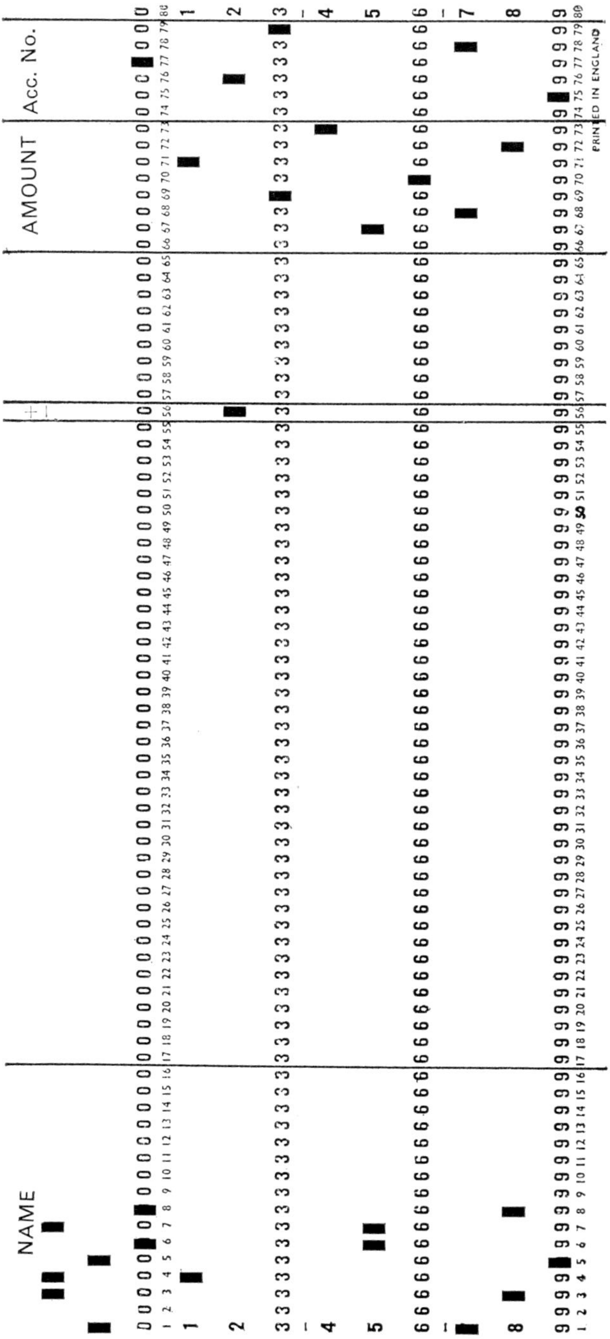

NAME

AMOUNT

Acc. No.

PRINTED IN ENGLAND

FIG. 1.5. PUNCHED CARD LAYOUT

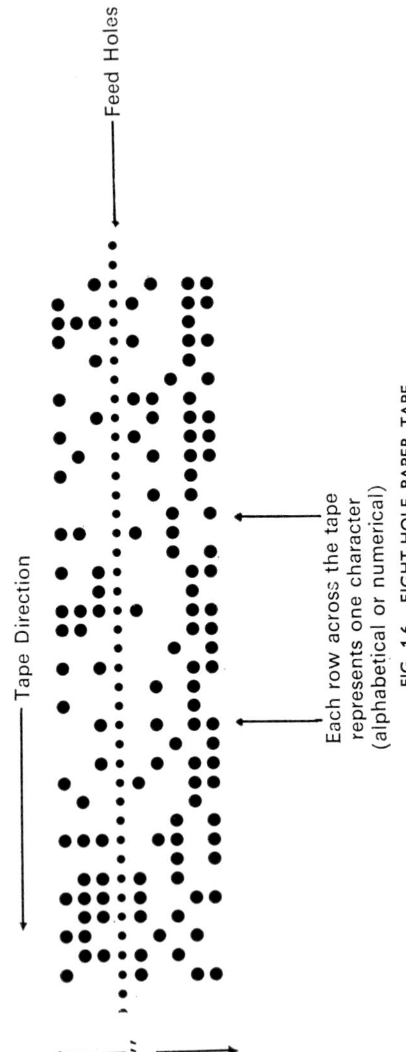

FIG. 1.6. EIGHT-HOLE PAPER TAPE

Output

The results of the computation may be printed out for inspection and use. The printer uses 'continuous stationery' which is fed under the print wheels in a continuous length, automatically driven by the computer.

For mathematical calculations the format and spacing of the print-out may not be of prime importance, but for commercial and accounting work the layout may have to be carefully planned so that the computer can insert figures into pre-printed forms. The format of the print-out is determined either by making the necessary electrical connections to the print character control circuits or by programming. A large part of the program may be devoted to the output print layout.

Where records are being revised or updated by the computer it is often unnecessary to print out the results, a revised set of cards, paper tapes or magnetic tapes being more convenient. The computer must then operate a card or paper tape punch and a magnetic tape unit as alternative forms of output. The input and output machinery is often called **peripheral equipment.**

Instructions and Data

As we have seen, information is stored as sequences of digits or **words,** a word being a row of digits representing either a number or an instruction. The computer can only store and handle numerical digits, so the instructions must be coded into numerical form.

For example:

1 may represent **add**
2 may represent **subtract**
3 may represent **multiply**
4 may represent **divide**
. . . etc.

This machine code is determined by the designer of the computer. The set of basic operations built into the machine, such that each can be performed by providing a direct single instruction, is known as the **instruction code.** Note that when an 'autocode' is used by the programmer, one autocode instruction may represent a large number of basic machine code instructions.

If we number the 'locations' of each word held in the store, we can refer to a location as n where the number n is its **address.** The information held in location n is written as (n), meaning the contents of n. If the number 41 is held in location 214 we may write this as

$$(214) = 41$$

i.e. the contents of location 214 is 41.

The accumulator can also hold a number or instruction, the contents of the accumulator being written as (A).

The minimum instruction code required by a computer to enable it to perform a useful calculation is:

(1) Add (n) to (A)
(2) Subtract (n) from (A)
(3) Write (n) in A
(4) Write (A) in location n
(5) Input to location n
(6) Print out (n)
(7) Stop.

There are several ways of representing a complete instruction as a 'word', which are classified according to the number of addresses or locations specified in it. The simplest type is the 'single address' instruction which has the form

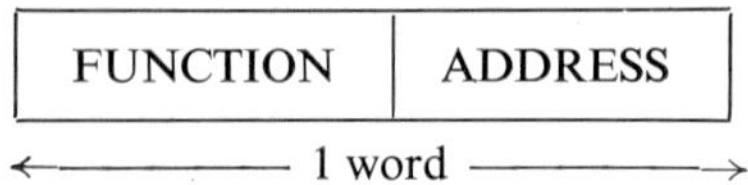

A fixed number of digits is allocated to define the 'function' and the rest used for the 'address'. In each of the frames a number occurs, the number in the address part representing a location in the store, the function number being one of the 'instruction code' numbers.

To add two numbers *a* and *b* together and to put the result in store location *c*, we require an instruction code such as

(1) Write the number in the specified address into the accumulator.
(2) Add the number in the specified address to the accumulator.
(3) Write (A) into the specified store location.

If, say, *a* is stored in location 6
b is stored in location 7
and the result is required in location 8,
the operation would require three instructions:

1	6	(write *a* into accumulator)
2	7	(add *b* to accumulator)
3	8	[write (A) into location 8.]

Single address systems are simple, but several instructions are required to perform an arithmetical operation. The number of instructions may be reduced by using 'multiple address' instructions such as

FUNCTION	ADDRESS 1	ADDRESS 2	RESULT

← 1 word →

This is a three-address instruction which takes the numbers in addresses 1 and 2 and adds, subtracts, multiplies or divides them, etc., according to the 'function' specified. The result is placed in the store location indicated in the 'result' frame.

The previous calculation may now be written as one instruction:

1	6	7	8

which is interpreted as **add** contents of **location 6** to **location 7** and put the result in **location 8**, function 1 meaning 'add'.

The Sequence of Operations

After an instruction has been obeyed, the machine must be told what to do next, *i.e.* it must select the address of the next instruction. Assuming that the instructions are numbered in sequence, a counter may be used to increase the instruction number by one after each operation.

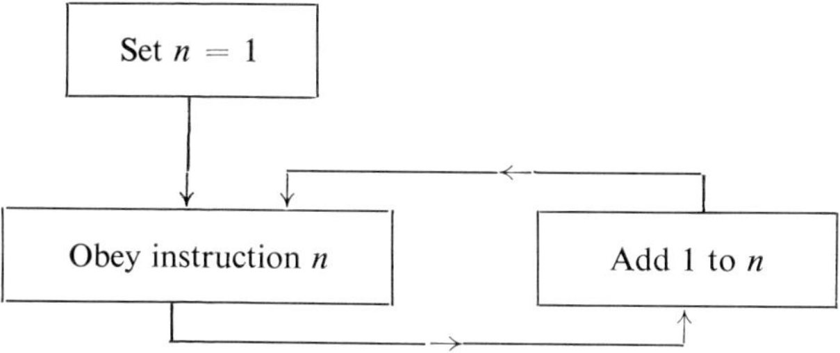

The computer will then obey the instructions in sequence 1, 2, 3, . . . etc., but will not be able to repeat instructions by performing 'loops'.

Loops are required even for simple programs, which enable the same set of instructions to be used over and over again. This means that the programmer can instruct the computer to perform a large number of repetitive operations by writing a few instructions. As an illustrative example consider the sequence of operations needed to find a certain page in a book. The pages may be turned over, starting at page 1, until the required page (say page number 117) is found.

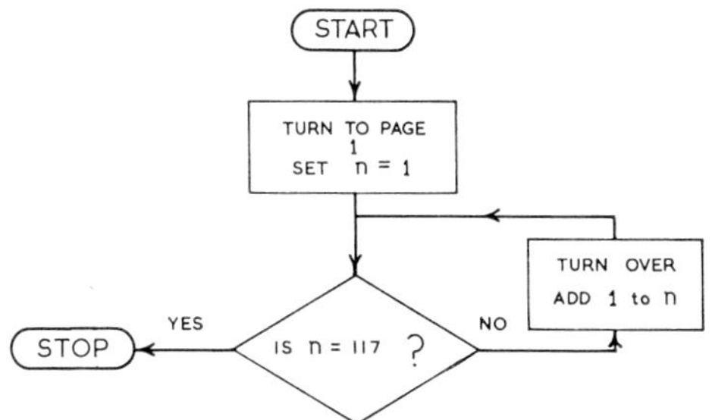

By using only four instructions we can now search through a book of any number of pages.

Problem 3. This is not the most efficient way of finding a page in a book. Can you devise a method using the minimum number of operations? Assume of course that the required page may be chosen at random, the above method is adequate for pages near the beginning.

(Answer is on page 174)

In the above example a further requirement is introduced, that of **branching.** A decision must be taken at 'Is $n = 117$?', alternative courses of action being possible after this point. The diagram branches put into two paths, and in fact this is the only way out of what would otherwise be an endless loop. It must be possible to **jump** to any instruction when requested to do so, rather than slavishly follow the set instructions in a sequential order.

To enable this to be done, the 'next instruction' address may be included in the instruction word.

OPERAND	FUNCTION	NEXT INSTRUCTION

← 1 word →

This is a 'one plus one' address type of instruction, being a single address instruction plus the next instruction address.
A typical instruction is

14	1	9

where function '1' means add to the accumulator. This instruction is then interpreted as

> **Add** the contents of **location 14** to the accumulator and then go to the instruction in **location 9.**

The 'next instruction' may be altered by the computer during a program by adding or subtracting any number. One of the most important properties of a computer is now revealed: IT IS POSSIBLE TO DO ARITHMETIC ON THE INSTRUCTIONS AS WELL AS ON THE NUMERICAL DATA, thus making possible a non-sequential operation including branches and jumps.

The Definition of a Computer

We now return to our original question: 'What is a computer?' In 1946 the logician John von Neumann formulated a set of principles which we may take to be the basis of our definition. These principles may be summarized as follows:

(1) Instructions are coded as numerical digits and stored in the machine.

(2) Data and instructions are stored together in the machine as 'words' and no distinction is made between them by the machine.

(3) Numbers are stored and manipulated in **binary** form (*i.e.* powers of two).

We may now loosely define a computer as a calculating machine built on von Neumann's principles. It will be seen that many calculating machines described as computers do not fulfil these requirements.

Calculating Machines

The small desk calculating machine is basically a mechanical or electrical adding machine working on digital principles. The essential parts are:

(a) A **setting register,** in which the numbers are inserted by mechanical levers or a keyboard;

(b) A **quotient register,** in which the number of operations performed is indicated; and

(c) A **product register,** in which the sum or difference of numbers in the setting register is formed.

The registers are either numbered wheels or electrical circuits which hold and indicate the numbers being used in the calculation.

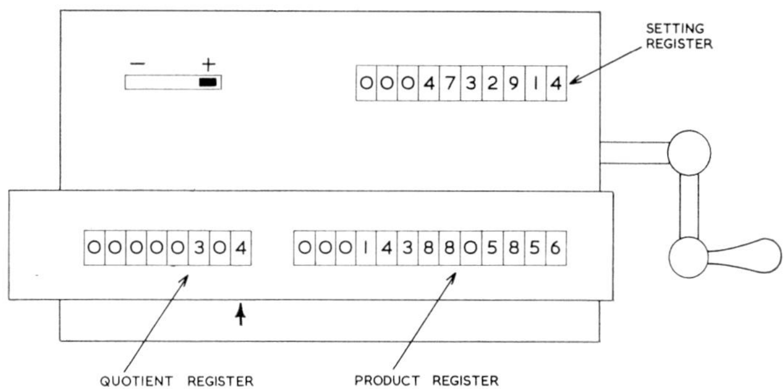

FIG. 1.7. TYPICAL ARRANGEMENT OF A DESK CALCULATOR

The machine behaves as follows.

> Turning the handle once in a clockwise direction **adds** the number in the **setting register** to the **product register.**
>
> The number of handle turns is recorded in the **quotient register.**
>
> Turning the handle once in an anticlockwise direction subtracts the number in the **setting register** from the **product register.**
>
> N.B. The number of anticlockwise turns is **subtracted** from the quotient register if the initial turn was clockwise; and **added** if the initial turn was anticlockwise. Some models have a '+ −' lever provided to override this if required.

The accuracy (and cost) of the machine depends upon the number of significant digits that can be held in the registers. For a typical small desk calculator the setting register may have 10 figures, the product register 13, and the quotient register 8.

'Back Transfer' allows the number in the product register to be transferred into the empty setting register. All registers can be 'cleared' or 'zeroed' by levers provided. The quotient and product registers are usually mounted on a carriage, movable with respect to the setting register, to enable units, tens, hundreds, etc. to be dealt with column by column.

Example. To multiply 481 by 342.

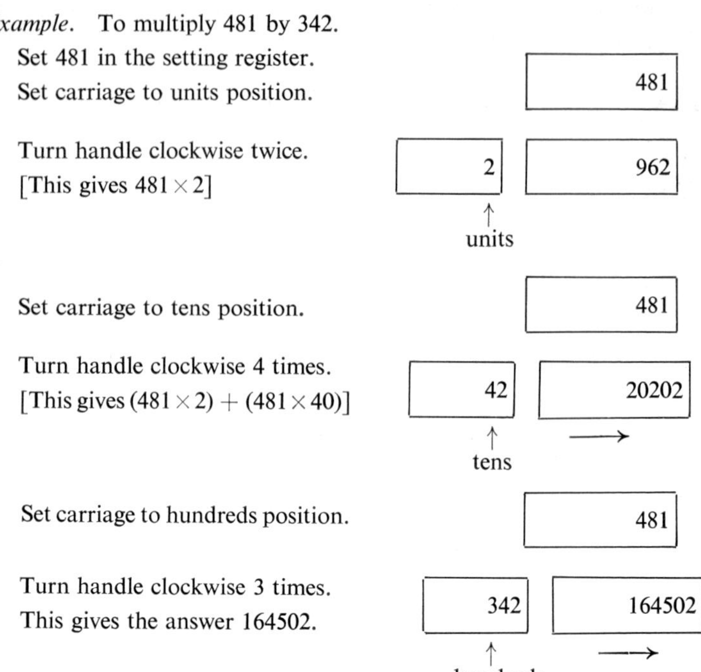

Set 481 in the setting register.
Set carriage to units position.
481
Turn handle clockwise twice.
[This gives 481 × 2]
2
962
units
Set carriage to tens position.
481
Turn handle clockwise 4 times.
[This gives (481 × 2) + (481 × 40)]
42
20202
tens
Set carriage to hundreds position.
481
Turn handle clockwise 3 times.
This gives the answer 164502.
342
164502
hundreds

The addition of a store to a calculator is possible, with stored instructions and the facility for executing simple repetitive loops, but unless the instructions are capable of being treated in exactly the same way as the numbers stored, it is not a computer in our sense of the word.

Examples (Chapter 1)

(1) Decode the paper tape in Fig. 1.6, using Appendix D (page 170). (Answer is on page 174)

(2) Sketch the punching required on both card and paper tape to represent your name, address, age and the date.

(3) Obtain some punched cards or tape and decode them.

2

A BRIEF HISTORY OF COMPUTERS

Aids to Calculation

The use of 'counters' was man's first attempt to assist his rather limited capacity for mental calculation. Although this is often considered to be his first step towards the computer it must be realized that the motives for using counters and bead frames were quite different from those that prompted the modern computer. Before the 16th century paper was expensive and almost a luxury, commercial arithmetic being performed by tally sticks or chalk marks on tables. Where we use pencil and paper as an aid to calculation our ancestors used the 'counter', a term which is still retained for tables in shops and offices.

About 1,500 years ago beads were strung on threads to form the 'abacus', which has been in extensive use in many parts of the world up to the present time.

In 1614 John Napier discovered logarithms and Professor Henry Briggs calculated logarithms to a base of 10 and published a set of tables in 1624. The original use of logarithms was to assist in the calculation of sines of angles for navigation and astronomy. This work is of interest to us for two reasons. Firstly, it led Edmund Gunter to produce a logarithmic scale on which multiplication and division could be performed by adding or subtracting distances with a pair of dividers. This could be said to be the first analogue computer. Later William Oughtred placed two logarithmic scales together to form the first slide-rule. Secondly, it was whilst studying a table of logarithms that the idea of an automatic calculating machine occurred to Babbage in 1812, who was at that time an undergraduate at Cambridge.

The first example of a machine specifically designed to remove the labour involved in calculating is that due to Pascal (1623–1662). Pascal replaced the beads of the abacus by cylinders with the numbers 0 to 9 engraved around their circumference. These were operated by numbered wheels on the front of the calculator, the carry digits being transmitted to the next highest column by a ratchet. The details of the mechanism are shown in Fig. 2.1.

This calculator could only add or subtract, but a machine built by Leibniz (1646–1716) could also multiply and divide. The principles involved in the machines of Pascal and Leibniz are still found in some present-day dial instruments and hand calculators.

The evolution of computers proceeded in two directions, one leading to analogue and the other to digital computers. The history of the two types will therefore be considered separately.

Early Analogue Computers

After the slide-rule, the next important mathematical machine was the planimeter, invented by Hermann in 1814. Its purpose is to measure the area of an irregular figure, but as it performs the mathematical operation of 'integration' it is a simple form of computer. The design of the

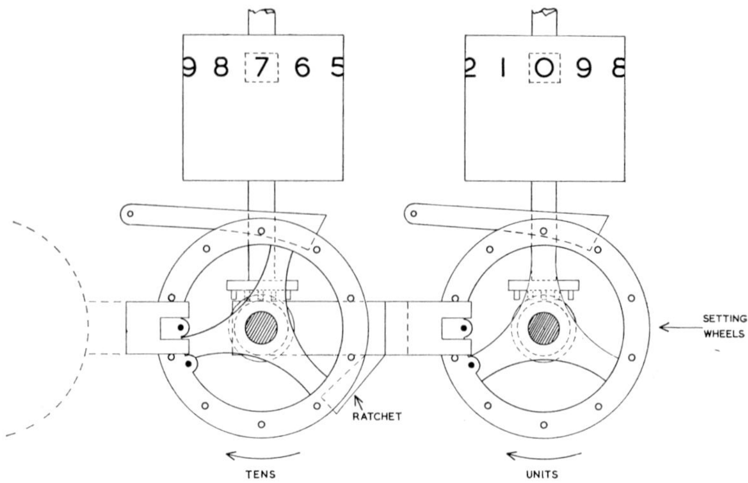

FIG. 2.1. PASCAL'S CALCULATOR (1642)

planimeter most frequently used today (Fig. 2.2) is due to Professor Amsler (1856). Between 1856 and 1885 it is said that 12,400 of these instruments were made. In operation the stylus is moved once round the figure, the area being indicated by a calibrated wheel.

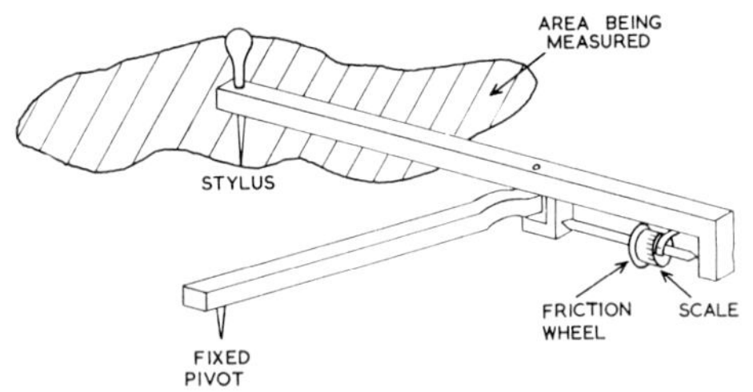

FIG. 2.2. AMSLER'S PLANIMETER

In 1845 Bashforth published the description of 'a machine for finding the roots of equations and tracing a variety of useful curves', a device for combining simple harmonic motions and producing a graph of the results. Sir William Thomson (Lord Kelvin) invented a machine based on similar principles in 1872 for the purpose of calculating tides. This machine, Fig. 2.3, could produce the yearly tidal figures for a given port in less than four hours.

In 1876 Kelvin's brother (Professor J. Thomson) made one of the most important discoveries in analogue computing, the Disc-Globe-and-Cylinder integrator. Fig. 2.4 shows the essential parts of the integrator, which behaves simply as an infinitely variable ratio gear. The disc is rotated, which rotates the sphere, which in turn drives the cylinder by

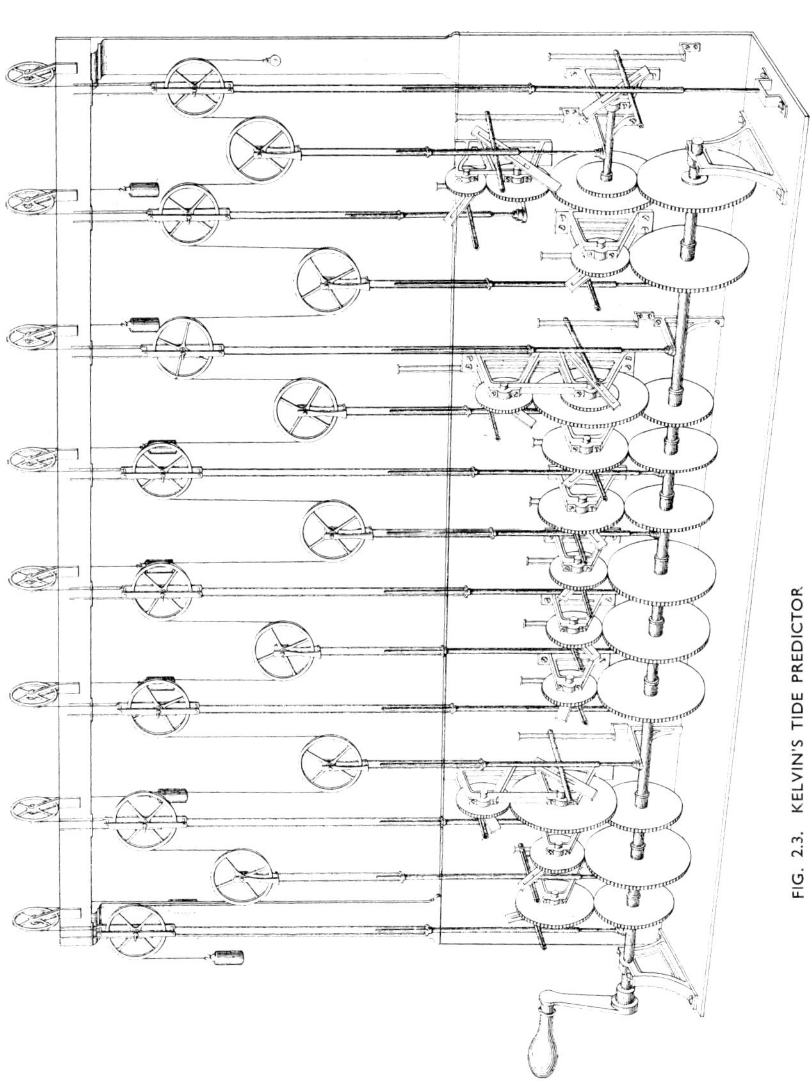

FIG. 2.3. KELVIN'S TIDE PREDICTOR

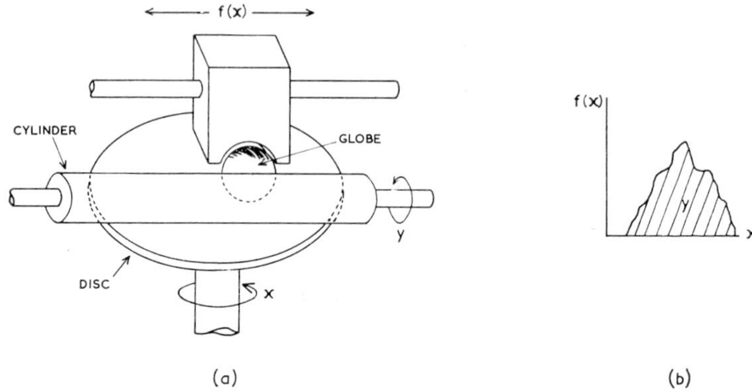

FIG. 2.4. DISC-GLOBE-AND-CYLINDER INTEGRATOR

frictional contact. The output is taken from the cylinder shaft. The position of the globe or sphere is controlled by the input to the machine, which controls the ratio between the disc and the cylinder rotations.

The operation of integration is that of finding the area under the graph of a function. Consider a function $f(x)$, (typical 'functions' of x are x^3, $\sin x$, $\log x$, . . . etc.). Fig. 2.4(b) shows the graph of such a function. To use the machine the disc is turned round proportional to x, whilst the sphere is moved to corresponding values of $f(x)$. The cylinder shaft rotation is then proportional to the area under the curve, y.

To the reader familiar with calculus the proof of this is simple.

Let the disc be rotated by a small amount dx.

Let dy be the corresponding output.

If the ratio of the shaft rotations is $f(x)$ then

$$dy = f(x).dx$$

$$\text{hence} \quad y = \int f(x).dx.$$

One of Kelvin's first uses for his brother's invention was to construct an 'harmonic analyser' comprising five such integrators for computing tables of

$$A + B \sin \theta + C \cos \theta + D \sin 2\theta + E \cos 2\theta$$

for the deviation of the compass in an iron ship. In a paper discussing its action he wrote: 'The object of this machine is to substitute brass for brain in the great mechanical labour of calculating.'*

Kelvin also described how several integrators could be connected together to solve differential equations, but apparently did not construct such a computer. This was first done by Dr. V. Bush in 1931. Inspired by Bush's success, Professor Hartree in 1935 built an analogue computer at Manchester University entirely out of Meccano parts. This prototype

* "Thomson on Tidal Instruments", *Proc. Inst. C.E.*, Vol. LXV, 1881.

was followed by larger models at Manchester and Cambridge using conventional engineering techniques.*

After 1948 electronic analogue computers, as described in Chapter 10, replaced mechanical computers because of their higher accuracy and greatly improved flexibility (Fig. 2.5).

Digital Computers:
The First Phase, 1820-1850

A major advance in the concept of digital computing took place in this period, although its importance was not fully realized until the second period of development, 1935–1960.

Charles Babbage (1791–1871) was the first man to appreciate that a truly automatic machine could perform calculations with more accuracy and speed than could a human calculator. However, some years elapsed after his first thoughts on the errors in logarithm tables before he was inspired to design his first machine. In 1821 he was verifying some calculations for the Royal Astronomical Society when he exclaimed, 'I wish to God these calculations had been executed by steam!'† By 1822 he had constructed his first 'difference-engine' to calculate tables of functions such as

$$x^2 + x + 41$$

and although not driven by steam the 'engine' was based on levers and gear-wheels.

The difference engine worked on the principle that a function of the form

$$ax^n + bx^{n-1} + \ldots . + px + q \qquad \text{(a polynomial)}$$

may be evaluated by finding the differences between adjacent terms in a table of values for the function.

Consider, as an example, the function $x^2 + x + 41$ as used by Babbage.

We tabulate this for a few values of x.

x	$x^2 + x + 41$	1st differences	2nd differences
		0	
0	41		2
		2	
1	43		2
		4	
2	47		2
		6	
3	53		2
		8	
4	61		2
		10	
5	71		

. . . etc.

* Crank, J., "The Differential Analyser" Longmans, 1947.

† Moseley, M., "Irascible Genius" Hutchinson 1964, p 65.

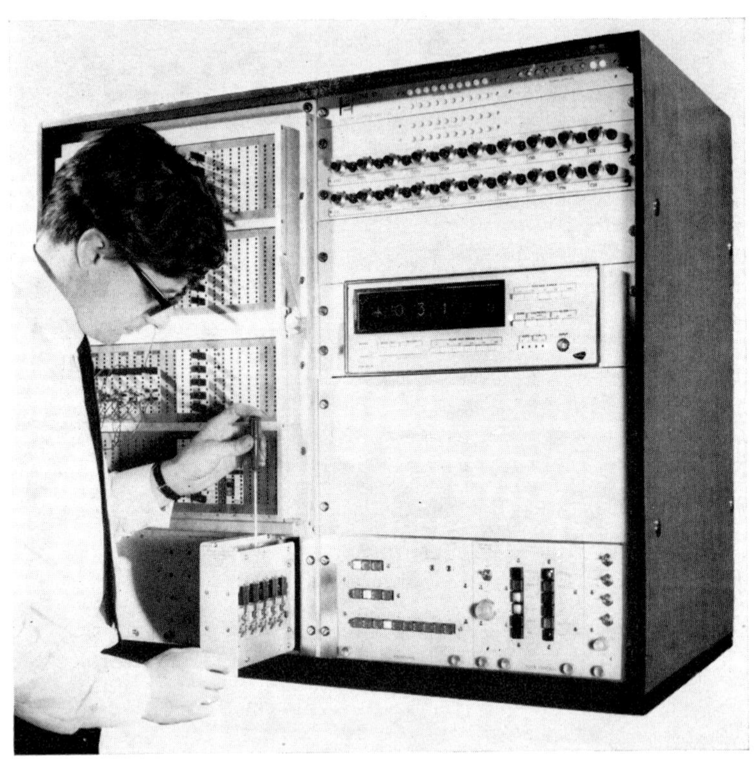

(*Reyrolle Parsons Automation Ltd*)

FIG. 2.5. ELECTRONIC ANALOGUE COMPUTER: MODERN TRANSISTORIZED VERSION

The first differences are those between adjacent values of the function, and the second differences are those between values of the first differences. For any polynomial, if the process is continued far enough, one of the difference columns will eventually contain the same number in each position.

Once this constant difference is found, the machine is set up to contain the first value of the function and the differences. In our example the numbers

41 0 2

are set in the engine. The second difference is added to the zero and the sum added to the current value of the function. This gives the next value 43. The engine now holds the numbers

43 2 2

The second difference is added to the first difference (now 2) and the sum again added to the current value, 43, to give the next value 47. The process is repeated as far as required.

Babbage first made a model using three numbered wheels to represent the function, two wheels for the first differences and one wheel for the second differences. A larger model giving six-figure accuracy was then made which produced 44 figures per minute (Fig. 2.6). The government was so impressed by the possibilities of such a machine that it undertook to finance a much larger version giving 20 significant figures and extending as far as the sixth differences.

Unfortunately, the machine was never completed owing to lack of money and considerable engineering difficulties. The fault was not entirely Babbage's; mainly responsible were the government's failure to provide the promised financial assistance, and disputes with his engineer Clement. Eventually, a difference engine was built by Scheutz with a capacity of 14 significant figures using fourth differences, showing that Babbage's claims for such a machine were not ill-founded.*

Fourteen years after commencing work on the machine, Babbage had conceived the idea of a general-purpose digital calculating machine which he called an 'Analytical Engine'. From 1842 to 1848 he worked on the design of this machine which embodied most of the principles considered essential in a modern computer. His machine was to have a store containing 1,000 fifty-digit numbers, and an arithmetic unit. 'Operations' and 'Variables' were to be fed in, and the numbers could be set into the store manually or by punched cards.

The idea of constructing a machine to perform a program of operations controlled by punched cards was due to Joseph Jacquard (1752–1834). Jacquard built a weaving loom in 1801 in which the movement of the threads was controlled by the holes in the cards. A hole caused a thread to be lifted and a blank space left it in a depressed position. Holes corresponding to the pattern required were punched on to a large number of cards which were strung together and fed over a rotating perforated box. An early print of the system is reproduced in Fig. 2.7.

* *Proc. Inst. C.E.*, Vols XV and XVI.

(*Crown Copyright, Science Museum, London*)

FIG. 2.6. BABBAGE'S DIFFERENCE-ENGINE (1822)

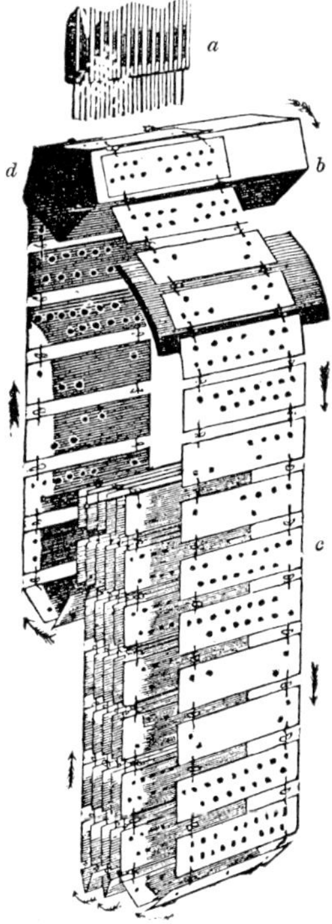

a, the bars attached to the threads of the warp; *b*, the box perforated with holes, corresponding with holes perforated in *c*, the pattern-cards. These cards, by which the weft is caused to produce the pattern on the web of silk or other material wove in the loom, pass upwards from *d*, over *b*, decending to *c*, and so on—at last again arriving at *d*, &c. They are loosely joined so as to readily fit the sides of the box.

FIG. 2.7. PUNCHED CARDS USED TO CONTROL JACQUARD'S LOOM

Babbage went to Lyons and examined the mechanism of Jacquard's loom for himself. He then decided that this method could be used to 'instruct' and control his analytical engine, and that mathematical tables could be fed into the store by similar means. He designed a method of automatically selecting type from boxes to enable the engine to print out its answers, rather than having an assistant copy down the numbers from the wheels as had been done on his difference-engine. Here he anticipated the line printer of the modern computer.

The British Government, having withdrawn their financial support from the difference-engine, refused to contribute anything to the analytical engine. Progress was slow and Babbage died before the machine was completed.

His ideas, however, were not forgotten and his son, H. P. Babbage, continued to support the digital computer after his father's death. In 1885 Hele Shaw published a paper on mechanical analogue integrators which H. P. Babbage criticized by writing: 'In digital computers there was absolute accuracy of result, and the same with all operators, and there were mechanical means for correcting, to a certain extent, slackness of the machinery. In the other instruments (analogue computers) all this was reversed'.

Hele Shaw wisely replied: 'Continuous and discontinuous calculating machines, as they had respectively been called, had entirely different kinds of operation to perform, and there was a wide field for the employment of both. All efforts to employ mere combinations of trains of wheelwork for such operations . . . had hitherto entirely failed.'*

Hele Shaw had the advantage of having constructed his machines: Babbage had not.

The First Programmer

The first programmer was a woman, the Countess of Lovelace daughter of Lord Byron. She first met Charles Babbage in 1831 at the age of fifteen and was fascinated by the mechanism of the difference-engine. She was a gifted mathematician and offered her services to Babbage in 1841, as what would now be called a programmer, and assisted him until her death in 1852.

Her understanding of computer programming was remarkable, and her methods were almost identical to the 'machine code' language programming of later electronic computers. Her work was completely original, indicating the degree of her mathematical genius. The problems she chose to solve were difficult and included programs for logarithms, square roots, simultaneous equations, real and imaginary roots of polynomials and Bernouilli numbers.

Perhaps her greatest gift to posterity was her translation of an Italian account of Babbage's computer, together with her own notes on the subject. Babbage himself left no written account.

Digital Computers:
The Second Phase, 1935-1960

About the year 1900 the traditional methods of calculating and data processing (*e.g.* clerical work, movement of documents, reading, typing, filing, etc.) were beginning to show signs of inadequacy. Large companies, banks, libraries and insurance organizations had to cope with an unprecedented amount of 'paper-work'. In the mathematical field, problems in astronomy, physics and engineering design were being left unsolved owing to the mental and physical labour involved in performing the calculations. These factors prompted developments which led to the revival of the general-purpose digital computer, but with one important difference—the machine was electrical instead of mechanical.

* *Proc. Inst. C.E.*, Vol. LXIV, 1885, pp 163-164.

Prior to the introduction of the electronic computer several inventions and discoveries were made which were to have a major effect on their design. The binary code (see Chapter 3) was known and used by Sir Francis Bacon in 1623. He claims to have discovered this whilst still a youth and later incorporated it into a cipher using letters of the alphabet.

Babbage had found difficulty in describing his complex mechanisms and had invented a 'mechanical notation' to make his work easier. This same difficulty was later encountered by the designers of electrical switching circuits. In 1854 George Boole had developed an algebra for dealing with the relationships between 'classes' or 'sets' of objects. He found that his algebra applied to 'statements' and 'propositions' equally well, thus reducing logic to algebraic equations. The work of both Boole and Babbage lay dormant for many years until technology had caught up with their ideas.

Several people had attempted to design an algebra for use with relay and switching circuits, but it was Shannon in 1938 who noticed that Boole's algebra could be used for this purpose.* Shannon's notation was the reverse of Boole's but proved to be a 'dual' of the same system. The computer algebra of today uses the original notation, and so important has Boole's work become that his book "Mathematical Analysis of Logic", originally published in 1847, was reprinted in 1948.

The storage of a large quantity of information in a machine was a problem encountered by Babbage and other early computer designers. An invention which eventually turned out to be one solution was the phonograph of Valdemar Poulsen. About 1900 Poulsen experimented with a machine (Fig. 2.8) in which signals were recorded by magnetizing

FIG. 2.8. POULSEN'S MAGNETIC DRUM RECORDER (*circa* 1900)

* Shannon, C. E., "A Symbolic Analysis of Relay and Contactor Circuits", *Trans. Amer. Inst. Elec. Engrs.*, 1938, Vol. 57, p 713.

the surface of a rotating drum. His drum was wound with fine steel wire to give a magnetic surface. Today a similar drum, with a magnetic oxide coating, is used as a store in many computers. Poulsen even anticipated the magnetic tape store by building a primitive tape recorder (Fig. 2.9) in which the tape was fed through at a rate of 1·6 feet per second. The large data banks built up to aid modern commerce are the result of Poulsen's inventions.

FIG. 2.9. POULSEN'S MAGNETIC TAPE RECORDER

In 1889 Dr. Hollerith in America used punched cards on a large scale for sorting and tabulating data. He would have been familiar with the work of Jacquard and Babbage as looms were working in his country and Babbage's reputation was probably higher in America than in England. (The American Government had even sought his advice on calculating machines). Hollerith's contribution was to show convincingly that punched cards could be used in data processing and that electrical contacts could be used to detect the holes in the cards. His first large-scale project was the U.S. census of 1890. Punched card machinery was manufactured and sold by the International Business Machines Corporation, and for some years the purely mathematical possibilities took second place to commercial arithmetic.

In 1937 the London Mathematical Society published a set of papers by Dr. A. M. Turing on the theory of a machine for solving almost any arithmetical problem.* Turing proved that there is a minimum number of functions that a machine requires to be able to solve a problem that could be solved by any other machine, however many functions it could perform. In other words he designed the simplest theoretical computer.

* Turing, A. M., "On Computable Numbers, with an Application to the Scheidungs Problem", *Proc. London Math. Soc.*, Vol. 42 (1937).

If Turing's machine could not solve a problem then no computer however large and sophisticated could solve it either. The work was purely mathematical and the construction of such a machine was never intended. However, it proved to be the beginning of modern computer philosophy, and led von Neumann to formulate his computer principles in 1946.

The Programmed Calculator

The limitation of early punched card equipment for calculating purposes was that the machine performed only one operation at a time on the data. This operation could be changed by the 'plug board' attached to the machine. A separate 'pass' of the cards was required for each operation. There was no provision for forming 'loops' (*i.e.* returning to data already handled) and only very simple decisions or tests could be applied.

To overcome these difficulties the manufacturers introduced a facility for performing a limited number of preset operations. This was the beginning of the 'stored program'. For example, the I.B.M. 604 would perform a 20-step program between card feeds, the program being laboriously set by making electrical connections on a plug board. This machine was later improved by adding a card reader enabling the program to be set by punched cards. The operation sequence was determined by reading in 'instruction cards' instead of by plugging. The machine was known as the Card Programmed Calculator. A limited amount of information could be stored on counter wheels and relays. McRae* describes this machine as 'A comparative failure . . . . a flamboyant prototype computer widely publicized in the late forties'.

From 1937 to 1944 H. Aiken of Harvard, in collaboration with I.B.M., was engaged in building a relay calculator out of desk calculators and adding machines. This was known as the Automatic Sequence Controlled Calculator. The program was determined by paper tape input and the facilities for forming branches and loops were very limited. The machine was very slow, in fact comparable with the speed estimated for Babbage's Analytical Engine (four seconds for a multiplication and 10 seconds for a division). Numbers were stored in decimal form by counter-wheels, and it had facilities for the usual arithmetical operations plus functions such as sines, cosines, and logarithms. Constants could be set into the machine manually as in Babbage's engine.

Some writers quote this machine as being the first computer but, although automatic, it did not store its program in the same form as its data and we must class it as a rather large and slow calculator. It lacked many of the refinements envisaged by Babbage, which supports the claim sometimes made for Aiken that he built his machine without being aware of Babbage's work. Booth states that his machine does lay claim to a certain distinction, 'it is most unlikely that any similar engine will be built again'.† Nevertheless, it was in continuous use during its life of fifteen years.

* McRae, T. W., "Impact of Computers on Accounting", Wiley, 1964.

† Booth, A. D., "Automation and Computing", Macmillan, 1959.

The next stage in development was to replace the slow electro-mechanical relays by electronics. In 1946, Eckert and Mauchly of the University of Pennsylvania completed the Electronic Numerical Integrator and Calculator (ENIAC) using 18,000 valves. This machine was designed to solve the trajectories of bombs and shells, and was not originally a general-purpose machine. It is interesting to note that Bashforth, referred to earlier in connection with analogue computers, had been engaged on similar work in the 19th century. Every valve was required to be in working order if the machine was to function, and this was one of the greatest troubles in operation. Despite its inherent unreliability, it could perform in 30 seconds a calculation in ballistics requiring 20 hours on a desk calculator. As 10 valves were needed to store each decimal digit, the storage capacity was far too small for general use. The original machine did not constitute a logical advance over Aiken's calculator, but by using electronics it advanced the engineering technology considerably. Later the machine was modified for more general problem solving.

The Universal Computer

Based on the work of Turing already referred to, von Neumann formulated the principles of universal computation in 1946.* This was the decisive theoretical step. The idea was to store the instructions along with the data such that either could be modified by arithmetical operations, thus allowing the computer to rewrite part of its own program as the computation proceeded. The universal digital computer was now theoretically created.

The race to produce the first machine based on these principles was now on. A prototype computer incorporating von Neumann's ideas was completed at Manchester University by Professor F. C. Williams, T. Kilburn and G. C. Tootill† in June 1948. Although small, this was the first truly automatic general-purpose computer. On a test program it took half-a-second to show that 314159265 and 271828138 were co-prime. Williams states that:

> 'There is nothing new in the idea, for the construction of an automatic computing machine was proposed by Charles Babbage as long ago as 1864'.

The paper by Williams and his associates is well worth reading, as it contains a clear account of the experimental machine's operation.

Other machines followed in rapid succession:

EDSAC, at Cambridge University, by Dr. M. V. Wilkes, completed in May 1949.

EDVAC, at the Institute of Advanced Studies, Princeton, by von Neumann in 1950.

ACE, at the National Physical Laboratory, built in 1950 by Womesley, Turing and Colebrook.

* Burks, A. W., Goldstine, H. A., von Neumann, J., "Preliminary Discussion of the Logical Design of an Electronic Computing Instrument". Institute for Advanced Study, Princeton, 1946.

† Williams, F. C., Kilburn, T., Tootill, G. C., "Universal High-Speed Digital Computers: A Small Scale Experimental Machine". *Proc. I.E.E.* Vol. 98, II, 1951, pp 13-28.

Whilst the basic principles had been established, technical difficulties were still to be overcome. The problem of bulk information storage with a quick access had not been solved until Williams introduced the Cathode-Ray-Tube Store in 1948. Mercury delay-lines had been used but were expensive and temperamental. Early magnetic drum stores were used in SEC, a London University computer, and in ERA 1101 built by Engineering Research Associates. The magnetic store has now entirely superseded the Williams tube store.

In 1951 the world's first commercial computer, LEO I, was built and operated by J. Lyons and Co. Ltd. for cost account analysis of their bakeries. The LEO computer was a developed form of Dr. Wilkes' EDSAC machine.

Later developments are not concerned so much with the 'logic' and principles of the computer as with engineering techniques and programming. In 1948 Dr. W. Shockley discovered the transistor, and it was not long before these were replacing valves in computers. This greatly reduced machine size and power consumption. Conventional wiring is now being replaced by 'integrated circuits' in which components and their interconnections are formed together. (Aiken's machine used over 500 miles of wire).

The core store has replaced the drum in some instances as it has a similar capacity but a much reduced access time. The main store is backed up by magnetic tapes and magnetic discs which, unlike the drum, may be removed from the computer for information storage.

The speed of operation has steadily improved since 1948. Early machines took 1·25 milliseconds to add two numbers together; this has been reduced to a few microseconds on modern machines.

Programming Developments

The first digital computers received their instructions in a form which directly operated the machines. This meant that the programmer had fully to understand the working of the machine with regard to storage and manipulation of data. Every movement of every number had to be specified and the basic steps were limited to those in the machine's 'instruction code' or repertoire. The number of basic instructions varied from about 20 to 60, and consisted of such operations as add, subtract, read, write, move from register to store, store to register, shift left, shift right, etc.

Program writing was a highly skilled operation and many of the first programmers were required to have a degree in mathematics. The programs took a long time to prepare and were so complicated that they were difficult to check and modify. The first step in simplifying programming was to use 'symbolic coding', *e.g.* using words that are interpreted by the computer as a numbered instruction.

The commonly used parts of all programs, such as read in and convert to binary, add, subtract, multiply, divide, take the square root, convert to decimal and print out, etc., were written out and kept as sub-routines to be used over and over again. The Cambridge University Mathematical Laboratory published a small library of sub-routines in 1951 for use on the EDSAC computer.

By 1957 ‘autocodes’ were being written which brought into operation a whole sub-routine by specifying only one input instruction. The input was called a ‘macro’ instruction which was interpreted by the computer as a larger number of ‘micro’ instructions, the system being called an ‘interpretive autocode’. The programming was becoming ‘problem-oriented’ rather than ‘machine-oriented’.

The programming languages using only terms which the machine could use directly were called ‘low-level languages’ and those which resembled ordinary English, with the usual mathematical notation, were called ‘high-level languages’.

The first high-level language was FORTRAN, developed by I.B.M. This ‘compiled’ or ‘assembled’ a machine code program, corresponding to the input program, before the actual computation commenced. The translation was done by the computer itself, which of course had to have the autocode written in machine code in the first instance.

In 1960 a report on ALGOL 60 was issued by a committee representing all the major countries using computers. The idea was to have a universal language which could be used on any machine. The work of implementing the code to a particular computer was the responsibility of the manufacturer.

For business and commercial programs, the COBOL language was devised in 1959, again as a universal language. Unfortunately neither ALGOL nor COBOL has become ‘universal’ in the sense that they can be used on any computer. Variations peculiar to specific machines have had to be created. Nevertheless, great simplification and standardization has resulted from the use of autocodes, and the academic requirements of a programmer are now much reduced. This has been essential in order to find the large number of programmers needed in the modern business and technological world.

3

NUMBER SYSTEMS

The Radix of a Number

In our normal decimal system of numbers 7142 represents

	7 thousands
plus	1 hundred
plus	4 tens
plus	2 units.

The four columns in the number represent units, tens, hundreds and thousands, which are powers of 10. We may therefore write 7142 as

$$7 \times 10^3 + 1 \times 10^2 + 4 \times 10^1 + 2 \times 10^0$$

10 is called the **radix** or the **base** of the system.

Although we are accustomed to dealing with numbers to a base of 10, there is no reason why other bases should not be used to form a number system. The greatest disadvantage in such a system would be our unfamiliarity with it for practical use.

In general, if we call the radix of any number x,

$$243 \text{ means } 2x^2 + 4x^1 + 3x^0$$

Example. If the radix is 5, the number 243 represents

$$2 \times 5^2 + 4 \times 5^1 + 3 \times 5^0$$

$$50 + 20 + 3 = 73 \text{ in our usual radix 10 system.}$$

Notice that the right-hand column **always** represents units, as x^0 is always 1 whatever the value of x. In dealing with numbers to a radix different from 10, it is usual to indicate the radix by a subscript. In the previous example we see that

$$243_5 = 73_{10}$$

To convert a number having a radix other than 10 to a number with radix 10 we may evaluate each digit in turn and sum the results, as in the last example.

One interesting fact now emerges: no digits larger than or equal to the radix need appear in any number. For example

$$\begin{aligned} 24_3 &= 2 \times 3^1 + 4 \times 3^0 \\ &= 2 \times 3 + 4 \times 1 \end{aligned}$$

Now 3 from the units column may be transferred left to the 3's column

$$= 3 \times 3 + 1$$

The 9 in the 3's column may now be transferred left to the 9's column

$$\begin{aligned} &= 1 \times 9 + 0 \times 3 + 1 \\ &= 101_3 \end{aligned}$$

In the familiar decimal system this is the same as saying that no number greater than 9 is required in any column.

Counting is possible with a number scale of any radix. The following table shows the first ten numbers in several systems.

Radix 10	2	3	5	8
1	1	1	1	1
2	10	2	2	2
3	11	10	3	3
4	100	11	4	4
5	101	12	10	5
6	110	20	11	6
7	111	21	12	7
8	1000	22	13	10
9	1001	100	14	11
10	1010	101	20	12

The particular number scales required in computing are those with bases of 10 (decimal), 2 (binary), and 8 (octal).

Why Computers Use the Binary System

To store a given amount of information the decimal system requires more storage capacity than the binary system. Storage capacity here means the number of **possible states** that each column or digit may have, multiplied by the number of digits. Storage space is valuable, so it is advantageous to use any system which reduces the number of possible states in the store.

For example, to hold a 3 figure decimal number in a machine requires a selection of 3 from a total of 30 digits: 10 for the units, 10 for the tens, and 10 for the hundreds, as each of the 3 figures may be anything from 0 to 9 inclusive.

100s	tens	units
0	0	0
1	1	1
2	2	2
3	3	3
4	4	4
5	5	5
6	6	6
7	7	7
8	8	8
9	9	9

30 possible states

It is more convenient in a computer to reduce the possible states from 10 (0 to 9) to 2 (0 or 1). Such a **binary** or two-state system is also more easily represented and manipulated by the machine.

To feed in data by punched cards or tape requires only the simple code

Blank = 0

Hole = 1

and a number may be represented by indicator lights as

Lamp OFF = 0

Lamp ON = 1

The electrical circuits used in the computer may be simplified to use 'two-state' devices that are either ON or OFF. Transistor circuitry is particularly convenient for this.

The number of columns or digits in the binary system will, however, be larger. To represent 999 as a decimal requires 3 digits but

$$999_{10} = 1111100111_2$$

and so 10 digits are required in binary. However, as each column can only have 2 states (0 or 1), only 20 possible states are required compared with 30 for the decimal system.

0	0	0	0	0	0	0	0	0	0
1	1	1	1	1	1	1	1	1	1

} 20 possible states

The information is held in the computer as a string of binary digits or **bits,** *e.g.*

0 0 0 0 1 0 0 1

⟵ 1 word ⟶

is an 8-bit word representing the number '9'.

If the input cards to the computer are punched in binary instead of decimal, each row or index position can hold a complete word. As there are now 12 words per card instead of 1, the card packs are reduced and the speed of input increased by a factor of 12.

The Handling of Binary Numbers

The main store of the computer (to be discussed in detail in Chapter 6) may hold from about 4,000 to 16,000 words in a small machine. These would be referred to as 4k and 16k stores respectively. The numbers and instructions that are to be used for an arithmetical operation are first written from the main store into a **register.** A register is a row of two-state transistor circuits each holding a '1' or a '0' depending on its switched condition. The number of these **bistable** circuits in a register is equal to the number of bits in a word. These bistable circuits can be switched from 1 to 0, or *vice versa*, by the application of an electrical pulse.

The access time is the time taken to move a word from the store into a register. Access to the main store takes an appreciable time (10 milliseconds is typical for a drum store), but access to a register is almost immediate and to reduce computing time several registers may be used to hold words temporarily whilst they are being used in a calculation. Eventually, the results of the calculation must be written back into the main store.

The number of significant figures available obviously depends upon the word length, the number of bits per word. The largest number that can be held in a register is its 'capacity' and will be represented in binary by a row of 'ones'.

$$1\ 1\ 1 = 7 \quad \text{(3 bits)}$$
$$1\ 1\ 1\ 1 = 15 \quad \text{(4 bits)}$$
$$1\ 1\ 1\ 1\ 1 = 31 \quad \text{(5 bits)}$$

and so on.

We may continue the sequence by doubling and adding 1.

In general, the number represented by a row of 'ones' is

$$2^{n-1} + \ldots + 2^4 + 2^3 + 2^2 + 2^1 + 2^0 = S_n$$

This is a geometric progression, where S_n is the sum of n terms. To find S_n, rearrange so that

$$S_n = 1 + 2 + 4 + 8 + \ldots + 2^{n-1} \quad \ldots\ldots\ldots\ldots \quad \textbf{(1)}$$

multiply by 2, $2S_n = 2 + 4 + 8 + \ldots + 2^{n-1} + 2^n$ .... **(2)**

subtract **(1)** from **(2)**, $2S_n - S_n = 2^n - 1$

all other terms cancelling.

$$\therefore\ S_n = 2^n - 1.$$

This is the capacity of an n bit register.

Example. Calculate the capacity of a 16 bit register.

Capacity $2^{16} - 1 = 65536 - 1 = 65535$

this being the largest number that can be represented using 16 binary digits.

The table below shows the capacities of registers having typical word lengths.

WORD LENGTH	CAPACITY
8	255
12	4095
16	65535
18	262143
32	4294967295
40	1099511627775

As a guide, we may say that 10 binary digits are approximately equivalent to 3 decimal digits, so that a 40 bit computer gives 12 significant figures, assuming that only one word is used for each number.

The Conversion of Numbers from One Scale to Another

Simple examples have already been given at the beginning of this chapter, but we must discuss the process of conversion in more detail. As conversion between binary and decimal is that most often required we shall consider this first.

To convert a decimal number to binary we must find the 'powers of two' that are contained in it. This may be done by the following process.

(1) If the number is **even** write 0;
If the number is **odd** write 1.

(2) Divide by 2 (ignoring any remainder).

(3) If the result is **even** write 0;
if the result is **odd** write 1.

(4) Go back to (2) and repeat until the number is reduced to unity.

The binary number is then formed by writing the 0s and 1s from left to right starting with the **last** number obtained.

Example. To convert 26_{10} to binary

	26	0
÷ 2	13	1
÷ 2	6	0
÷ 2	3	1
÷ 2	1	1

↑ read $\therefore\ 26_{10} = 11010_2$

This process or algorithm may be called the 'Russian Peasants' method, as it is based on a method of reducing multiplication to simple addition reputedly used by the Russian peasants up to this century.

If the reader cannot see why it works, the proof is given below.

Let the number be N. We require the values of a, b, c, etc. in the binary form $2^n x + \ldots + 8d + 4c + 2b + a$.

$$N = \underbrace{2^n x + \ldots + 8d + 4c + 2b}_{\text{even}} + a$$

a is 0 if N is **even**
a is 1 if N is **odd**

$$\div 2 \qquad \underbrace{2^{n-1} x + \ldots 4d + 2c}_{\text{even}} + b$$

b is 0 if number is **even**
b is 1 if number is **odd**

$$\div 2 \qquad 2^{n-2} x + \ldots + 2d + c$$

c is 0 if number is **even**
c is 1 if number is **odd**

. . . etc.

Hence the binary number is evaluated, the least significant digits being obtained **first.**

We may now check the binary equivalent of 999 given earlier.

999	1
499	1
249	1
124	0
62	0
31	1
15	1
7	1
3	1
1	1

↑ read $\therefore\ 999_{10} = 1111100111_2$

To convert binary numbers to decimals we reverse the process, starting with 1 at the most significant binary digit and doubling for each term, adding 1 when the corresponding binary digit is 1.

Example. Convert 11010_2 to decimal form.

↓		
1	1	
1	3	$[(2 \times 1) + 1]$
0	6	$[2 \times 3]$
1	13	$[(2 \times 6) + 1]$
0	26	$[2 \times 13]$

$\therefore\ 11010_2 = 26_{10}$

Similarly for 1111100111_2:

↓	
1	1
1	3
1	7
1	15
1	31
0	62
0	124
1	249
1	499
1	999

$\therefore\ 1111100111_2 = 999_{10}$

The Use of the Octal Scale

The octal scale is a useful shorthand way of writing binary numbers. If the digits of a binary number are subdivided into groups of three, and each group converted to decimal, we have a more compact way of expressing the number.

Example.

$$\underbrace{1\ 0\ 1}_{5}\quad \underbrace{0\ 1\ 1}_{3}\quad \underbrace{0\ 0\ 1}_{1}\quad \underbrace{1\ 1\ 1}_{7}\quad \underbrace{0\ 0\ 0}_{0}$$

Note that each group represents the number of units, eights, sixty-fours, . . . etc. in binary, hence the result 53170 is the **octal** form of the number.

$$\ldots\ \underbrace{256,\ 128,\ 64,}_{64}\ \underbrace{32,\ 16,\ 8,}_{8}\ \underbrace{4,\ 2,\ 1}_{1}$$

Binary columns (top row); Octal columns (bottom row)

Consider our number 999 again. We know that

$$999_{10} = 1111100111_2$$

Subdividing the binary number into groups of three

$$\underbrace{1}_{1}\ \underbrace{111}_{7}\ \underbrace{100}_{4}\ \underbrace{111}_{7}$$

Therefore $999_{10} = 1747_8$

This is a compact way of writing a binary number and as such is a useful aid to programmers. It is easier to write

4573106

than 100101111011001000110

and only the binary numbers from 0 to 7 need be memorized.

Conversion from decimal to octal is possible by a method similar to that used for decimal to binary.

To express 247_{10} in octal form

$$247 \div 8 = 30 \quad + 7 \text{ remainder}$$

$$30 \div 8 = 3 \quad + 6 \text{ remainder}$$

$$3 \div 8 = 0 \quad + 3 \text{ remainder}$$

$$\therefore\ 247_{10} = 367_8$$

This is now easily converted to binary by inspection,

$$\overbrace{011}^{3}\quad \overbrace{110}^{6}\quad \overbrace{111}^{7}$$

$$\therefore\ 247_{10} = 011110111_2$$

Binary Arithmetic

The computer must be able to perform arithmetic on the binary numbers contained in it. For addition the simple rules are

$$\begin{aligned} 0 + 0 &= 0 \\ 0 + 1 &= 1 \\ 1 + 0 &= 1 \\ 1 + 1 &= 0 \quad \text{and carry 1} \end{aligned}$$

Example.

$$\begin{array}{r} 0\,1\,1\,0\,1 \\ +\quad 1\,0\,1\,1\,0 \\ \hline 1\,0\,0\,0\,1\,1 \\ \hline \end{array} \qquad \text{which in decimals is} \qquad \begin{array}{r} 13 \\ +\quad 22 \\ \hline 35 \\ \hline \end{array}$$

Subtraction is just as simple, remembering now to add 2 to a column in order to subtract from a lower number, carrying 1 over to the next column.

Example.

$$\begin{array}{r} 1\,0\,0\,0\,1\,1 \\ -\quad 1\,1\,0\,1 \\ \hline 1\,0\,1\,1\,0 \\ \hline \end{array} \qquad \text{or} \qquad \begin{array}{r} 35 \\ -\quad 13 \\ \hline 22 \\ \hline \end{array}$$

Multiplication is as for decimals but remembering to add the partial products in binary form.

Example.

$$\begin{array}{r} 1\,1\,1 \\ \times\quad 1\,0\,1 \\ \hline 1\,1\,1\,0\,0 \\ 0\,0\,0\,0 \\ 1\,1\,1 \\ \hline 1\,0\,0\,0\,1\,1 \\ \hline \end{array} \qquad \text{which is} \qquad \begin{array}{r} 7 \\ \times\quad 5 \\ \hline 35 \\ \hline \end{array}$$

Division follows a similar pattern, with binary subtraction to find the remainder.

Example.

$$\begin{array}{r} 1\,1\,1 \\ 1\,0\,1 \,\big)\, \overline{1\,0\,0\,0\,1\,1} \\ 1\,0\,1 \\ \hline 1\,1\,1 \\ 1\,0\,1 \\ \hline 1\,0\,1 \\ 1\,0\,1 \\ \hline \cdots \end{array} \qquad \text{or} \qquad \begin{array}{r} 7 \\ 5\,\big)\,\overline{35} \end{array}$$

Apart from the addition operation, these methods are not directly suitable for use by a computer. The actual methods used will be described in Chapter 7.

Shifting and Binary Fractions

If a decimal point is moved one place to the left or right a number is divided or multiplied by 10. In binary, the shifting of the 'binary point' changes a number by a factor of **2**.

$$
\begin{aligned}
1000\cdot0 &= 8\\
100\cdot0 &= 4\\
10\cdot0 &= 2\\
1\cdot0 &= 1
\end{aligned}
$$

Obviously we may continue

$$
\begin{aligned}
0\cdot1 &= \tfrac{1}{2}\\
0\cdot01 &= \tfrac{1}{4}\\
0\cdot001 &= \tfrac{1}{8}
\end{aligned}
$$

. . . etc.

For example, $7\frac{1}{4}$ is 111·01 in binary.

The integer (whole number) part and the fractional part must be converted into binary separately. To convert decimal fractions to binary, multiply by 2, and if the integer part is **even** (including zero) write 0, and if **odd** write 1. Continue until no fractional part remains.

Example To find the binary form of $0{\cdot}75_{10}$

			Read
	0·75		
× 2	1·50	1	↓
× 2	3·00	1	

$\therefore\ 075_{10} = 0{\cdot}11_2$

Unless the fraction can be expressed as the sum of halves, quarters, eighths, etc., the binary fraction will never terminate.

Example.

			Read
	0·014		
× 2	0·028	0	↓
× 2	0·056	0	
× 2	0·112	0	
× 2	0·224	0	
× 2	0·448	0	
× 2	0·896	0	
× 2	1·792	1	
× 2	3·584	1	
× 2	7·168	1	
× 2	14·336	0	
× 2	28·672	0	
× 2	57·344	1	

. . . etc.

$\therefore\ 0{\cdot}014_{10} = 0{\cdot}000000111001\ .\ .\ .\ .\ ._2$

or 0·0071 . . . . . in octal.

This does not terminate and illustrates one of the difficulties of using binary fractions. As the computer will have a limited word length this necessitates approximating or 'truncating' by leaving off the least significant digits. In the last example, although we have calculated the answer to 12 binary places, it represents only 0·013916 instead of 0·014 (check this!).

Unfortunately, such decimal fractions as 0·1 and 0·01 which are often used as steps or 'increments' in a program are non-terminating in binary.

$$0{\cdot}1_{10} = 0{\cdot}0001\dot{1}00\dot{1}1001100110011\ldots_2 \quad \text{etc.}$$
$$= 0{\cdot}6314 \quad \text{in octal.}$$

This explains why the computer may print out an answer 2·9999998 when the correct answer is known to be 3·0 exactly.

The reader should now be able to derive a method of converting binary fractions to decimal fractions. If not, consider this example where we repeatedly divide by 2, adding 1 for every corresponding binary digit.

To convert $0{\cdot}10010_2$ to decimal form.

0		
1	1	
0	0·5	[1 ÷ 2]
0	0·25	[0·5 ÷ 2]
1	1·125	[(0·25 ÷ 2) + 1]
↑ ·		
0	0·5625	[1·125 ÷ 2]

$$\therefore\ 0{\cdot}10010_2 = 0{\cdot}5625_{10}$$

Negative Numbers

The computer must be able to handle both positive and negative numbers, and yet it can use only two characters '0' and '1'. The simplest (but least convenient) system of indicating the sign is by means of a 'sign digit' preceding the number, *e.g.*

(0) 0 0 0 1 0 1 = +5
(1) 0 0 0 1 0 1 = −5
↑
sign digit

The sign digit must not be interpreted as part of the binary place system.

A far better way, enabling subtraction to be performed automatically by the computer, is by using 'complements'. This is familiar to us in the way in which shop assistants give change. If you purchase an article for 53½p and tender £1, the assistant continues counting up from 53½p until £1 is reached. The 'change', 46½p, is the complement of 53½p. In this way subtraction is replaced by addition.

An example will first be given using decimal numbers, but it must be remembered that the machine would use binary. Consider a 3-digit system with a range 000 to 999, any digit carried over into the fourth column being discarded (as in a mileometer or counter). Suppose we wish to calculate

$$391 - 210$$

we first find the **complement** of 210 and **add** it to 391. The complement of a number is found by subtracting it from zero.

```
     0 0 0
  -  2 1 0
  ---------
 (1) 7 9 0
  ---------
```

Discard this ↑

Therefore the complement of 210 is 790.

Now add it to 391

```
     3 9 1
  +  7 9 0
  ---------
 (1) 1 8 1
  ---------
```

Discard this ↑

and the answer 181 is found.

We may therefore represent a negative number in the computer by its complement, and in adding it to any other number its sign is automatically taken into account.

Now, using binary numbers and assuming an 8-bit word length

$$5 = 00000101$$

The complement of 5 will be

```
   00000000
 - 00000101
 ----------
   11111011   which represents -5.
 ----------
```

Check this by subtracting 5 from 12, *i.e.* adding the complement of 5 to 12.

```
        12  =     00001100
        -5  =     11111011
                -----------
adding         (1)00000111
                -----------
```

Discard this ↑

This is known as the 'twos complement' method.

To make use of this system the computer must be able to produce complements by its electrical circuitry. One operation that the computer can easily do is to **invert** a number, *i.e.* write 0 for 1 and 1 for 0.

$$\text{If} \quad N = 1001100$$

$$\text{the inverse} \quad \overline{N} = 0110011$$

We now see that $N + \overline{N}$ is **always** a row of '1's. But a row of n '1's represents $2^n - 1$ (see page 34).

$$\therefore \; N + \overline{N} = 2^n - 1$$

2^n represents one more than the capacity of the n-bit register and would be indicated by a row of '0's. (Again, compare with a counter reading 9999; one more resets it back to 0000).

$$\therefore \; N + \overline{N} + 1 = \text{row of zeros}$$

$$\overline{N} + 1 = \text{row of zeros} - N$$

BUT THIS IS THE COMPLEMENT OF N. Hence we have the following rule:

TO FIND THE COMPLEMENT OF A NUMBER, INVERT AND ADD 1.

This operation can be performed by the computer.

We now have a problem. In the decimal example given earlier we saw that 790 was the complement of 210 and represented −210. How then do we represent the number 790? The answer is that we cannot do so without extending the capacity of the register, the range of positive numbers being limited to exactly half the word capacity.

Consider a 3-bit binary system

0 0 0	=	0	positive
0 0 1	=	1	
0 1 0	=	2	
0 1 1	=	3	
1 0 0	=	−4	negative
1 0 1	=	−3	
1 1 0	=	−2	
1 1 1	=	−1	

In general, for an n-bit binary number,
the positive range is 00 . . . 0 to 011 . . . 11 (0 to $2^{n-1} - 1$)
and the negative range is 10 . . . 0 to 11 . . . 1 (-2^{n-1} to -1).

One of the standard tests used in a computer program is to see if a number is positive or negative. We now see that this can be done by **examining the most significant digit only**; if it is 0 the number is positive, if it is 1 the number is negative. Again, we may call the first digit the 'sign digit' but in the system of complements it now forms part of the binary number.

Range and Accuracy

The order of magnitude of a number is expressed in one of two ways.

(i) FIXED POINT WORKING. No account of the decimal or binary point is taken until the answer is produced, the computer working in integers.

This is suitable for data processing, stock control, accounting, etc., where integers are used throughout. In accounting, all quantities would be reduced to pence as the basic unit. We have seen that the range of an n-bit computer is $\pm 2^{n-1}-1$ which for a 32-bit word is

$$\pm 2^{31}-1 = \pm 2{,}147{,}483{,}647$$

or approximately 2×10^9.

Fractional values are not possible over this range.

(ii) FLOATING POINT WORKING. Numbers are expressed in the form

$$A \times 10^E$$

where the **argument** A is a decimal fraction, and the **exponent** E is the power of 10 by which it is multiplied. The exponent, which may be positive or negative, indicates the position of the decimal point.

Example.

A	E	
71420	3	represents $0{\cdot}71420 \times 10^3$ or 714·20
−71420	3	represents −714·20
71420	−3	represents 0·00071420
−71420	−3	represents −0·00071420

Numbers such as $0{\cdot}0046 \times 10^{-3}$ are optimised by writing them as $0{\cdot}4600 \times 10^{-5}$ giving the maximum number of significant figures. (This makes the representation of zero an interesting problem).

In binary form the number is held in the computer in two parts a and b, a number being of the form

$$2^a \times b$$

where b lies in the ranges -1 to $-\frac{1}{2}$ and $\frac{1}{2}$ to 1 for the optimised form.

Now see what is possible in our 32-bit computer. Allocate 8 bits to a, one being used as the sign digit. Allocate 24 bits to b, one being used as the sign digit.

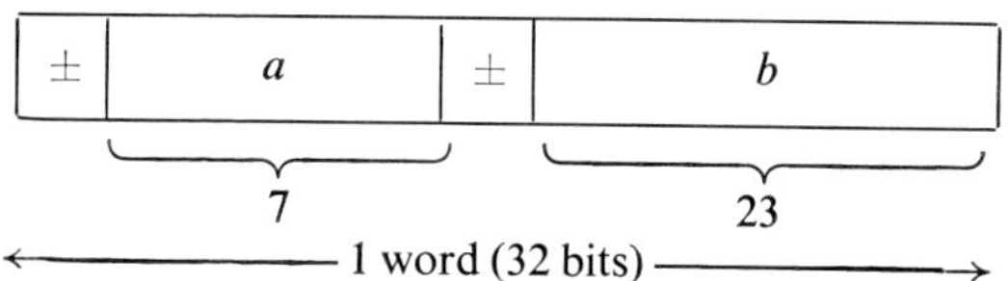

$2^a \times b$ now has the range $\pm 2^{127}$ determined by a, with 23 significant binary figures determined by b. The decimal equivalent of this is $\pm 3 \times 10^{38}$ to 7 significant figures, quantities as small as 10^{-38} being possible. Floating point arithmetic is used for mathematical, scientific and technical problems.

Examples (Chapter 3)

(1) Convert the following numbers to binary.

(a) 21
(b) 90
(c) 123
(d) $4\frac{1}{2}$
(e) $6\frac{7}{8}$
(f) 12·125.

(2) Convert the following binary numbers to decimal.

(a) 10111
(b) 111101
(c) 10111·011
(d) 111·111
(e) 10001010101
(f) 010111010.

(3) How many binary digits are required to represent a decimal range of

(a) 0 to 10,000
(b) −10,000 to +10,000?

(4) What is the decimal capacity of a 24-bit binary register in

(a) positive integer form;
(b) complementaty negative form;
(c) positive form with 12 integer bits and 12 fractional bits;
(d) complementary negative form with 12 integer bits and 12 fractional bits?

(5) Convert $0{\cdot}035_{10}$ to binary and octal form. What will be the percentage error if the number of binary digits is limited to 12?

(6) Convert the following octal numbers to binary and decimal form.

(a) 172_8
(b) $26{\cdot}3_8$
(c) 1022_8
(d) $1{\cdot}32_8$.

(7) Convert the following decimal numbers to 10-bit binary numbers using complementary negatives.

(a) 43
(b) 79
(c) 241
(d) 819
(e) −27
(f) −34.

(8) Convert the following 10-bit complementary negative binary numbers to decimal form.

(a) 0001011011
(b) 0011110000
(c) 1110000111
(d) 1111111000
(e) 1100000001.

(9) Multiply 10111000_2 by

(a) 4
(b) $\frac{1}{4}$
(c) 40.

Convert your answers to octal form.

(Answers are on pages 174/175)

4

BOOLEAN ALGEBRA

Why is it Needed ?

The operation of a digital computer is a complicated sequence of arithmetical activities automatically controlled by electrical circuitry. Data is being moved back and forth, into and out of the store, numbers are being tested, decisions made and answers punched or printed. In many instances several operations are being performed simultaneously, all accurately synchronized and interrelated.

A complete circuit diagram of a computer, even if it were available, would be so complicated and extensive as to completely mask the simple underlying principles, and the traditional methods of circuit design would fail or lead the designer to incorporate many redundant components. It is sometimes possible to use the same circuit and components to perform several different functions if one can be sure that they will not be required simultaneously. The designer and service engineer would find their task almost impossible if they had to rely solely on a conventional diagram.

However, if the detailed electrical circuitry is omitted from the diagram, which instead presents only the flow of data (electrical pulses) and shows the operations performed on the data, the understanding of the machine's behaviour is greatly simplified. Such an outline drawing is called a **logic diagram.** (Logic is the derivation of conclusions from a given set of data, determined by a set of rules).

If the designer recites the operations required, he finds that they are connected by conjunctions such as

AND OR NOT NOR etc.

These are called **logical operations.**

For example, 'Close switches A **and** B when C **and** D but **not** E **and** F are energized'.

By using these logical operations to define the interaction of the binary pulses it is possible to write down the behaviour of the computer circuits in a simple form. In the next chapter we shall discuss the transistor circuits that represent these logical operations, but first we must produce the rules for combining them. These can be written down in mathematical form using *Boolean Algebra**, sometimes called a **switching algebra.**

* George Boole (1815-1864), "An Investigation of the Laws of Thought", London, 1854.

The Algebra of Circuits

(1) The *AND* operation.

Consider a circuit with two switches in series (Fig. 4.1) an output being produced only when p **and** q are closed.

FIG. 4.1.

Now let $p = 0$ represent an open switch

$p = 1$ represent a closed switch

where $r = 1$ implies an output pulse and $r = 0$ implies no output.

Then $r = p$ **and** q means that $r = 1$ if (and only if) $p = 1$ **and** $q = 1$.

If either p or q is 0, then $r = 0$.

This is often shown as a table

$p =$	0	1	0	1
$q =$	0	0	1	1
$r =$	0	0	0	1

called a **truth table** as Boole's original work on the algebra was concerned with determining whether a statement was true or false (equivalent to our 1 and 0).

If we look at the table it appears that the **and** operation behaves as a **multiplication,** for

$$0 \times 0 = 0$$
$$1 \times 0 = 0$$
$$0 \times 1 = 0$$
$$1 \times 1 = 1$$

and so the operation is sometimes written as $r = p.q$.

(2) The *OR* operation.

Consider two switches in parallel (Fig. 4.2) an output r being obtained when either p **or** q (or both) is closed.

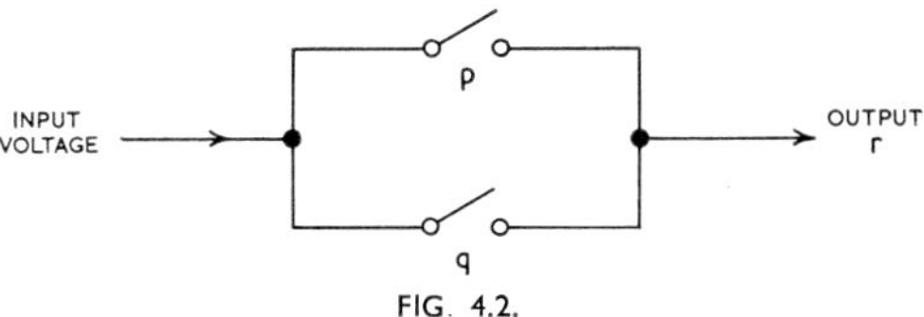

FIG. 4.2.

The truth table is

$p =$	0	1	0	1
$q =$	0	0	1	1
$r =$	0	1	1	1

The **or** operation is similar to **addition** except for the result when $p = 1$ and $q = 1$ (which would be 0 in binary arithmetic). This is an inclusive-or operation as the conditions for $r = 1$ include the case where both p and q are 1.

The operation is sometimes written as

$$r = p + q$$

although it is not quite the same as binary addition.

In the computer, $p\ q\ r$ . . . etc. are not open-and-closed switches but electrical pulses representing 0s and 1s. Applying pulses p and q to an **and** or **or** element produces an output pulse r.

In the logical diagram the elements are given the symbols as shown in Fig. 4.3.

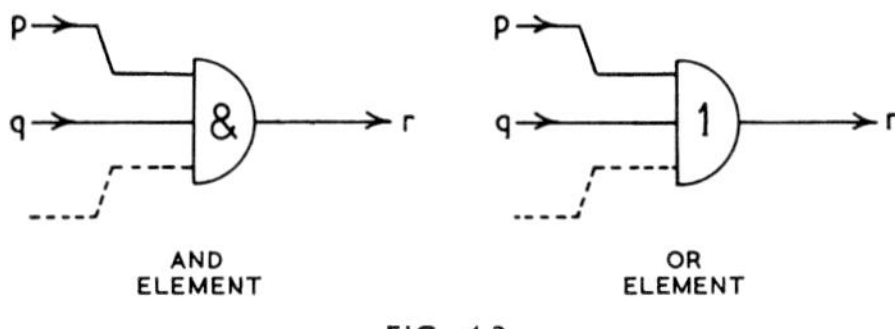

FIG. 4.3.

The '1' in the **or** symbol implies that any one input is sufficient to produce an output r. The number of inputs is not restricted to two.

(3) The *NOT* operation.

This is an **inversion** or **negation** operation, *i.e.* the output is 1 when the input is 0 and *vice versa*. The logical symbol is as in Fig. 4.4 and the operation is written

$$r = \bar{p}$$

r is 'not p', or the opposite of p.

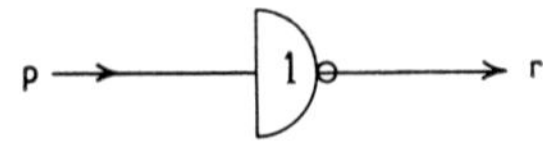

FIG. 4.4. *NOT* ELEMENT

The truth table is

$p =$	0	1
$r =$	1	0

(4) The *NOR* operation.

$$r = \overline{p + q}$$

meaning neither p **nor** q.

The truth table is

$p =$	0	1	0	1
$q =$	0	0	1	1
$r =$	1	0	0	0

and the logical symbol is shown in Fig. 4.5.

FIG. 4.5. *NOR* ELEMENT

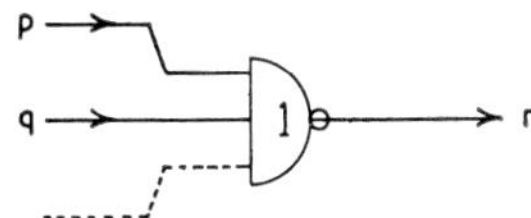

(5) The *NOT–AND* operation. (*NAND* operation)

$$r = \overline{p.q}$$

meaning not p and q.

Here the truth table is

$p =$	0	1	0	1
$q =$	0	0	1	1
$r =$	1	1	1	0

and there is an output except when all the inputs are present.

The symbol is shown in Fig. 4.6.

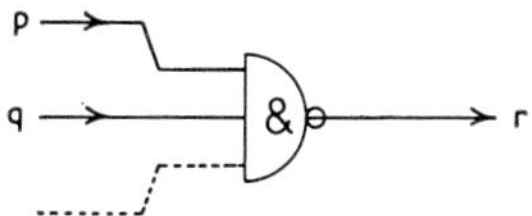

FIG. 4.6. *NOT-AND* ELEMENT

Boolean Algebra

Summarizing the most important operations so far discussed we have:

$p.q$ means p and q

$p + q$ means p or q

$\bar{p}$ means not p

We shall now write algebraic equations using these symbols, and determine the rules of the algebra.

Some of the more useful identities are shown below.

$$p + q = q + p \quad \ldots\ldots\ldots \quad (1)$$

$$p.q = q.p \quad \ldots\ldots\ldots \quad (2)$$

$$p + (q + s) = (p + q) + s \quad \ldots\ldots\ldots \quad (3)$$

$$p.(q.s) = (p.q).s \quad \ldots\ldots\ldots \quad (4)$$

$$p.(q + s) = p.q + p.s \quad \ldots\ldots\ldots \quad (5)$$

$$\overline{\overline{p}} = p \quad \ldots\ldots\ldots \quad (6)$$

Up to this point the Boolean Algebra behaves as 'normal' algebra, but **it will not always do so.** Equations **(1)** to **(5)** can be verified by drawing the switching circuits that they represent.

For the first equation (Fig. 4.7) it is obvious that the order of p and q is immaterial (it is commutative).

FIG. 4.7.

Problem 1. Draw the switching circuits represented by equations **(2)**, **(3)**, **(4)** and **(5)** and hence verify the equations.

The following Boolean identities have no equivalents in ordinary algebra.

$$p + p = p \quad \ldots\ldots\ldots \quad (7)$$

$$p + \overline{p} = 1 \quad \ldots\ldots\ldots \quad (8)$$

$$p.p = p \quad \ldots\ldots\ldots \quad (9)$$

$$p.\overline{p} = 0 \quad \ldots\ldots\ldots \quad (10)$$

These are easily verified by considering the circuits they represent, *e.g.* **(7)** states that p **or** p is p, *i.e.* two identical switches in parallel are equivalent to one switch.

Equations **(8)** and **(10)** are illustrated below in Fig. 4.8.

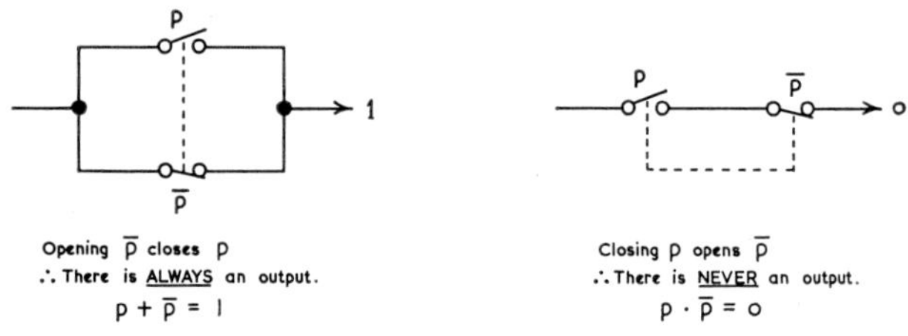

FIG. 4.8.

Equation (**9**) represents two identical switches in series which may obviously be replaced by one.

Two theorems in Boolean Algebra which are extremely useful for circuit simplification are **De Morgan's Theorems.**

$$\overline{p.q} = \bar{p} + \bar{q} \quad \ldots\ldots\ldots\ldots\ldots\ldots \quad \mathbf{(11)}$$

$$\overline{p + q} = \bar{p}.\bar{q} \quad \ldots\ldots\ldots\ldots\ldots\ldots \quad \mathbf{(12)}$$

These may be seen to be true by considering examples involving the choice of two articles. For instance, in a restaurant you may have peas or carrots, but not both, *i.e.* you may **not** have peas **and** carrots. Let p be peas and q be carrots, then

$\overline{p.q}$ means **not** peas **and** carrots.

You must therefore decide which you will not have, **not** peas **or not** carrots.

This is $\bar{p} + \bar{q}$

$$\therefore \overline{p.q} = \bar{p} + \bar{q} \quad \ldots\ldots\ldots\ldots\ldots\ldots \mathbf{(11)}$$

Equation (**12**) may be similarly verified.

Alternative symbols for logical operations are given in Appendix A.

Circuit Simplification

By writing the Boolean equation for a circuit, it is often possible to simplify it by using the identities (**1**) to (**12**) just described.

Example 1. Consider two **not** elements in series, Fig. 4.9.

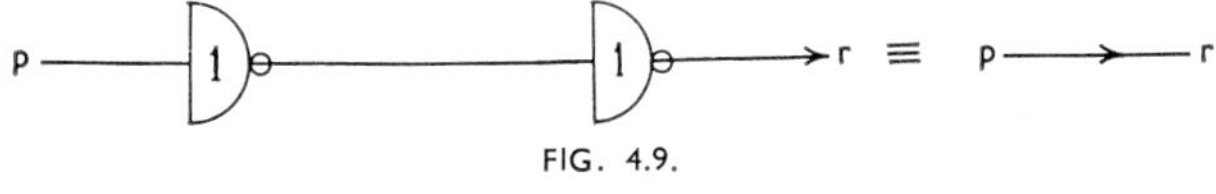

FIG. 4.9.

Then r = **not not** p

$= \bar{\bar{p}}$

$= p$ by (**6**)

and hence the circuit may be replaced by a piece of wire, as the output is always equal to the input.

Problem 2. Simplify the circuits in Fig. 4.10. (Answer are on page 175).

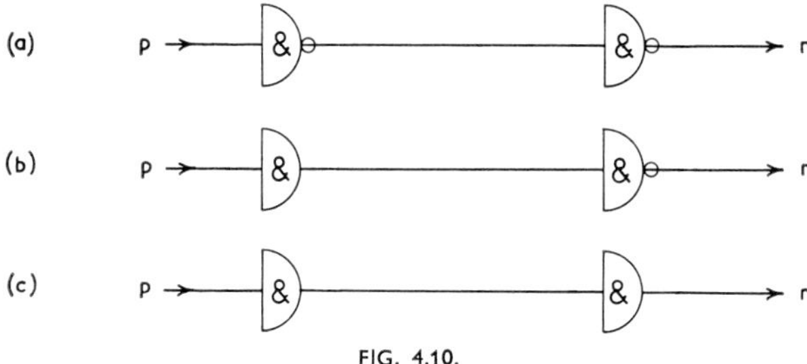

FIG. 4.10.

Example 2.

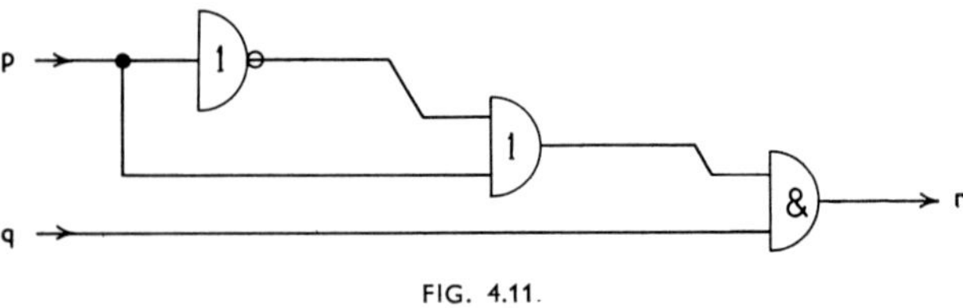

FIG. 4.11.

The Boolean equation for Fig. 4.11 is

$$r = (\bar{p} + p).q \qquad (r \text{ is not } p \text{ or } p\text{, and } q)$$

$$\text{But } \bar{p} + p = 1 \qquad \text{by } (\mathbf{8})$$

$$\therefore r = 1.q \qquad (r \text{ is 1 when 1 and } q \text{ are 1})$$

$$\text{and } r = q \qquad (r \text{ is 1 when } q \text{ is 1})$$

Again, the elements are redundant, and a piece of wire connecting q to r is sufficient.

Example 3. To simplify Fig. 4.12(a).

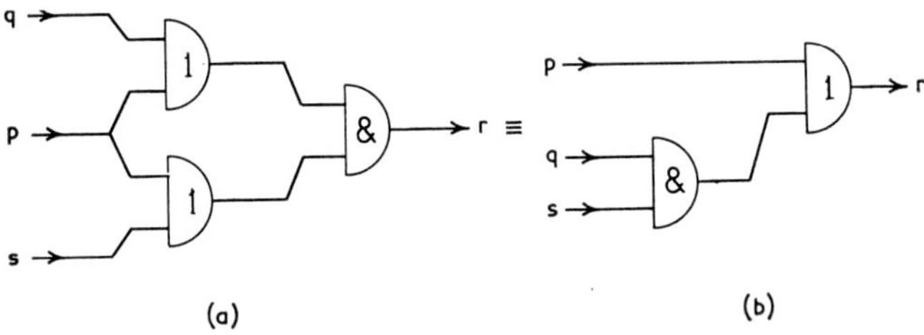

FIG. 4.12.

$$\begin{aligned} r &= (q + p).(p + s) \\ &= q.p + q.s + p.p + p.s \\ &= q.p + q.s + p + p.s \qquad \text{as } p.p = p \text{ by } (\mathbf{9}) \end{aligned}$$

Taking p out as a factor,

$$r = p.(q + 1 + s) + q.s$$

Now $(q + 1 + s)$ is always 1 whatever the state of q or s

$$\therefore r = p + q.s$$

and hence the simplified circuit is as Fig. 4.12(b).

Problem 3. Simplify the circuits shown in Fig. 4.13.

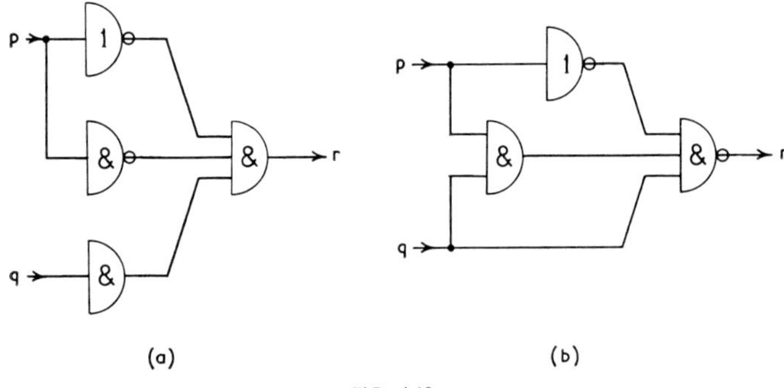

FIG. 4.13.

(Answers are on page 175)

Circuits involving combinations of **or, nor, and, not–and,** are simplified by using De Morgan's theorems, **(11)** and **(12)**.

Example 4. To simplify Fig. 4.14.

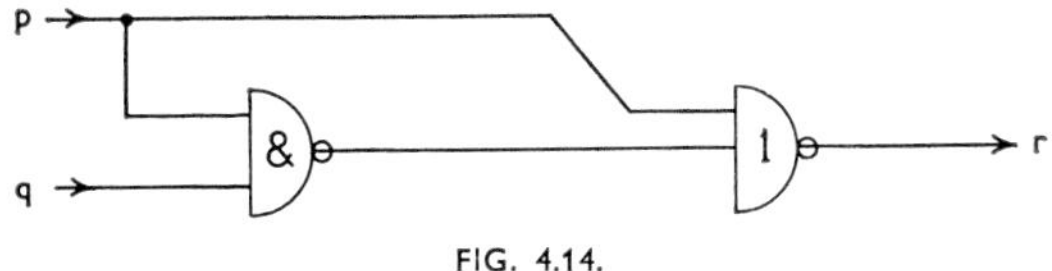

FIG. 4.14.

$$r = \overline{(\overline{p}.q) + p}$$

$$= \overline{\overline{p.q.\overline{p}}} \qquad \text{writing } p = \overline{\overline{p}} \text{ and using } \mathbf{(12)}$$

$$= p.q.\overline{p} \qquad \text{by } \mathbf{(6)}$$

$$= p.\overline{p}.q \qquad \text{by } \mathbf{(2)}$$

$$= 0.q \qquad \text{as } p.\overline{p} = 0 \text{ by } \mathbf{(10)}$$

$$= 0$$

$\therefore$ r is always 0, and the circuit is completely redundant.

Example 5. Simplify Fig. 4.15(a).

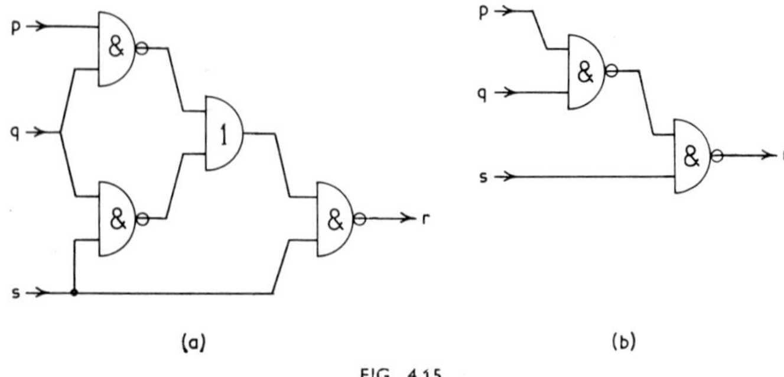

FIG. 4.15.

The Boolean equation is

$$
\begin{aligned}
r &= \overline{\left(\overline{p.q} + \overline{q.s}\right).s} & \\
&= \overline{\left(\bar{p} + \bar{q} + \bar{q} + \bar{s}\right).s} & \text{by } \mathbf{(11)} \\
&= \overline{\left(\bar{p} + \bar{q} + \bar{s}\right).s} & \text{by } \mathbf{(7)} \\
&= \overline{\left(\bar{p} + \bar{q}\right).\bar{s} + \bar{s}.s} & \text{by } \mathbf{(5)} \\
&= \overline{\left(\bar{p} + \bar{q}\right).s} & \text{by } \mathbf{(10)} \\
&= \overline{\left(\overline{p.q}\right).s} & \text{by } \mathbf{(11)}
\end{aligned}
$$

the circuit of which is as Fig. 4.15(b).

Computer Logic

The adding circuit.

The computer must be able to add binary numbers according to the rules:

$$
\begin{aligned}
0 + 0 &= 0 \\
0 + 1 &= 1 \\
1 + 0 &= 1 \\
1 + 1 &= 0 \quad \text{and carry 1.}
\end{aligned}
$$

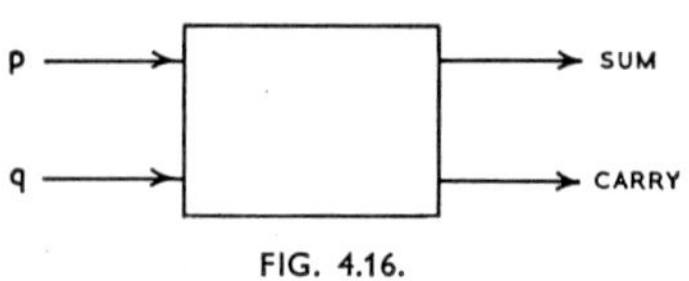

FIG. 4.16.

Representing an adder by Fig. 4.16, the sum digit is produced in accordance with the truth table:

p =	0	1	0	1
q =	0	0	1	1
sum =	0	1	1	0

The Boolean equation is therefore

$$(p.\bar{q}) + (q.\bar{p}) = \text{sum}$$

and the logic circuit is shown in Fig. 4.17.

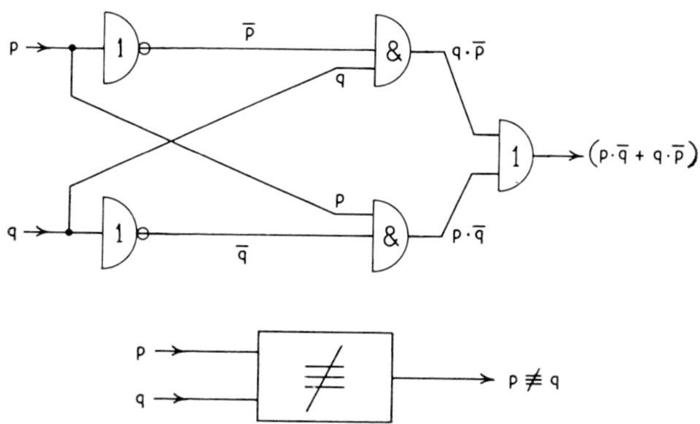

FIG. 4.17. NON-EQUIVALENCE CIRCUIT

This is referred to as a 'non-equivalence' circuit because an output pulse appears only when p and q are in different states. It is also known as an **exclusive–or** circuit (compare the truth table with that for the **inclusive–or** logic element, page 48).

The carry digit appears only when both inputs p and q are 1, hence the truth table:

p =	0	1	0	1
q =	0	0	1	1
carry =	0	0	0	1

The Boolean equation is

$$p.q = \text{carry}$$

and the logic circuit is shown in Fig. 4.18.

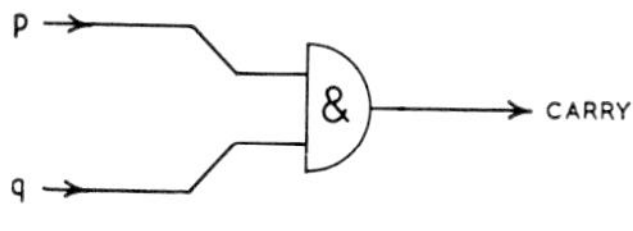

FIG. 4.18.

Problem 4. Show that the circuit in Fig. 4.19 is also a non-equivalence circuit. (Answer is on page 175.)

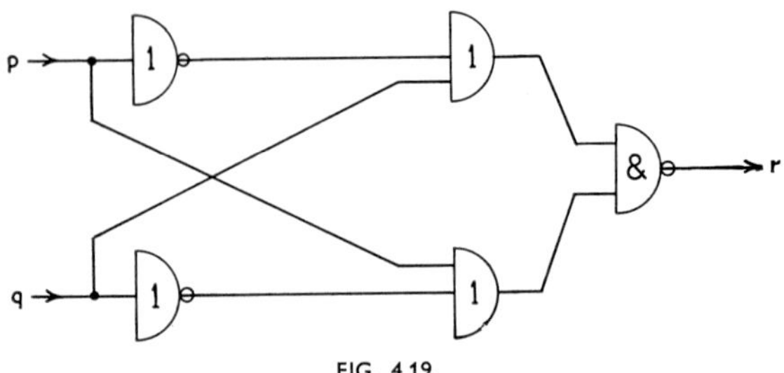

FIG. 4.19.

We now combine the 'sum' and 'carry' circuits in Fig. 4.20 to give a **half-adder.**

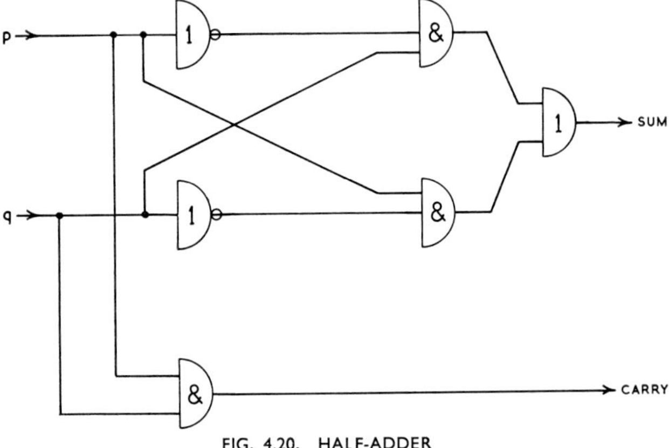

FIG. 4.20. HALF-ADDER

In an addition process the carry digit must be added to the sum of the digits in the next column, and so the adder must be capable of accepting **three** inputs, *p*, *q*, and the carry from the previous column. The circuit in Fig. 4.20 accepts only two inputs and is therefore known as a half-adder. Two half-adders are required to make a three-input or **full adder.**

If *p* and *q* are the digits to be added, and *c* is carried over from the previous column, the arithmetic table for the full adder is

p	q	c		
$0 + 0 + 0$			$= 0$	
$1 + 0 + 0$			$= 1$	
$0 + 1 + 0$			$= 1$	
$1 + 1 + 0$			$= 0$	and carry 1
$0 + 0 + 1$			$= 1$	
$1 + 0 + 1$			$= 0$	and carry 1
$0 + 1 + 1$			$= 0$	and carry 1
$1 + 1 + 1$			$= 1$	and carry 1

Note that the carry digit may be produced by the sum of p and q, q and c, or by p and c. The full adder can be constructed as in Fig. 4.21.

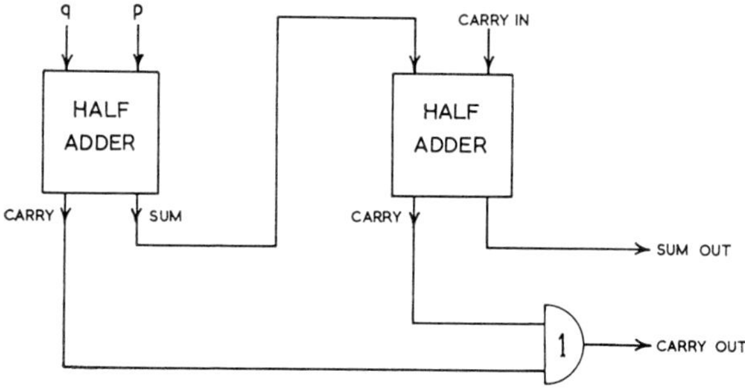

FIG. 4.21. FULL ADDER

The complete logical diagram is shown in Fig. 4.22 (overleaf).

This is not the simplest form of adder, and one using fewer logical elements will be given in the next section.

Standardization of Logic Circuits

It is possible to perform all the arithmetical operations using only one type of logic element. This enables manufacturers to concentrate on the mass production of standard circuits and facilitates servicing and the stocking of spare plug-in circuits.

(1) *NOR* logic.

Fig. 4.23 (page 59) shows the arrangement of **nor** elements to produce **not, or, and,** and **not–and** circuits.

The reader should verify these circuits by applying 0s and 1s to the inputs and constructing the truth tables.

Fig. 4.24 shows a half-adder made from **nor** elements. Again, a truth table should be constructed for all possible values of p and q.

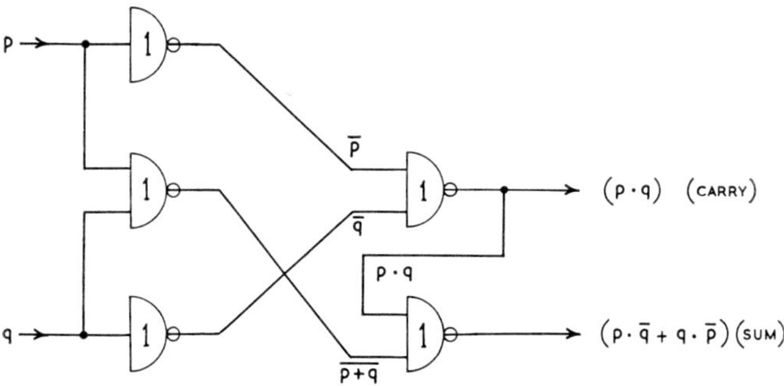

FIG. 4.24. A *NOR* LOGIC HALF-ADDER

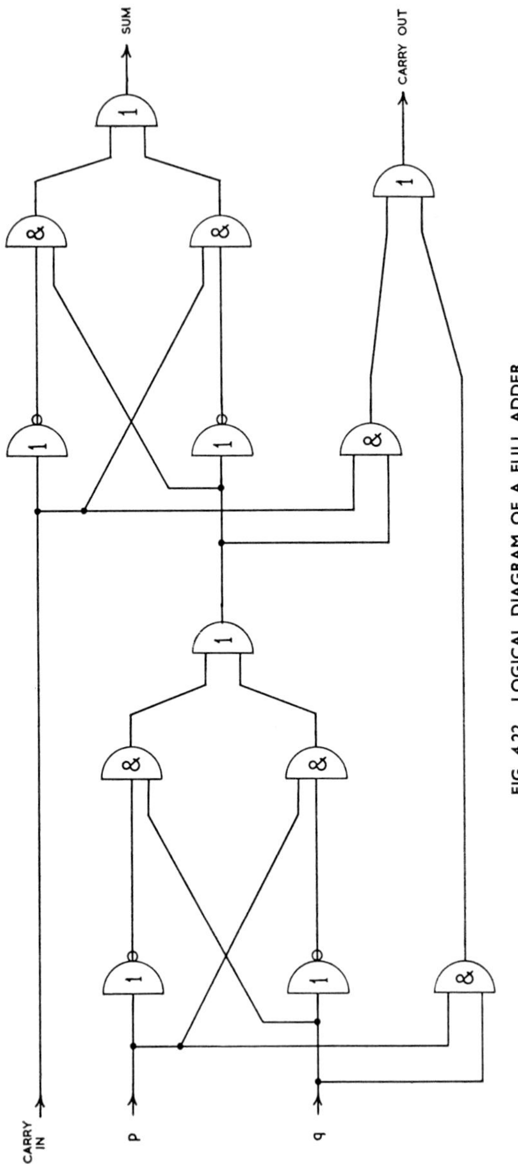

FIG. 4.22. LOGICAL DIAGRAM OF A FULL ADDER

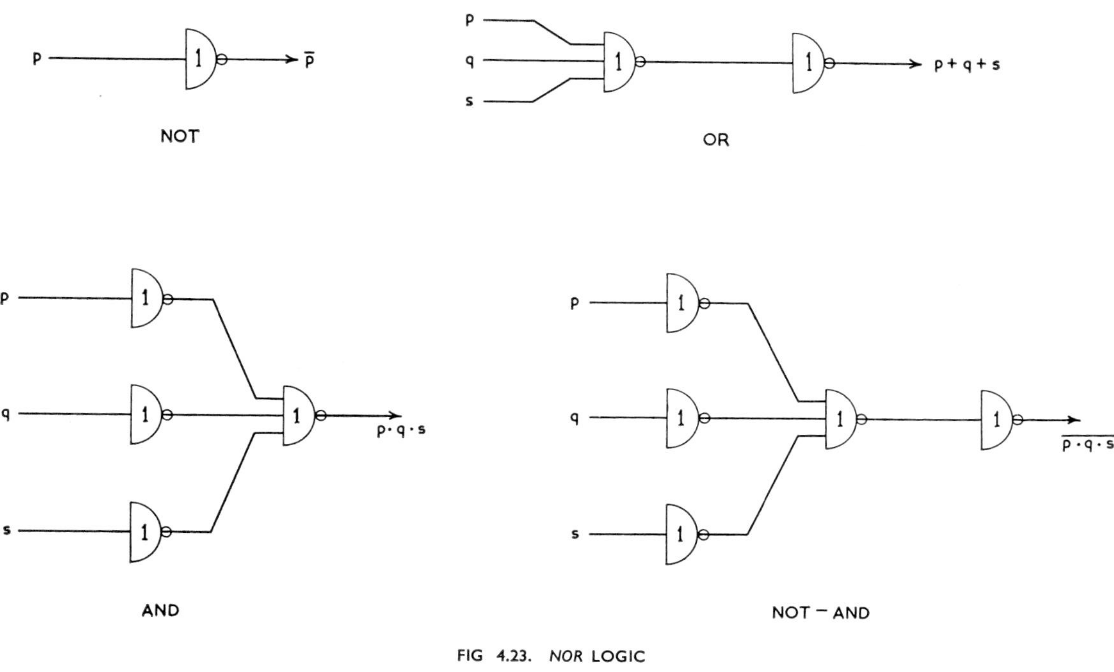

FIG 4.23. *NOR* LOGIC

(2) *NOT–AND* logic.

Fig. 4.25 shows the **not, and, or, nor,** and **half-adder** circuits constructed from **not–and** elements only.

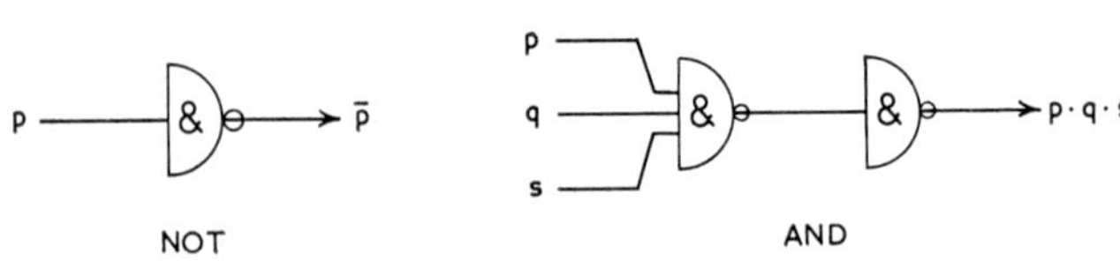

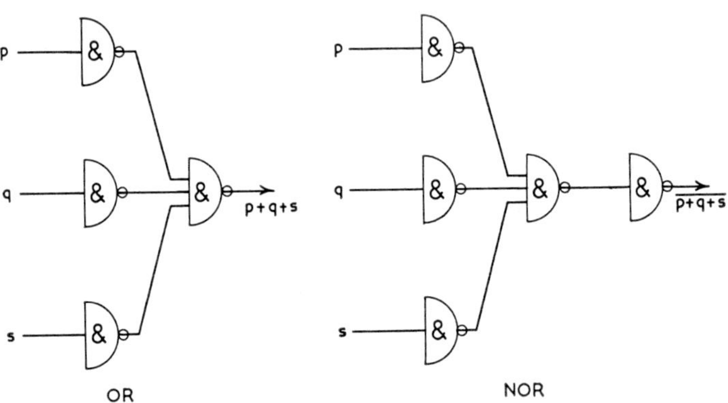

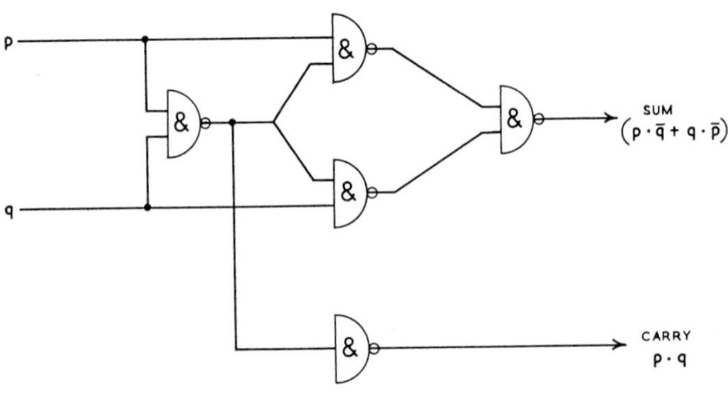

FIG. 4.25. *NOT-AND (NAND)* LOGIC

Problem 5. Check that the circuits in Fig. 4.25 perform their correct functions.

The factors influencing the choice between **nor** and **not–and** logic will be discussed in Chapter 5.

Examples (Chapter 4)

Simplify the circuits in Nos. 1 to 4.

(1)

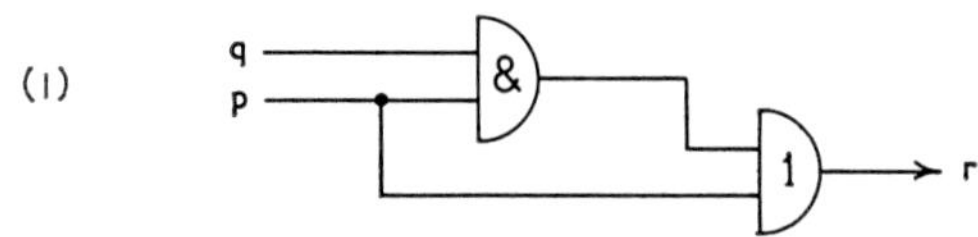

(2)

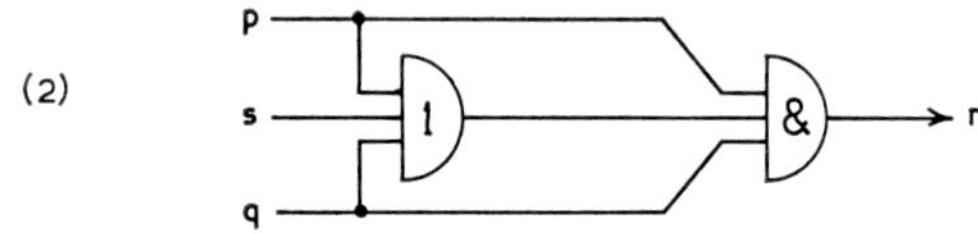

(3)

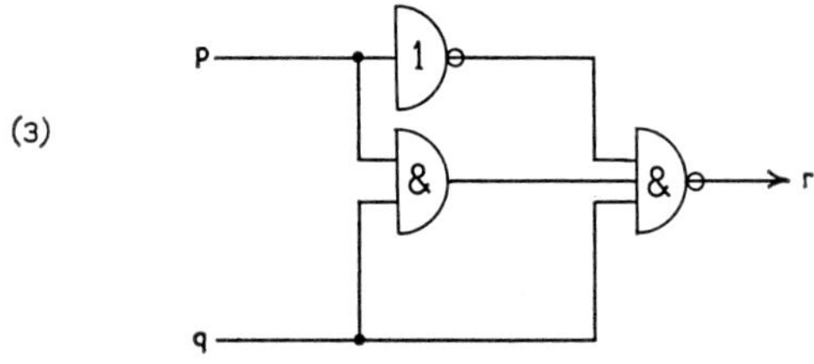

(4)

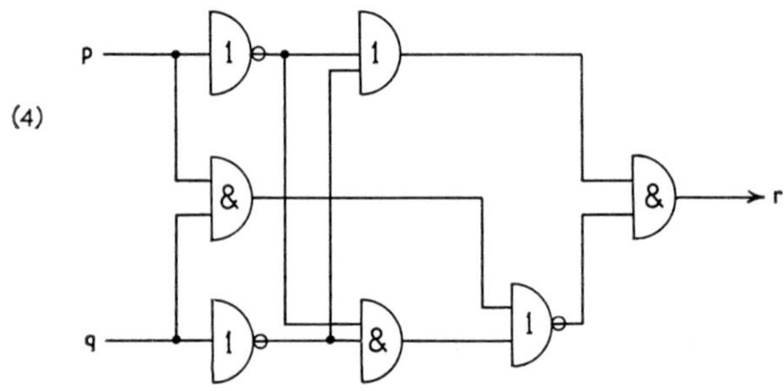

Simplify the following Boolean expressions and draw the logic circuits for the results:

(5) $r = (p + q).(\bar{p} + q).(\bar{p} + \bar{q})$

(6) $r = (\bar{p} + \bar{q}).\bar{p}.(p + p.q)$

(7) $r = (p + q).(p + s) + (q.s)$

(8) $r = (A + B + C).(A + D + E) + (A + B) + B.(B + C)$

(Answers are on page 176)

5

COMPUTER CIRCUITRY

Positive and Negative Logic

The electrical pulses representing the binary information in a computer are usually about 6 to 10 volts in amplitude. Any number (say nine) may be held in the computer in two alternative forms as shown in Fig. 5.1.

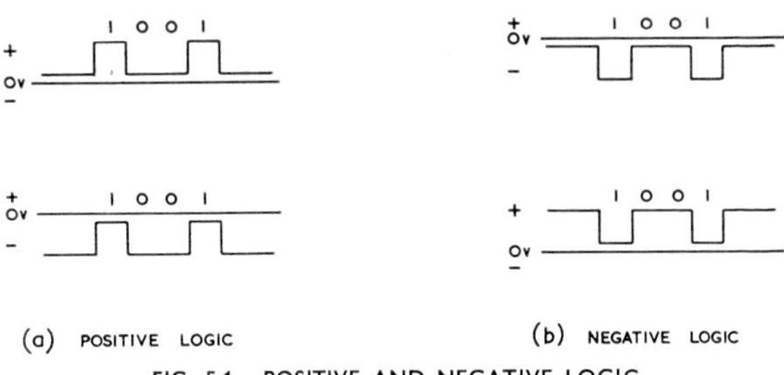

FIG. 5.1. POSITIVE AND NEGATIVE LOGIC

An inspection of Fig. 5.1 shows that if the **more** positive potential represents the 1, the system is said to have **positive logic.** If the **less** positive potential represents the 1, the system is said to have **negative logic.** The behaviour of a given logic circuit is entirely different for positive and negative logic.

For example, a circuit which behaves as an **and** circuit with positive logic will produce an output 1 when all the inputs are 1, *i.e.* all inputs positive produce a positive output. Using negative logic, this same circuit condition represents all the inputs at 0 producing an output of 0. If one input is 1 the output goes negative, representing 1, this behaving as an **or** circuit.

Similarly, a positive logic **or** circuit behaves as an **and** circuit when used with negative logic. The relationship between the logic functions in the two systems is found by interchanging the 0s and 1s in the truth table.

Problem 1. Show that a positive logic **not–and** circuit is a negative logic **nor** circuit.

The Transistor as a Switch

Many computer circuits incorporate transistors acting as high-speed switches. These circuits are used to perform the logical operations, in registers, and to generate the pulses necessary for controlling and timing the computer. We may consider the transistor as a three-terminal switch, a p-n-p type operating from a negative voltage supply, and an n-p-n type operating from a positive voltage supply.

Fig. 5.2(a) shows an n-p-n transistor with the emitter, e, connected to the 'common' terminal and the collector, c, connected to a positive supply *via* a load resistor R_L. If the transistor base terminal, b, is given a small

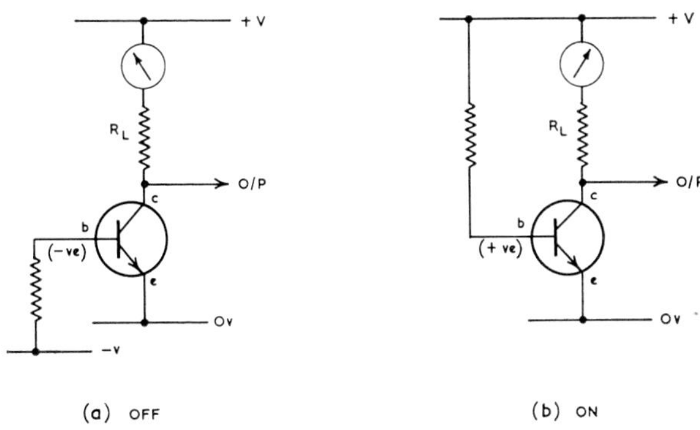

FIG. 5.2. THE TRANSISTOR AS A SWITCH

negative potential only a small 'leakage' current flows in the emitter-collector circuit and the transistor is said to be switched OFF.

When the base potential is made positive, as in Fig. 5.2(b), the transistor conducts and a current flows in the emitter-collector circuit. The transistor is then switched ON. As the collector voltage changes from $+V$ when the transistor is off to approximately zero when the transistor is on, the collector voltage is used as an output indicating the state of the circuit.

The polarities of all voltages are reversed if p-n-p transistors are used.

Registers

Reference has been made to a **register** which temporarily holds a string of 0s and 1s representing a number or instruction. Each digit is held by a **bistable circuit** which may be switched into one of two stable conditions, one representing 0, the other 1. A bistable circuit consists of two transistor switches connected so that the output of one goes to the input of the other (Fig. 5.3).

On switching on, one transistor will turn on before the other as the components cannot be exactly matched. If TR_1, Fig. 5.3, conducts first the point A will be reduced to a low voltage thereby allowing the negative

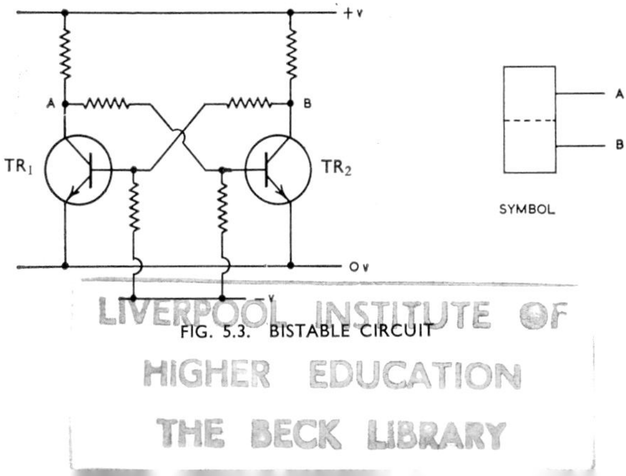

FIG. 5.3. BISTABLE CIRCUIT

supply to hold TR_2 in the OFF condition. This leaves B at +V volts which is applied to the base of TR_1 holding it in the ON state. Hence TR_1 ON, TR_2 OFF, is a stable state. Let this represent the digit 0.

Similarly, if TR_2 is ON and TR_1 OFF, this state is also stable and will represent 1. If the output is taken from point B a voltage here represents 0, and no voltage represents 1. Note that it is impossible for both transistors to be in the same state at the same time.

Provision must now be made to 'write' a digit into the circuit, and to 'reset' or 'clear' it.

Fig. 5.4 shows the **set** and **reset** connections required. If a negative pulse is applied to the set terminal, TR_1 is turned OFF, TR_2 is consequently

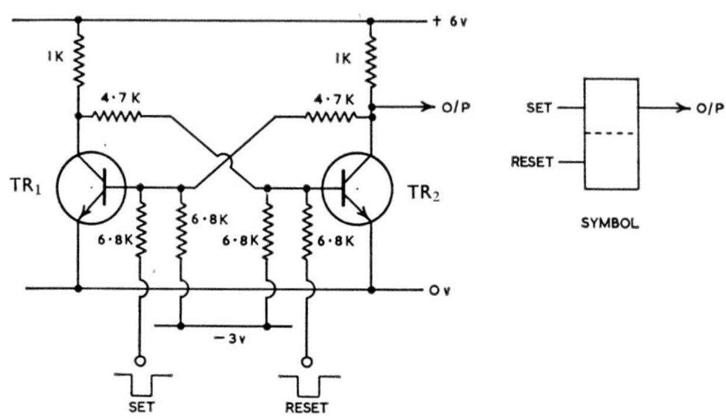

FIG. 5.4. COMPLETE BISTABLE CIRCUIT (NEGATIVE LOGIC)

turned ON and the circuit holds a 1 digit. Fig. 5.5 shows how a row of bistable circuits is arranged to form a complete binary register. To clear a number held in a register, a negative pulse is applied to the **reset** terminal of each bistable circuit, turning the TR_2 transistors OFF and leaving a 0 digit in each position.

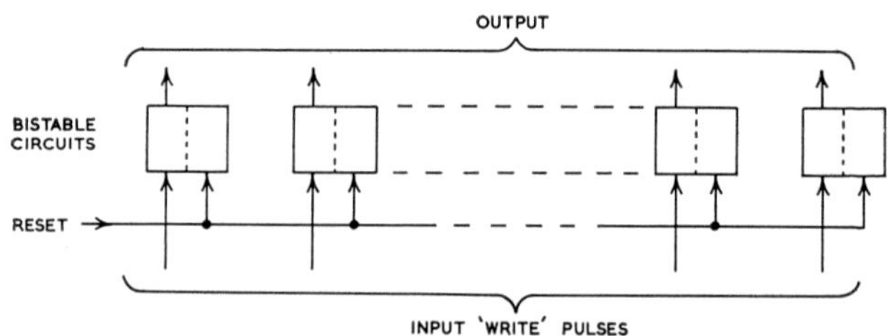

FIG. 5.5. BLOCK DIAGRAM OF A BINARY REGISTER

Serial and Parallel Modes

A number may be processed in a computer in either **serial** or **parallel** mode. In the **serial** form a word is a sequence of pulses which occur one after the other in time, rather like the dots and dashes of a morse code transmission [Fig. 5.6(a)]. The least significant digit arrives first. This is

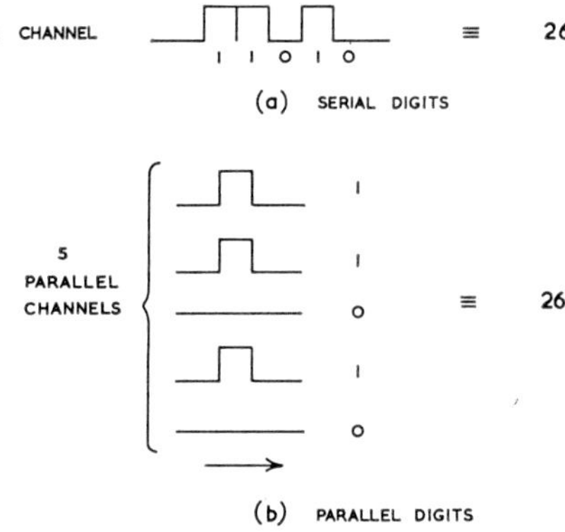

FIG. 5.6. SERIAL AND PARALLEL DIGITS

the simplest system but slow compared with parallel representation as each digit is processed separately.

In the **parallel** form the pulses that form a word occur simultaneously along separate channels, Fig. 5.6(b). In this case the arithmetic is much quicker (approximately n times quicker for an n-bit word) but requires n times as many circuits to deal with the number.

Shift Registers

Whilst the arrangement in Fig. 5.5 is suitable for accepting parallel binary numbers, serial numbers must be fed into a register one digit at a time. The pulses are applied to one end of a register, each digit shifting along until the transfer of data is complete.

The bistable circuits that make up the register are so connected that their outputs are coupled to the inputs of the adjacent right-hand circuits whenever a **shift pulse** is applied. The input pulses are fed into the left-hand bistable circuit and all digits transferred one place to the right for every shift pulse. The contents of the extreme right-hand bistable circuit are lost, or fed as an output to some other part of the computer. It is possible to feed the digits back into the left-hand end of the same register and re-circulate the number.

Fig. 5.7 shows a 4-bit word being transferred into a register by 4 shift pulses. Notice that a shift pulse must be present for **each** digit being transferred, whether it is a 0 or 1.

Problem 2. You are provided with a 32-bit shift register which transfers a digit any number of places to the right. How would you transfer a digit in the right-hand half of the register

(a) one place to the left;

(b) 10 places to the left?

(Answer is on page 176)

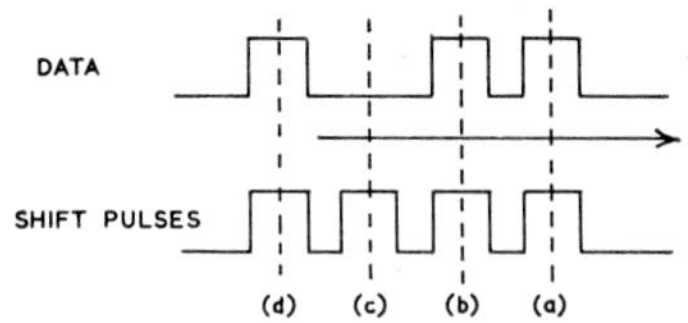

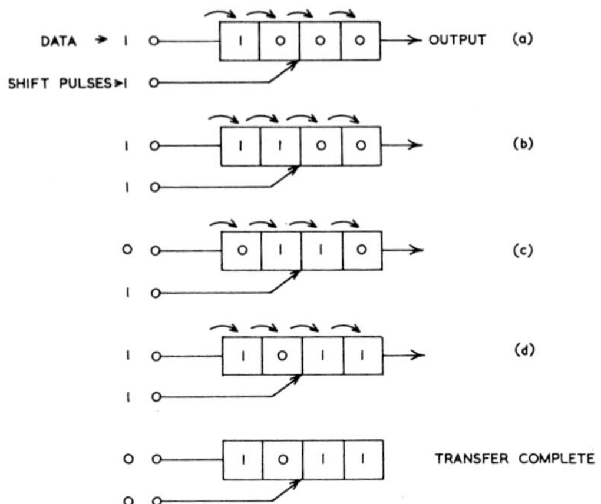

FIG. 5.7. 4-BIT SHIFT REGISTER

Monostable and Multivibrator Circuits

Two variations in the circuit of Fig. 5.3 are often used in a computer. The **monostable** circuit, as its name implies, has only one stable state. A capacitor is connected between the collector of one transistor, say TR_2, and the base of the other, TR_1, as in Fig. 5.8.

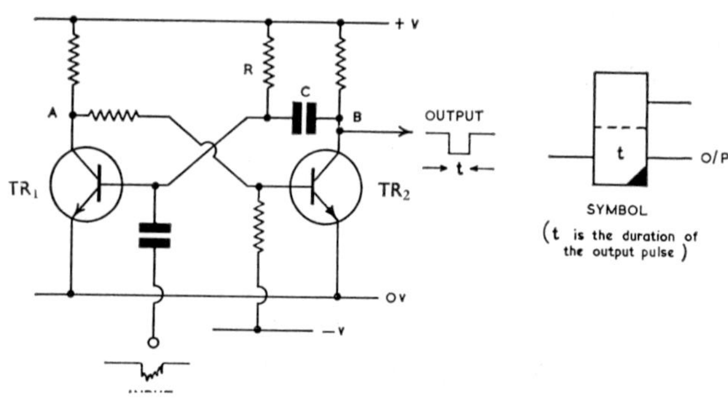

FIG. 5.8. MONOSTABLE CIRCUIT

The base of TR_1 is now taken to the positive supply *via* resistor R, ensuring that TR_1 is ON and hence that TR_2 is OFF. A negative input pulse applied to the base of TR_1 turns it OFF, and TR_2 ON. This condition is not stable however, as the low potential at B is not maintained at the base of TR_1. C is slowly charged through R and the base potential of TR_1 goes steadily more positive until TR_1 turns ON, hence TR_2 turns OFF again. Because of this action the circuit is known as a 'flip-flop'.

Its use is to provide a good square pulse of given duration from an input pulse which may be ragged or of variable duration. The output pulse duration, or 'width', is approximately 0·7 RC seconds.

The second variation to this circuit converts it into a square wave generator or **multivibrator,** Fig. 5.9. Both states are now unstable and the transistors turn on and off alternately. The action is continuous and

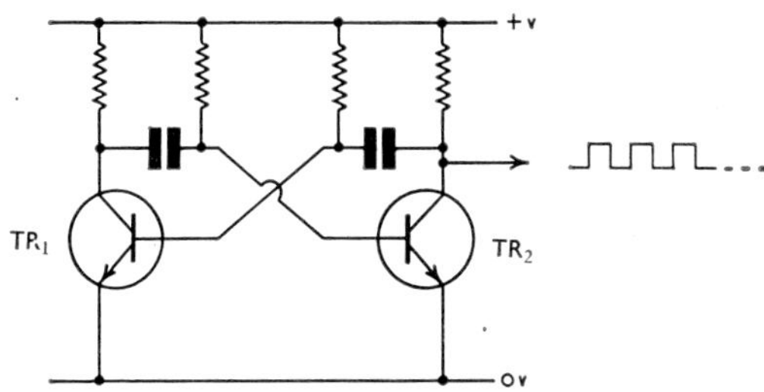

FIG. 5.9. MULTIVIBRATOR CIRCUIT (ASTABLE CIRCUIT)

no input is required to start the operation, but pulses may be applied to the base of a transistor to synchronize the output to the frequency of the computer. The multivibrator is used to generate timing pulses, shift pulses, etc.

Block Representation of Bistable Circuits

As the bistable and flip-flop circuits are extensively used in computers and industrial logic equipment it is convenient to represent them in block form. In many cases the circuits are built from logic elements rather than from the basic components shown in Fig. 5.4. Several forms of the circuit exist, the most common being described below.

(1) The S-R flip-flop, Fig. 5.10, is operated by applying **set** and **reset** pulses and is in fact the circuit previously described in Fig. 5.4. We now

FIG. 5.10. S-R FLIP-FLOP

consider it from a different viewpoint. Examination of Fig. 5.4 will show that the circuit is in fact two **nor** circuits connected together, the input of one connected to the output of the other.

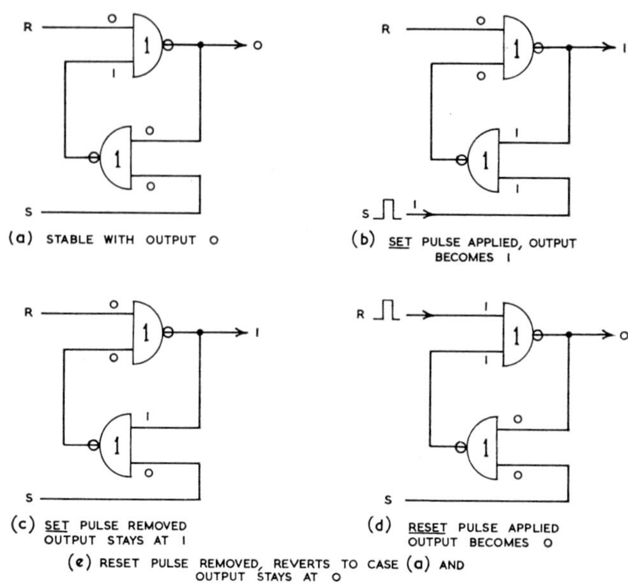

5.11. OPERATION OF THE S-R FLIP-FLOP IN *NOR* LOGIC

The complete circuit is shown in Fig. 5.11 in the different states during its operation.

The input S is a **set** pulse which sets the output to 1. If the output is already 1, S does nothing.

The input R is a **reset** pulse which sets the output to 0. If the output is already 0, R does nothing.

The reader should check that the **nor** elements in Fig. 5.11 fulfil these conditions, remembering that a **nor** element has an output 0 when one or more of the inputs is 1. The signal levels representing 0s and 1s are shown on the diagrams.

(2) The T flip-flop, so-called because of its trigger action, has one input as shown in Fig. 5.12. The state of the circuit is changed each time an input pulse is applied.

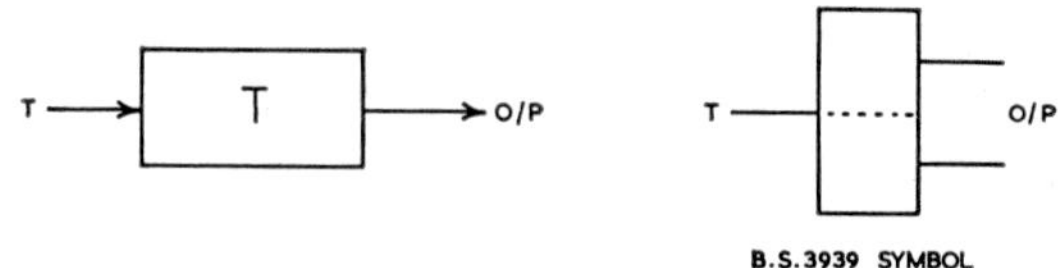

FIG. 5.12. T FLIP-FLOP

Fig. 5.13 shows a possible circuit using an S-R flip-flop. The input pulse is 'steered' to either the set or reset input depending upon the polarity of the charge on the capacitors. One capacitor voltage is in

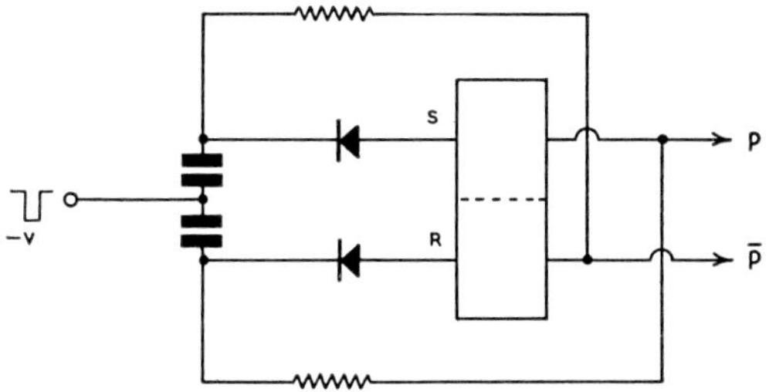

FIG. 5.13. T FLIP-FLOP MADE FROM AN S-R CIRCUIT (NEGATIVE LOGIC)

opposition to the trigger pulse and blocks it, the other is in series-aiding and allows the pulse to pass to the S-R circuit. The polarity is determined by the previous state of the S-R flip-flop. The T flip-flop is the basis of many counting circuits.

(3) The J-K flip-flop (Fig. 5.14).

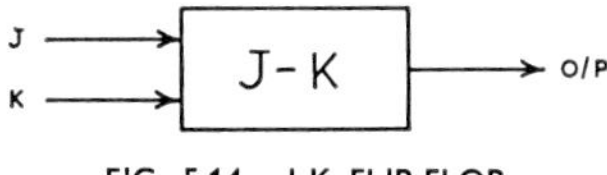

FIG. 5.14. J-K FLIP-FLOP

One of the disadvantages of the S-R circuit is that its behaviour is uncertain if **both** set and reset inputs are energized. The J-K flip-flop overcomes this difficulty by changing the state of the output whenever this occurs. Hence, we may convert the J-K flip-flop into a T flip-flop by simply connecting the inputs together and feeding them with the trigger pulse. In all other respects the J-K circuit behaves as an S-R circuit, J being the set input and K the reset input.

Gates

In many parts of the computer we require to switch the various lines of communication on and off by applying a control pulse. This was done by relays in the early electromechanical calculators but for the speed and reliability required in modern machines these are out of the question. The switching is now performed electrically by **gates.** An **and** element, Fig. 5.15, will act as a simple gate.

If a control pulse is present the **in** pulse completes the requirements

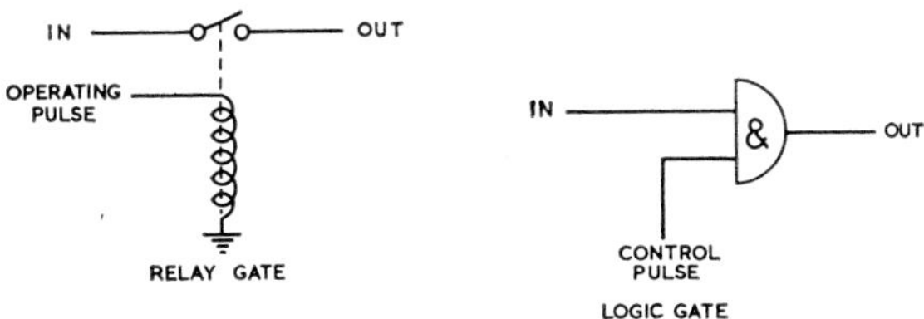

FIG. 5.15. THE *AND* GATE

for an output pulse to appear. The gate is **open.** Without the control pulse no output can occur and the gate is **closed.**

Masks

A mask is used to select certain digits from a word. It may happen that a word contains several small items of information, such as

Name
Account No.
Type of Account
District
Branch No.
Amount.

To find the total of all transactions handled by a particular branch the computer must extract the branch number and amount. The mask is a word containing 1s in the digit positions corresponding to the required data, and zeros in all other positions. The mask and the data word are compared digit for digit, and fed into an **and** gate. Only the data corresponding to the 1s in the mask are produced as an output.

Fig. 5.16 shows the diagrammatic arrangements for serial and parallel masking operations for an 8-bit word, the 3rd to 6th digits inclusive being extracted from the word.

Diode Logic Circuits

Circuits performing the logical operations may be constructed using diode rectifiers or transistors. The circuits are then classified as **diode logic** and **transistor logic.** Fig. 5.17 shows a diode logic circuit for the **or** function with positive logic.

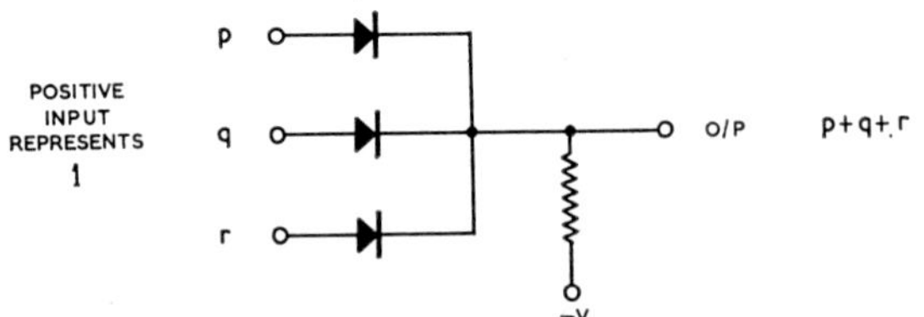

FIG. 5.17. DIODE *OR* LOGIC CIRCUIT (POSITIVE LOGIC)

With the inputs at zero volts the diodes all conduct and the output is consequently zero. If *p* **or** *q* **or** *r* is positive, representing 1, the output is positive, 1, the diodes preventing feedback to the zero inputs. Hence the circuit behaves as an **or** element.

Consider the operation with negative logic. If the inputs represent 0s they are all at a positive potential and the output is positive, representing 0. All inputs must be at zero volts (*i.e.* all 1s) before the output falls to zero, representing 1. Hence the circuit behaves as an **and** element.

The converse of this is the circuit of Fig. 5.18 in which all inputs zero ensures that all diodes conduct and the output is zero. All inputs must be

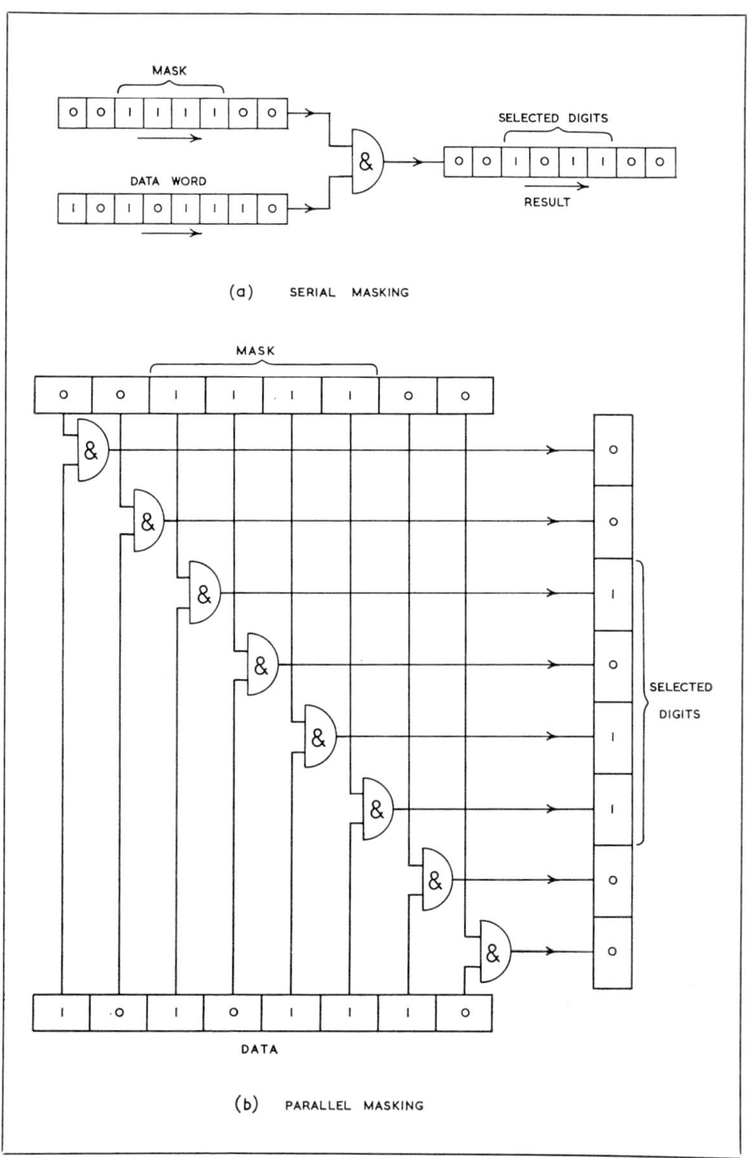

FIG. 5.16. SELECTING DIGITS BY A MASK

positive before the output will go positive, and the circuit is an **and** element in positive logic.

Problem 3. Show that the circuit of Fig. 5.18 is an **or** circuit when used with negative logic.

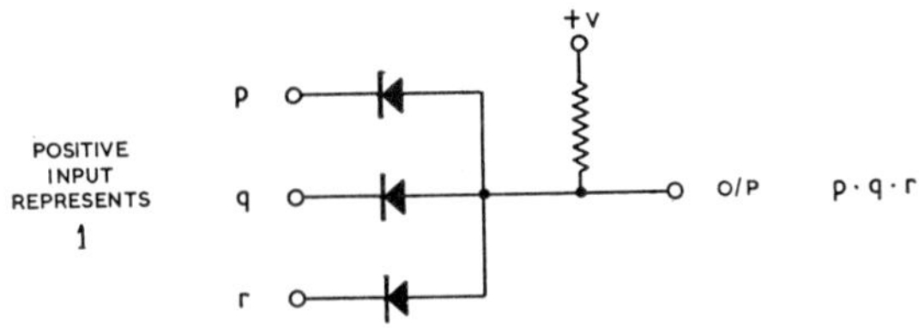

FIG. 5.18. DIODE *AND* LOGIC CIRCUIT (POSITIVE LOGIC)

Transistor Logic Circuits

The simplest transistor logic circuit is the **not** element of Fig. 5.19. Note that an n-p-n transistor is being used in this case, although a p-n-p type could be used with a reversal of the supply polarities.

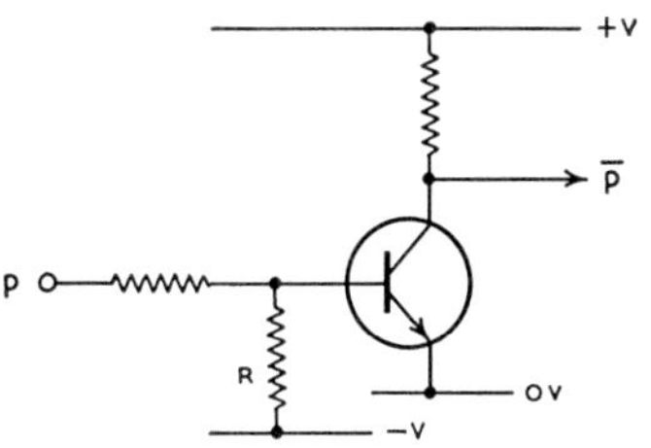

FIG. 5.19. TRANSISTOR *NOT* CIRCUIT (POSITIVE LOGIC)

Using positive logic, if p is at zero volts representing 0, the transistor is held OFF by the negative base supply and the output is positive representing 1. Let R be adjusted so that a positive input will turn the transistor ON, making the output zero representing 0. The circuit then performs as a **not** element, or a pulse inverter changing 0 to 1 and 1 to 0. The action is typical of a single transistor which may be invariably considered as an inverting or **negating** device giving an output $\bar{p}$ for an input p. Several inputs may be applied, as in Fig. 5.20.

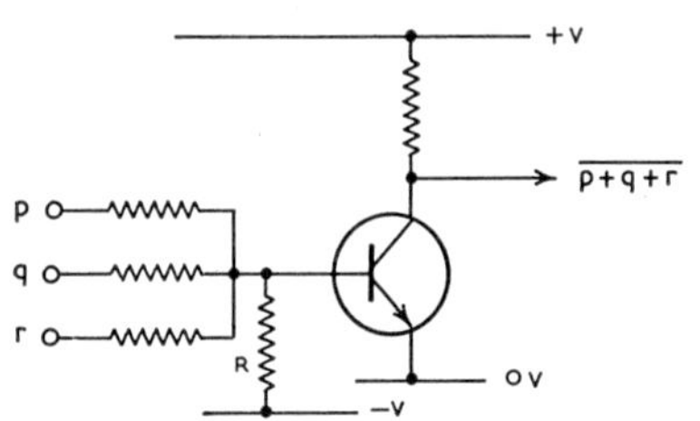

FIG. 5.20. TRANSISTOR *NOR* CIRCUIT (POSITIVE LOGIC)

The output is zero, representing 0, when the transistor is ON, *i.e.* when one or more inputs are present. The only condition that allows the transistor to turn OFF and give an output 1 is when no inputs are present. Hence the circuit may be used as a **nor** element, giving an output 1 when neither p **nor** q **nor** r are present.

Problem 4. Show that the circuit of Fig. 5.20 is a **not–and** circuit when used with negative logic.

If the value of R is adjusted so that more than one input is required to turn on the transistor, the circuit can be made to perform other logical operations. For example, assume in Fig. 5.20 that the value of R is reduced so that all the inputs must be positive before the transistor turns on. The output is then 1 unless p **and** q **and** r **are all** 1s. The circuit is a **not–and** element giving an output $\overline{p.q.r}$.

Problem 5. What is the behaviour of the circuit in these circumstances, using negative logic?

(Answer is on page 176)

Diode–Transistor Logic

The diode logic circuits of Figs. 5.17 and 5.18 are limited to performing the **and** and **or** functions. If, however, the outputs from these circuits are 'inverted' by a **not** element, the results are **not–and** and **nor** functions respectively.

Fig. 5.21 shows the symbolic and actual circuits for these functions, a simple transistor **not** circuit being used to invert the outputs from the diode logic. In Fig. 5.21(a) an additional negative supply is taken to the base of the transistor to ensure that it fully turns OFF when p, q and r are at zero voltage. This supply also decreases the turn-off time of the transistor.

One advantage of the diode-transistor logic over the resistor-transistor logic of Fig. 5.20 is that in the former the inputs are completely isolated from one another by the diodes, whereas in the latter the inputs are interconnected by the input resistors, and it is possible for one input signal to be fed back along another input line.

Encoders and Decoders

To 'encode' means to apply a code to numbers, instructions or other data. To convert from decimal to binary is to 'encode' the decimal data. One method of converting information from decimal to binary is by means of the diode matrix encoder shown in Fig. 5.22.

The matrix consists of two sets of parallel wires with diode interconnections. When a positive pulse is applied to one of the decimal inputs the appropriate lines are energized through the diodes which are connected so that the binary combination appears at the output. The diodes are necessary to prevent feedback from one binary line to another. Note that this circuit is **not** reversible: a binary input will not give a decimal output.

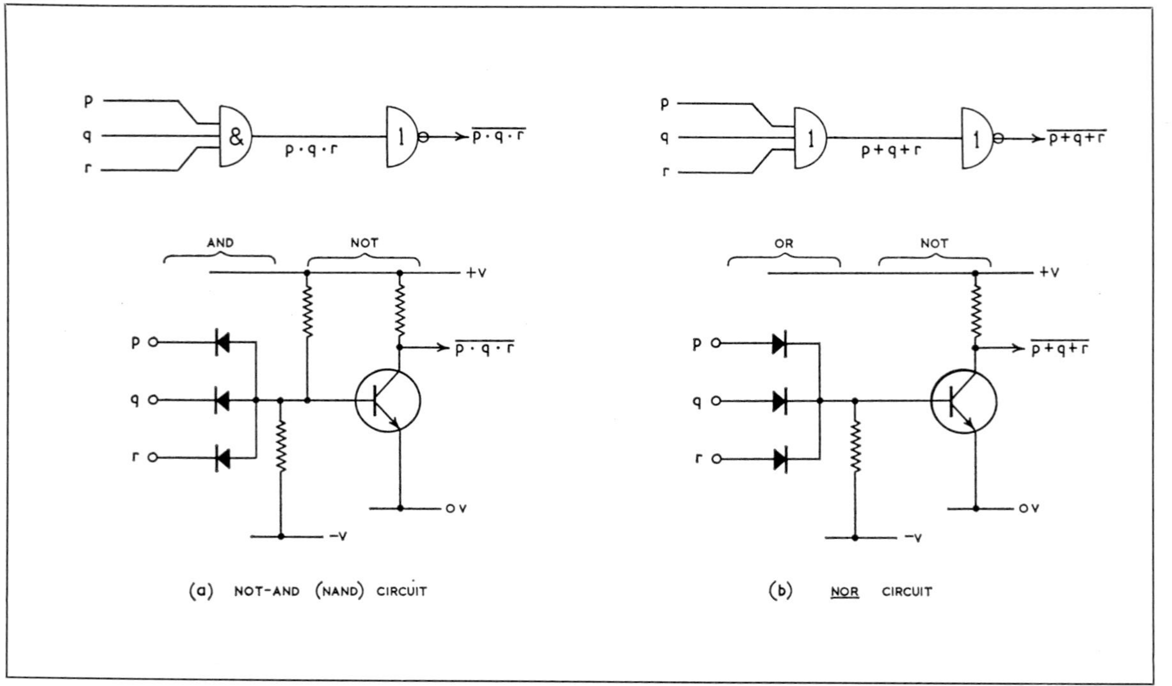

FIG. 5.21. DIODE-TRANSISTOR LOGIC CIRCUITS (POSITIVE LOGIC)

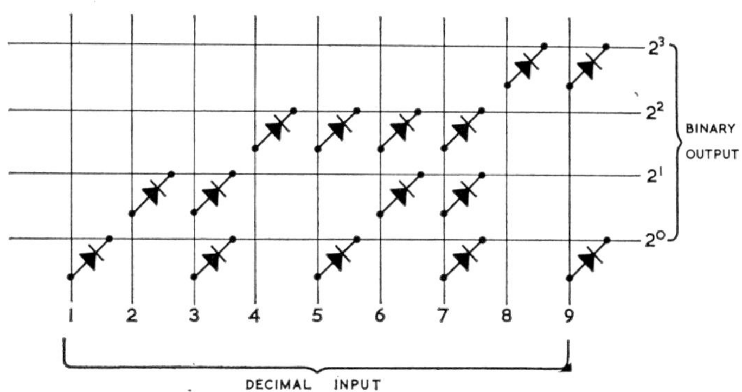

FIG. 5.22. DIODE MATRIX DECIMAL-BINARY ENCODER

Problem 6. Draw the circuit of a diode matrix to convert the decimal numbers 10, 20, 30, 40, 50, 60, 70, 80, 90, to binary.

(Answer is on page 176)

To 'decode' means to reverse the process of encoding, *e.g.* to convert the binary information back into decimal form. A parallel binary-to-decimal decoder is shown in Fig. 5.23 (overleaf). The binary input is made available in its normal and inverted form, and thc combination of 0s and 1s corresponding to a decimal number is fed into an **and** circuit to produce a decimal output.

In many computers the encoding and decoding is done by programming and not by the circuits shown here. This enables numbers in serial form to be converted using the arithmetic circuits of the computer (see Chapter 7).

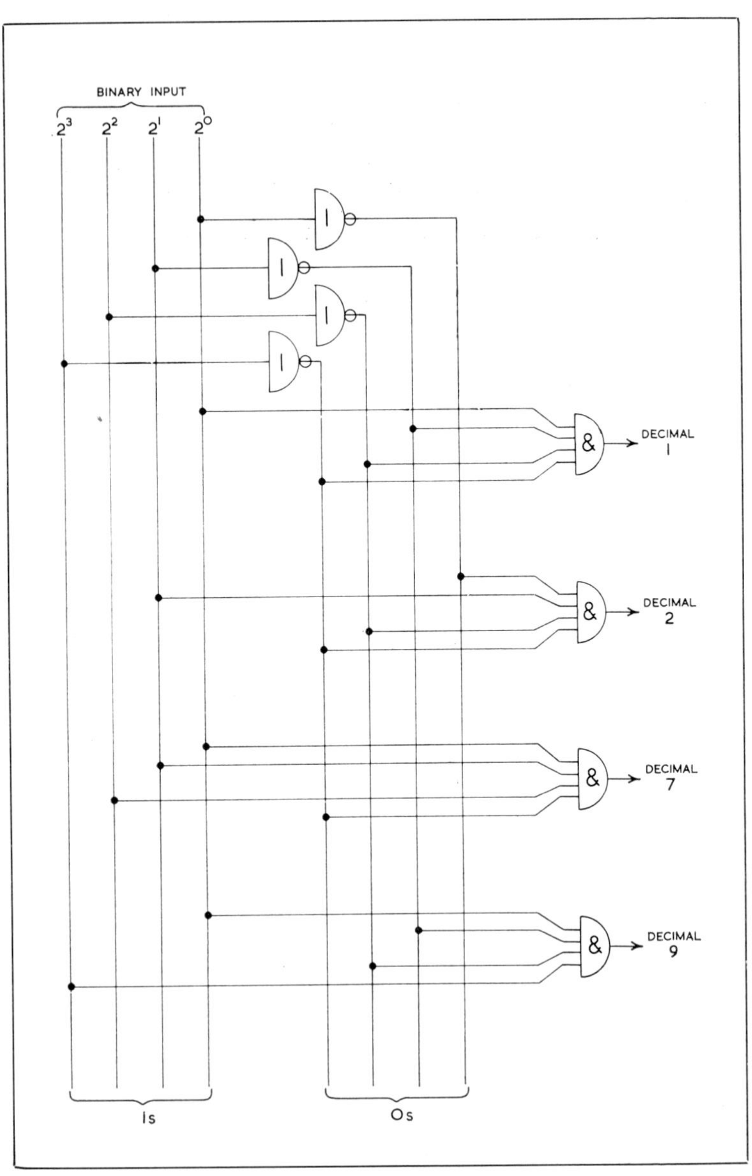

FIG. 5.23. BINARY-TO-DECIMAL DECODER

6

THE COMPUTER STORE

MANY techniques have been tried in attempting to store a quantity of information in a computer. The majority of stores are now based on the principle of magnetic recording, using ferrite cores, drums or tape. The number of words stored, or **capacity,** and the speed with which the information may be written into or read out of the store, called the **access time,** are equally important. We may classify storage systems according to either of these properties.

IMMEDIATE ACCESS STORES (I.A.S.). These are fast stores in which the access times, although not immediate, are measured in microseconds. The capacity of such a store may be several thousand words.

QUICK ACCESS STORES. In which the access times are measured in milliseconds, *e.g.* a rotating magnetic drum or disc holding 4,000 to 100,000 words.

SLOW ACCESS STORES. The access times here may be seconds or even minutes. They are usually of very high capacity (millions of words), and are used as backing stores to support and feed information into the faster stores prior to processing. In this category are magnetic tapes, paper tapes and punched cards.

The registers described in Chapter 5 may be considered as immediate access stores of one word capacity. To build a computer using only registers would be prohibitive both in cost and size with present-day techniques.

The Magnetic Core Store

In this store each binary digit is stored by magnetizing a small ferrite bead or **core.** When the core is magnetized with one polarity it represents 0, and if the magnetization is reversed it represents 1. An unmagnetized core is not used to represent a digit and is in an indeterminate state.

The ferrite cores are very small (Fig. 6.1) and are magnetized by passing current through wires on to which they are threaded. Plated wire

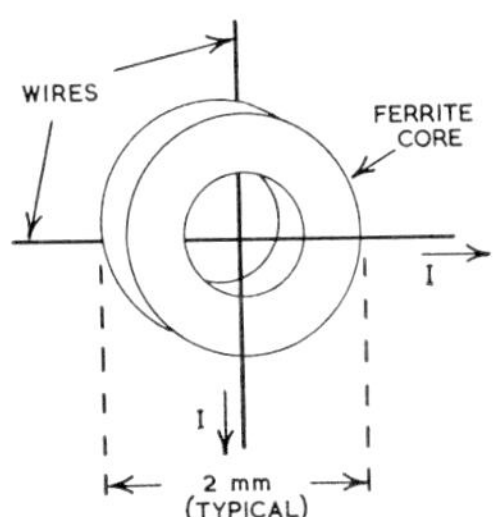

FIG. 6.1. A FERRITE CORE

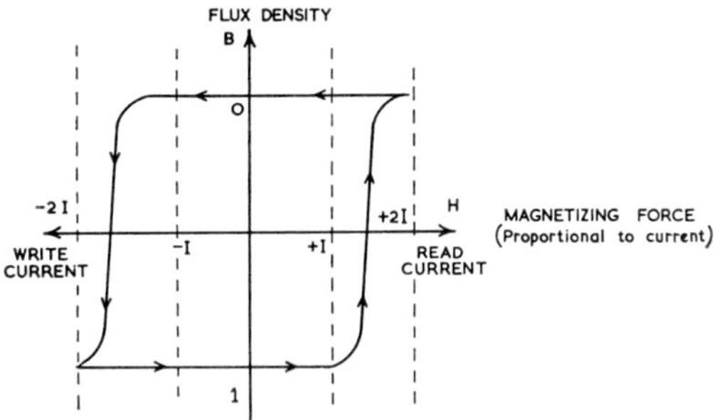

FIG. 6.2. FERRITE MAGNETIC CHARACTERISTICS (*B-H* LOOP)

is at present being developed to replace the threaded cores, a continuous length of wire acting as a row of cores.

The magnetic properties of the ferrite material used are illustrated in Fig. 6.2 in which the variation in magnetic flux density with wire current is shown. This *B-H* curve shows the characteristic 'square loop' required for successful store operation. The direction of the wire current determines whether reading from the core or writing into the core takes place.

With no current in the magnetizing wires a core remains magnetized at either the point marked 0 or the point marked 1. If the wire current is limited to $\pm I$ amperes it can be seen that no change in flux density is possible. It requires a current of $2I$ amperes to change the state of magnetization from 0 to 1, or 1 to 0.

This property is made use of in **addressing** the store, or selecting the required digit. The cores are assembled in the form of a **matrix** as in Fig. 6.3, two wires passing through each core. A typical matrix has 64 wires in each direction and can therefore store 4,096 digits, one on each core at the intersections of the wires.

To read the digit held in a particular location, a **read** current pulse of I amperes is passed simultaneously through the two wires which intersect at the required core. For example, Fig. 6.3 shows core B being selected by passing current through wires x_2 and y_1, the effective current through

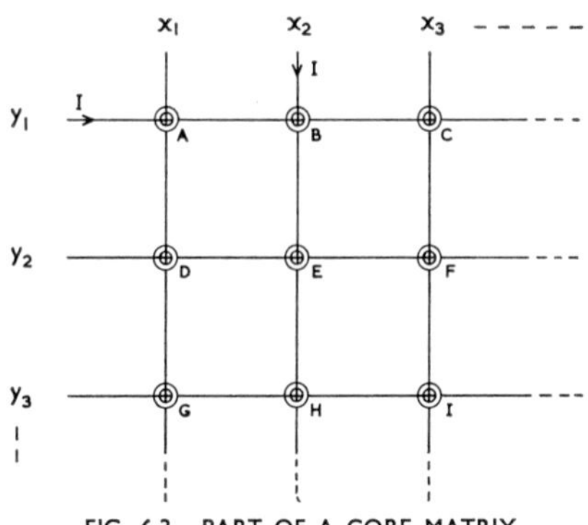

FIG. 6.3. PART OF A CORE MATRIX

the core being $2I$ amperes. Although cores A, C, E and H have a current I passing through one of their wires they remain unaffected; Fig. 6.2 shows that this is insufficient to change their magnetic state.

As core B is linked by both current-carrying wires it may have its magnetization reversed or remain unaffected depending upon its initial state. If the core contains a 0, the read pulse does not change the state of the core (Fig. 6.4) and no change in magnetic flux occurs.

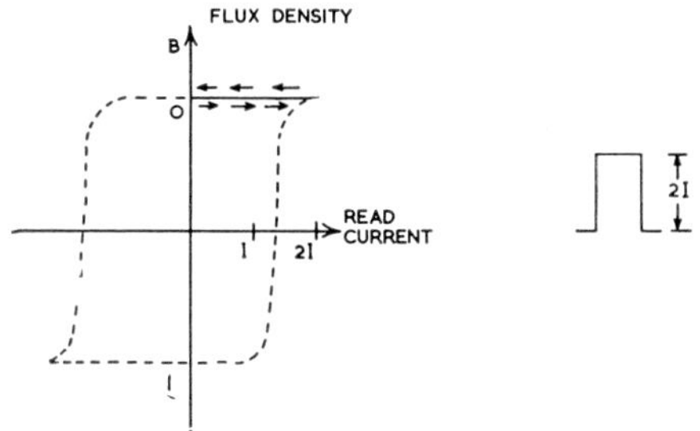

FIG. 6.4. NO FLUX CHANGE IF CORE IS AT 0

If the core contains a 1, the read pulse changes the core from 1 to 0 (Fig. 6.5).

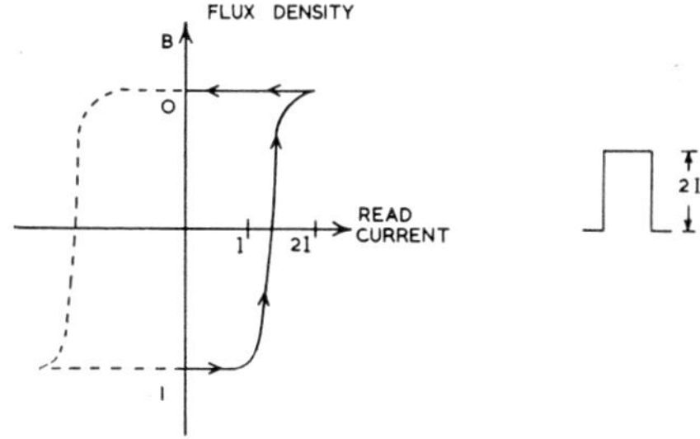

FIG. 6.5. FLUX CHANGE IF THE CORE IS AT 1

This change in flux is used to induce a voltage in a **read wire** which is threaded through all the cores in the matrix (Fig. 6.6). This induced

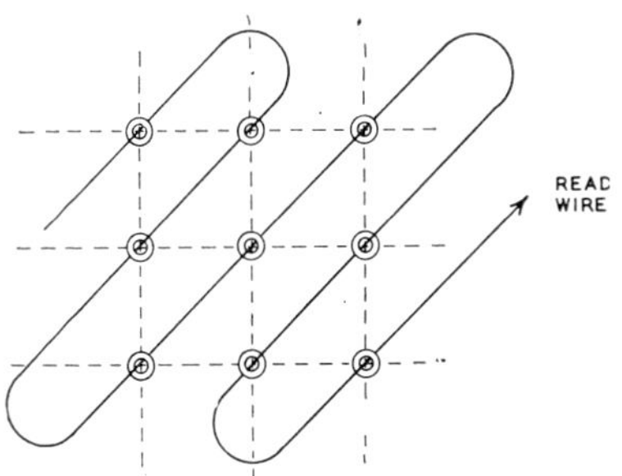

FIG. 6.6. THE READ WIRE

voltage pulse is amplified and forms the output of the store. The read wire detects any change in flux which takes place, but as only one core can change state at any one time there is no ambiguity as to which core is being read. In practice there is a small voltage induced by each core as the magnetic 'loop' is not quite square. This is cancelled to zero by winding the read wire in the reverse direction for half the cores on the matrix.

It will be seen that the 1 held by the core in Fig. 6.5 has been replaced by 0, and the original information is lost. To overcome this the output must be written back into the core. The complete operation is done by applying a **read-write** pulse (Fig. 6.7) which takes the core magnetization right round the *B-H* loop and back to 1 again.

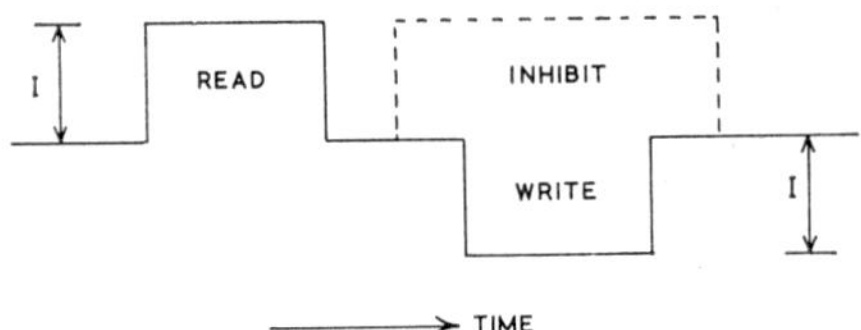

FIG. 6.7. THE READ-WRITE PULSE

The write pulse is only required when the core contains a 1 and must be **inhibited,** or cancelled out, if the core contains a 0. An inhibit pulse, shown dotted in Fig. 6.7, is applied to the cores to reduce the write pulse to an ineffective level. Notice that it overlaps the write pulse in duration to ensure no 'breakthrough' of the write pulse.

An inhibit wire is then added to the matrix, threading all the cores in opposition to the write pulse, Fig. 6.8. As the inhibit current pulse is limited to *I* amperes it has no effect on the unselected cores.

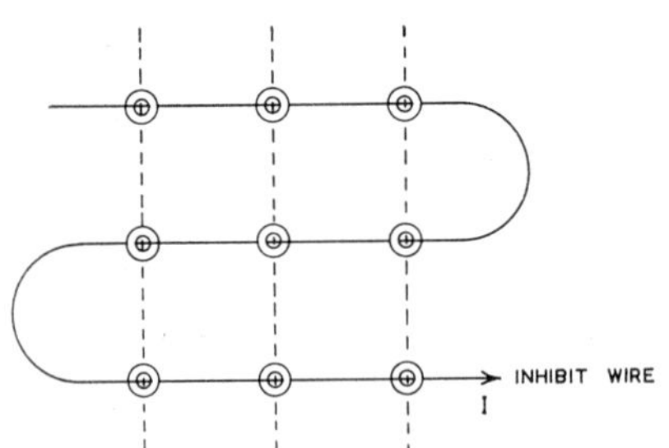

FIG. 6.8. THE INHIBIT WIRE

A photograph of an actual core matrix is shown in Fig. 6.9.

The circuitry associated with the store is shown in Fig. 6.10, only the selected core being included for clarity.

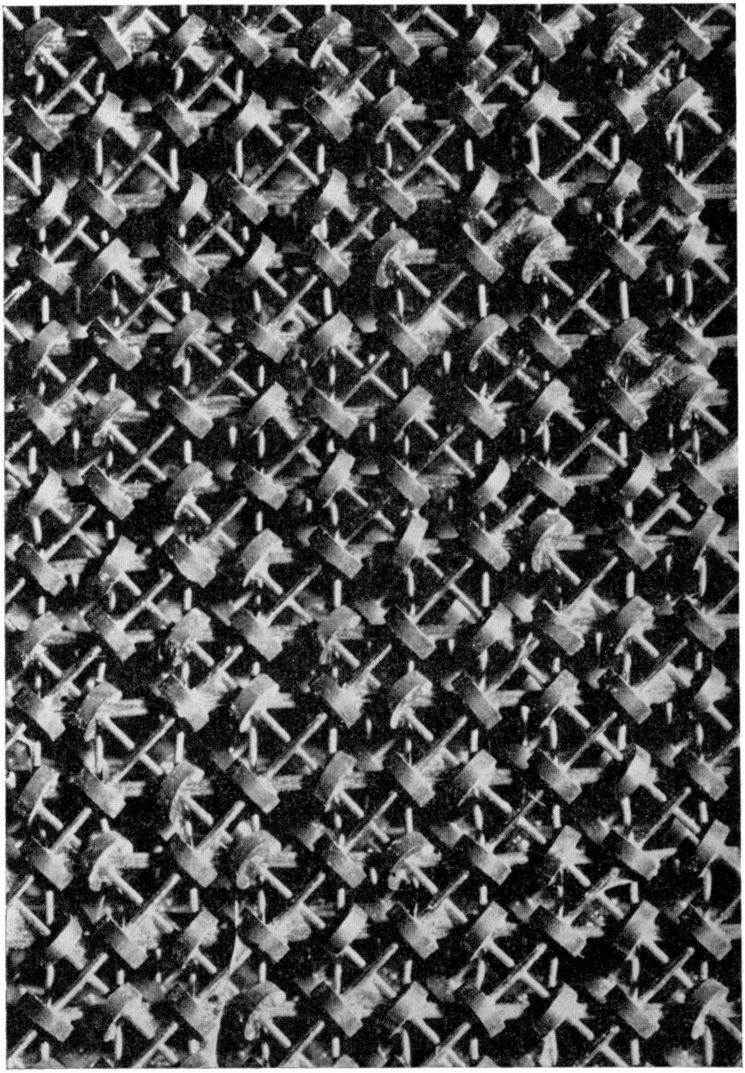

FIG. 6.9. PART OF A CORE MATRIX (ENLARGED)

(I.C.L. London)

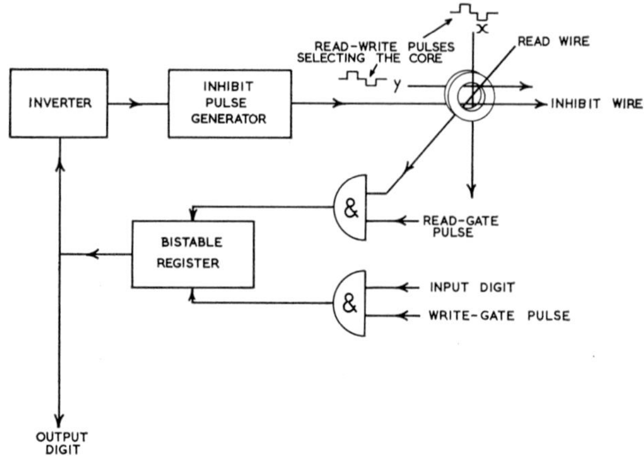

FIG. 6.10. SCHEMATIC DIAGRAM OF CORE STORE CIRCUIT

The complete action of the store is now as follows:

(a) To **Read Out** the contents of a particular address or location.

A read gate pulse is applied, connecting the read wire to the register. The required core is addressed by applying a read-write pulse to the appropriate x and y wires.

If the core contains a 0 no flux change occurs, no voltage is induced in the read wire and 0 is put into the register.

This is the output from the store.

The pulse is inverted to give 1 and applied to the inhibit pulse generator which cancels the **write** pulse and so leaves the 0 in the core.

If the core contains a 1 the flux in the core is reversed and the voltage induced in the read wire puts 1 into the register.

Again this is used as the output.

The core now contains 0. The output is inverted to 0 and no inhibit pulse is generated, allowing the write pulse to remagnetize the core to 1, replacing the original information back into the store.

(b) To **Write** a binary digit into the store.

A write gate pulse is applied, connecting the input to the register. The required core is addressed by applying a read-write pulse to the appropriate x and y wires. The **read** pulse puts a 0 into the core.

If the input digit is 0 it is inverted to 1 and the inhibit pulse cancels the **write** pulse. Hence 0 is left in the core.

If the input is 1 this is inverted to 0 and no inhibit pulse is generated. The **write** pulse then puts a 1 back into the store.

It should be emphasized that this is a simplified description of the operation, aspects such as pulse amplification and synchronization having been omitted.

The complete store consists of an assembly of matrices, the number of such matrices being equal to the number of bits in a word. One matrix is allocated to each digit position in a word. In Fig. 6.11 the matrices are shown assembled side by side with the address wires interconnected.

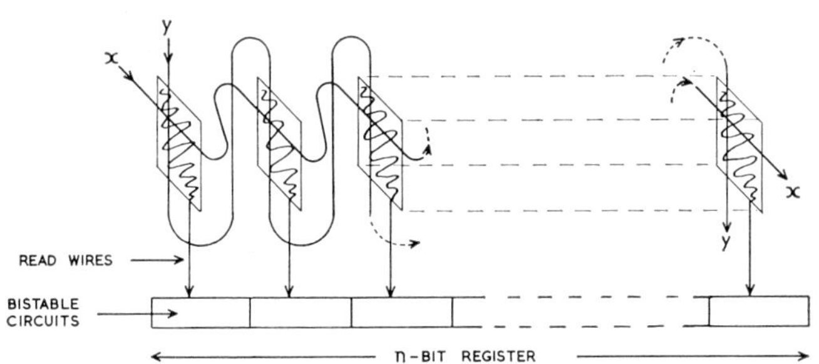

FIG. 6.11. ASSEMBLY OF *n* MATRICES TO FORM AN *n*-BIT WORD LENGTH STORE

The *x* and *y* address wires for each matrix are connected in series, *i.e.* wires locating the address *p,q* on one matrix locate *p,q* on **all** matrices. Hence a pair of read-write pulses reads (or writes) the whole word simultaneously. As the word is read in or out in parallel form, and as no delay due to searching through the store for the location is involved, the core store is an Immediate Access Store (I.A.S.).

The read wires from each matrix are connected to the store register which then indicates the contents of the selected location. As the output will usually consist of a mixture of 0s and 1s the inhibit wires for each matrix must be kept separate and cannot be interconnected.

Example. If a core store has a word length of 32 bits and a capacity of 8,100 words, it could consist of 32 matrices each with 90 *x* wires and 90 *y* wires.

The Magnetic Drum Store

In this store binary digits are magnetically recorded on to the surface of a revolving drum. The basic principle is similar to that for a tape recorder and is a development of the early drum recorder of Poulsen (see page 25). In the computer drum store the speech or music is replaced by pulses representing 0s and and 1s.

A metal drum, typically 0·2 m in diameter and 0·3 m long, is mounted on a shaft and driven by an electric motor at 2,000 to 6,000 r.p.m. The surface of the drum is coated with a layer of magnetic oxide which is magnetized by recording heads placed in close proximity to the surface.

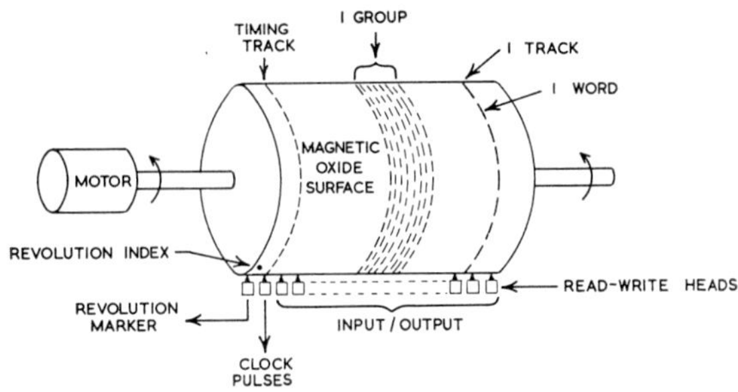

FIG. 6.12. A DRUM STORE

Fig. 6.12 shows the general arrangement.

As in the core store, 0s and 1s are distinguished by the polarity of the magnetization, an unmagnetized drum surface representing neither 0 nor 1. Fig. 6.13 indicates the way in which the magnetic flux is distributed on the surface and shows a diagrammatic view of a **read-write** head.

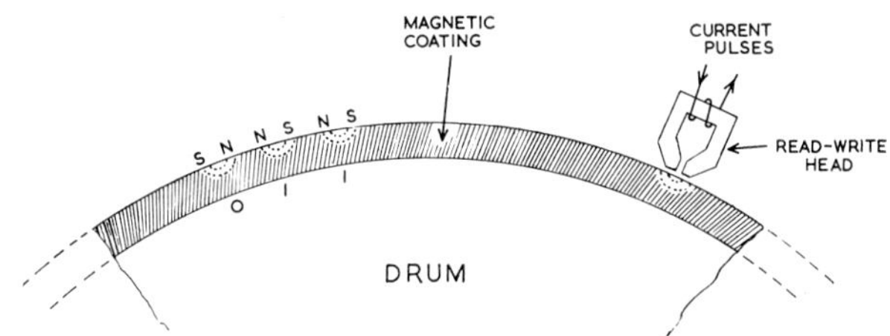

FIG 6.13. PULSES RECORDED ON A DRUM SURFACE

Each head records and reads information on one **track** round the periphery of the drum. The drum has several hundred tracks, each storing pulses at a density of about 2,000 per metre.

Example. A drum with 256 tracks, each holding 32 words, has a capacity of $256 \times 32 = 8{,}192$ words.

If the words are recorded round the drum in tracks as described, the information is handled in serial form, the pulses following one after the other as the drum rotates. It is possible to read and write words on to the drum in parallel form. In this case the number of read-write heads must be equal to the word length, and the word recorded along the length of the drum as in Fig. 6.14. All the digits of a word may now be written, or read, simultaneously.

To return to serial operation, in order to locate a word on the drum the address must specify

(i) the track; and

(ii) the position round the track, or **word.**

As the location has to be addressed in binary code, the drum tracks are **grouped** to assist the programmer. The address is now given in three

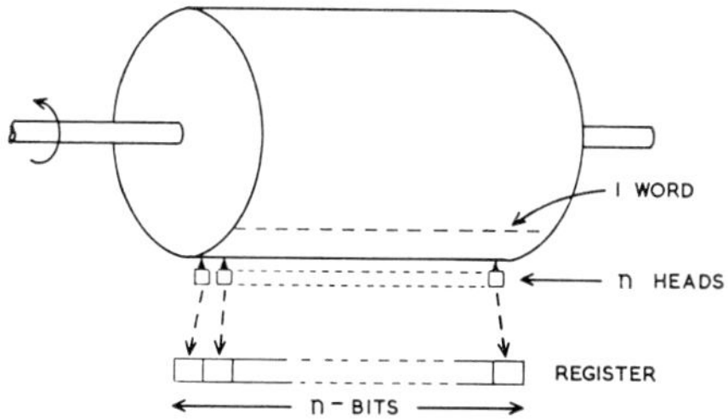

FIG. 6.14. PARALLEL FORM *n*-BIT DRUM

parts, the **group,** the **track,** and the **word.** As an example of addressing suppose that a drum has 16 words per track, 16 tracks per group, and 16 groups in all. The capacity of the drum will be

$$16 \times 16 \times 16 = 4{,}096 \text{ words.}$$

No programmer or service engineer can be expected to remember all the binary numbers up to 4,096, and so each location is referred to by its group, track, and word. Each of these is numbered 0 to 15 inclusive and so only the binary numbers up to 15 need be memorized.

Example. Let the location required by 2,847.

There are 256 words in each group of tracks (16 × 16) and so the required location is in group

$$\frac{2{,}847}{256} = 11, \text{ plus a remainder of } 31.$$

As there are 16 words per track, the required track in the selected group will be

$$\frac{31}{16} = 1, \text{ plus a remainder of } 15.$$

The required address is therefore Group 11, Track 1, Word 15. Expressed in binary, this is

1 0 1 1, 0 0 0 1, 1 1 1 1

But this is the binary number for 2,847, and so we have correctly addressed the drum without using any number above 15.

In practice, the address is never referred to in absolute terms (*i.e.* 2,847) but always as 11, 1, 15, and the calculation given is only an explanation of the theory.

Problem 1. A drum has 8 groups of 8 tracks, with 8 words per track. Find the address of the 1st, 404th and the last locations in terms of group, track and word. Convert these to binary addresses. What is the capacity of the drum?

(Answer is on page 177)

Access Time

Unlike the core store, information on the drum may not be immediately available. Track selection is virtually immediate but if the word required has just passed under the read-write head a complete drum revolution must elapse before access to it can be obtained. On the other hand, if the word required is just about to pass under the head no delay is introduced at all.

If we assume that the words are randomly distributed on the drum, the access times will lie between these two extremes. We define the **average access time** as the time taken for the drum to move half a revolution.

Example. If a drum rotates at 3,000 r.p.m., the time for one revolution is 20 milliseconds. Hence the average access time is 10 milliseconds.

In some cases the programmer can locate his data and instructions on the drum so that they appear at the read-write heads just at the time they are required, thus reducing access time to a minimum. This is known as **optimising.** The importance of this should not be underestimated, as a saving of (say) 12 ms in each of 100,000 arithmetical operations shortens the program running time by 20 minutes.

Synchronization of the Drum

In reading or writing a word on to the drum, the track is selected by a switching circuit similar in principle to an automatic telephone exchange. The selection of the **word** on the track is more difficult as the input-output circuit must be closed just before the required word passes under the read-write head and opened immediately after the last digit of the word has passed under the head. The timing of the switches or gates must be synchronized with the position of the drum as it revolves at high speed.

The problem of synchronization is simplified by deriving the computer timing pulses or **clock pulses,** from the drum itself. This means that the timing of the computer's operations is determined by the drum speed; if the drum runs slow the whole computer runs slow. The drum may be driven by a simple electric motor, as within reasonable limits its speed is non-critical.

One track of the drum has a complete set of pulses permanently stored on it corresponding to the individual digit positions of each word. If for example, there are 32 words of 16 digits per track, the timing track has 512 pulses together with the spaces required to separate each word.

Fig. 6.12 shows the timing track producing the clock pulses, the output of which represents a sequence of 1s as shown in Fig. 6.15.

One further pulse is required. As we label the words round each track from (say) 0 to 31, we must decide upon a datum line corresponding to word 0. In other words we require a **marker pulse** at every revolution of the drum to indicate when to start counting the words. This is produced as shown in Figs. 6.12 and 6.15.

The action of locating a word on the drum is now described with reference to Fig. 6.16.

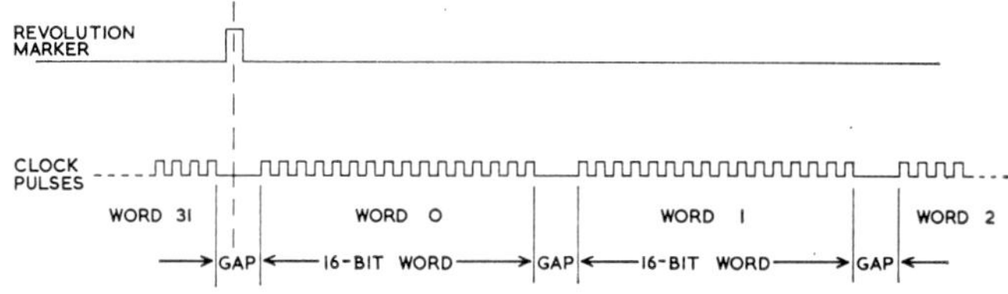

FIG. 6.15. THE CLOCK AND REVOLUTION MARKER PULSES

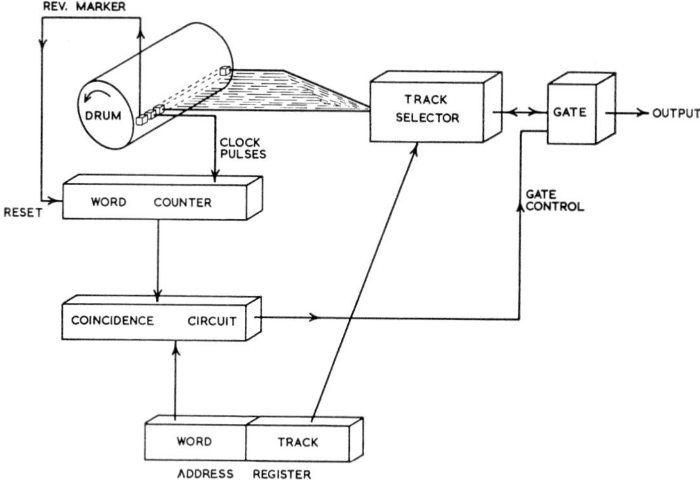

FIG. 6.16. DRUM ADDRESS SYSTEM

(1) The required location is loaded into the address register.

(2) The track selector connects the required track to the input-output gate. This gate is closed allowing no signals to pass in or out.

(3) The marker pulse starts the word counter.

(4) As the drum rotates the word counter registers the number of complete words that pass under the read-write heads by counting the clock pulses and dividing by the number of pulses per word.

(5) When the number in the word counter is the same as that in the address register the coincidence circuit provides an output signal which opens the gate.

(6) Information can now flow in or out of the drum for exactly one word time.

(7) At the end of this word, the word counter increases its contents by one, coincidence is lost, the gate control ceases and the gate closes.

The operation is now complete, the information being written or read from the required address in the store. If more than one drum is used, or if a combination of drum, disc and magnetic tape stores is used, the synchronization problems will obviously be much more difficult.

Magnetic Tape Stores

Based on the principle of the tape recorder, large reels of magnetic tape are used to store millions of characters of information. They may store complete programs indefinitely, and used as **data banks** store statistical data such as stores inventories, payrolls, insurance payments, credit payments, bank accounts, income tax details, etc.

The access time for the information may be relatively long unless the data is **sorted** and used in the order in which it is stored on the tape. Several minutes may be required to scan the tape from end to end, and it is obviously a slow process to keep dodging from one part of the tape to another at random. (The disc store described next is, by comparison, a random access store).

The Disc Store

The drum store has a reasonably quick access time, but a limited capacity; the magnetic tape store has a very large capacity with a slow access time. The disc store was developed to have the advantages of both, giving large capacity with quick access.

In a disc store the magnetic coating is applied to flat discs rather like gramophone records. The disc surface records the data on a large number of concentric circular tracks. Discs may be interchangeable in some designs, unlike the drum which is not removable. Several discs are usually mounted on one spindle to form a 'cartridge', Fig. 6.17.

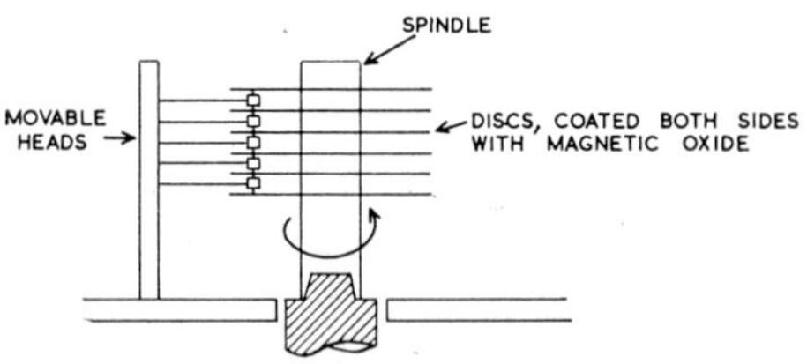

FIG. 6.17. A DISC STORE

Large disc stores can have a capacity of several million words. Access time is kept to below one second by using 'random access' techniques. Unlike magnetic tape, which has to be scanned in sequence as it runs through the machine, random access is achieved on discs by specifying the disc, track and word, the data being extracted without a sequential search through the stored data.

Volatile and Non-volatile Stores

If the information in a store is lost when the computer is switched off the store is said to be **volatile;** if the information is retained it is **non-volatile.** The core, drum and disc stores are examples of non-volatile stores, the information remaining indefinitely until deliberately (or accidentally) erased. A register is a volatile store, as the bistable circuits lose their information when the supplies are removed.

Backing Stores

A disc or drum may be used as a **backing store** for a core store. This is particularly useful when the computer is running several programs together. If a delay occurs in one program (human intervention, awaiting instructions or data, faulty program or similar causes) the computer switches to another program and proceeds to execute it. In this mode of operation, known as **time-sharing,** the maximum use is made of the computer.

However, the program being run will need a reasonable amount of high-speed core store and if one program is delayed for any length of time the associated part of the core store is not available for use by the other programs. To avoid this, core store data for the delayed program is off-loaded into the drum store. When the program is ready to run again the data is transferred back into the core store for processing (Fig. 6.18).

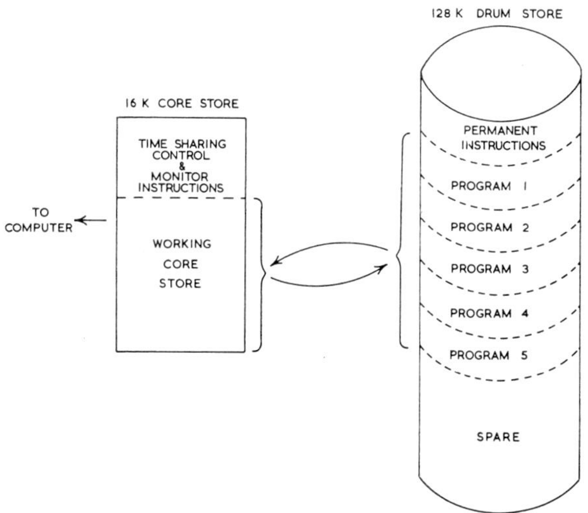

FIG. 6.18. A CORE STORE BACKED BY A DRUM STORE FOR TIME-SHARING OPERATION

Examples (Chapter 6)

(1) A core store has a capacity of 4,096 words, each 24 bits long. What is the number of

(a) Cores;

(b) Matrices;

(c) Read wires;

(d) Inhibit wires?

(2) A drum store has 32 words of 24 bits round each track. If there are 512 tracks and the speed of rotation is 4,000 r.p.m., calculate

(a) The total store capacity;

(b) The average access time;

(c) The density of recorded digits if the drum diameter is 0·15 m;

(d) The pulse repetition frequency.

(3) A drum has 24 words per track. If 10 numbers are stored sequentially on one track calculate the least and the greatest times that could be taken to read the numbers in order. The average access time is 10 ms.

(Answers are on page 177)

7

COMPUTER FUNCTIONS

In Chapter 5 it was shown that the binary numbers in a computer may be in either **serial** or **parallel** form. The arithmetic circuits are different for each of these two forms.

Parallel Addition

Fig. 7.1 shows a complete parallel adder; for an *n*-bit word *n* full adders are required.

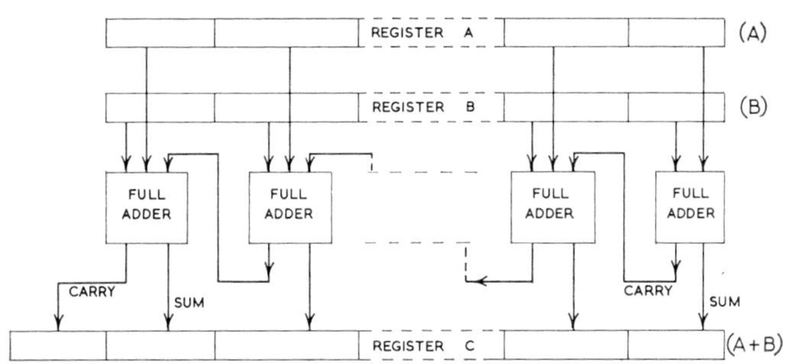

FIG. 7.1. COMPLETE PARALLEL ADDER

Serial Addition

Fig. 7.2 shows a serial adder. A sequence of shift pulses moves the digits one at a time from the registers A and B into the adder, the least

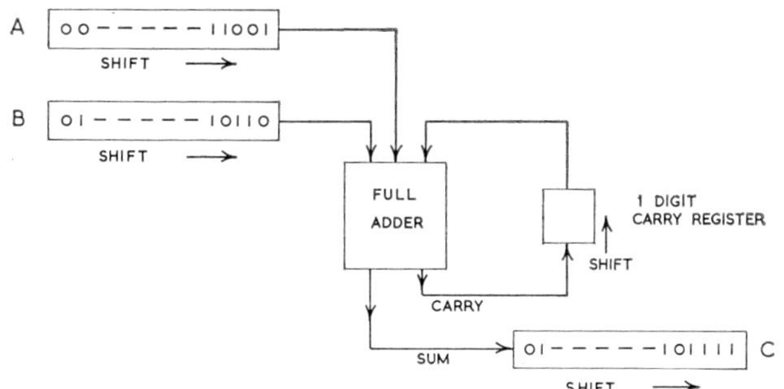

FIG. 7.2. COMPLETE SERIAL ADDER

significant digit first. Any carry-digit is stored in a single bistable register, the following shift pulse returning it to be added to the **next** pair of digits (Fig. 7.2). The sum is formed digit by digit in register C. When the transfer of digits from A to B is complete the answer is in the correct position in C.

Subtraction

If the numbers are represented in complementary-negative form (see Chapter 3) the addition circuits of the previous sections will automatically perform a subtraction (Fig. 7.3).

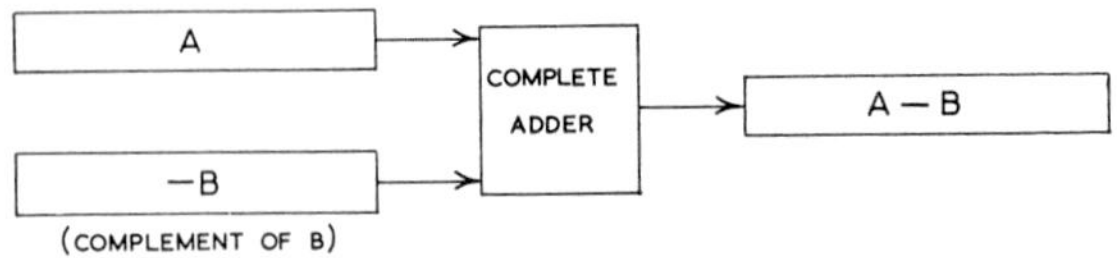

FIG. 7.3. SUBTRACTION

In Chapter 3 the rule for forming the complement of a number was shown to be 'invert and add one'. By modifying the circuit it is possible to subtract without previously forming the complement. If we wish to subtract B from A, as in Fig. 7.3, A and B are fed into the registers but the output of B is inverted by a **not** logic circuit before being passed into the adder (Fig. 7.4). This has the effect of adding A to the inverse of B. But the complement requires that we not only invert B but add 1. This 1 is added by presetting the carry register to 1 **before** the subtraction is performed.

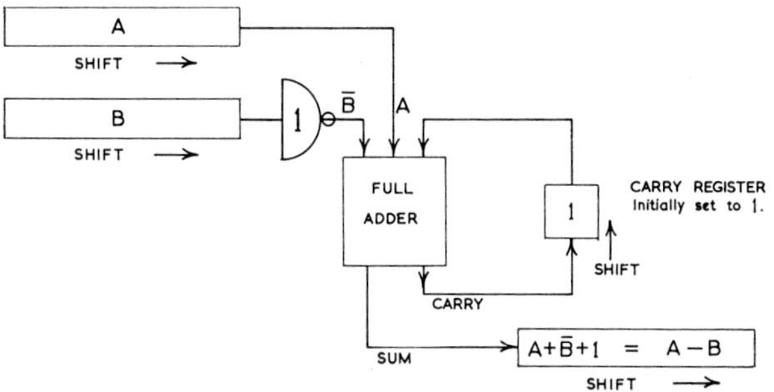

FIG. 7.4. COMPLETE SERIAL SUBTRACTOR

Problem 1. Sketch a modified form of Fig. 7.1 to perform parallel subtraction.

(Answer is on page 177)

As an example of subtraction, consider 25 − 11 = 14. (Fig. 7.5).

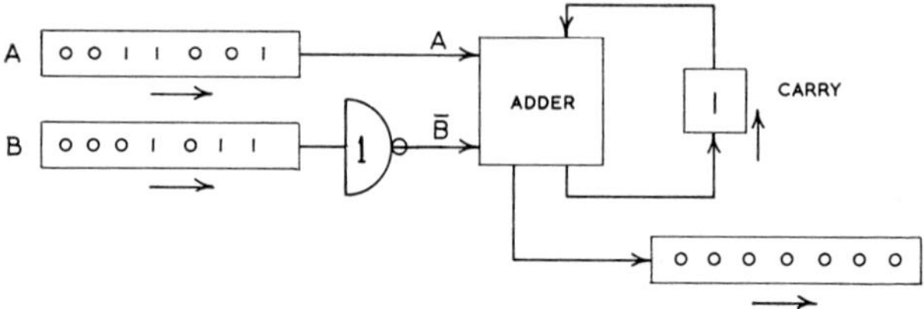

FIG. 7.5. THE SUBTRACTION OF 11 FROM 25

Put 0 0 1 1 0 0 1 in A

Put 0 0 0 1 0 1 1 in B

As each shift pulse is applied to the registers the right-hand digits of the registers A and B are fed into the adder. The following table shows the state of A, $\overline{B}$ and the result for each step of the operation. (Arrows indicate a carry digit).

Shift Pulse	A	$\overline{B}$	Carry	Result
1	1	0	1	0
2	0	0	1	1
3	0	1	0	1
4	1	0	0	1
5	1	1	0	0
6	0	1	1	0
7	0	1	1	0

Therefore the result is 0 0 0 1 1 1 0 $= 14_{10}$

Multiplication

One simple way to multiply two numbers together would be by the repeated addition of one number to itself a given number of times, *e.g.* 12 × 3 could be obtained by adding 12 to itself three times.

In Fig. 7.6 the number in A is added into the result register and also recirculated back into A. To multiply the number in A by n this operation is repeated n times. The cumulative sum is built up in the result register. A simple counter circuit, initially containing n, stops the operation at the appropriate time.

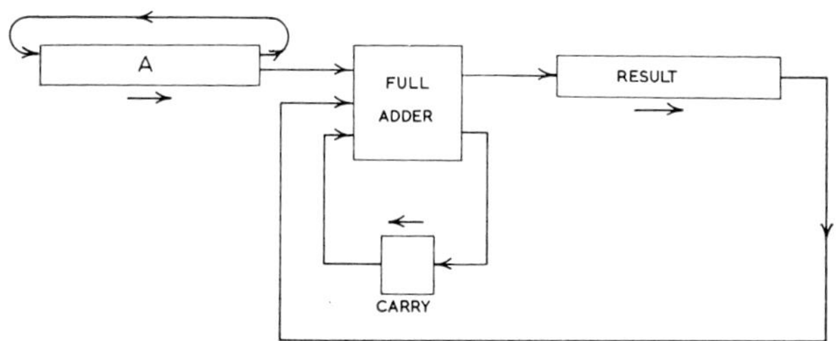

FIG. 7.6. SLOW MULTIPLICATION BY REPEATED ADDITION

Although simple, this method takes too long to perform. For example, to multiply 48,127 by 29,630 would require at least 29,630 separate additions. If there were 32 bits per word the number of shift pulses required would be 29,630 × 32 = 948,160. At a pulse repetition rate of 100,000 per second the multiplication would take about 10 seconds.

An improvement in multiplying speed may be obtained by using a technique similar to ordinary long multiplication *e.g.* for 12 × 3

1 1 0 0	multiplicand, 12
1 1	multiplier, 3
1 1 0 0	12×2^0 } The partial products
1 1 0 0 0	12×2^1
1 0 0 1 0 0	The total product, 36

In this case we form a partial product for each digit of the multiplier and sum them to obtain the answer. The procedure may be summarized as follows:

(a) If a 1 appears in the least significant position of the multiplier, the multiplicand is added into the product register; if a 0, nothing is added.

(b) The multiplicand is shifted one place to the left.

(c) The operation is repeated using the next highest multiplier digit.

The total product is therefore built up in the product register. A diagram of such a multiplier is shown in Fig. 7.7.

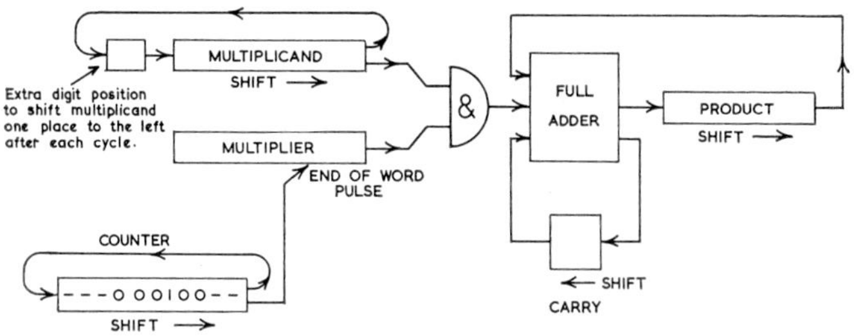

FIG. 7.7. FAST MULTIPLIER

If the least significant (right-hand) digit in the multiplier is 1, the **and** gate allows the multiplicand to be added into the product register. If the digit is 0 the **and** gate remains closed. In either case the multiplicand is recycled back into its own register.

The shift of one place to the left is achieved by adding an extra digit position to the multiplicand register. For example, if the word length is 32 digits, the multiplicand register has 33 positions and after 32 shift pulses the multiplicand has not been recycled back into its original position, but remains displaced one place to the left.

The counter recycles a word containing zeros in all positions but one. At the end of every complete word this pulse appears as an output and shifts the multiplier one place to the right. The next partial product is then added using the appropriate multiplier digit.

The time taken to perform a multiplication is now independent of the numbers used, and again assuming a 32-bit word length and a repetition rate of 100,000 pulses per second, the multiplication time is

$$\frac{32 \times 32}{100{,}000} = 0{\cdot}01024 \text{ seconds}$$

or approximately 10 milliseconds.

Division

Division could be performed by repeated subtraction. For example, if 11 is to be divided by 3, 3 is subtracted from 11 until the remainder is less than 3. The number of subtractions is the quotient, 3, with 2 as the remainder. However, this is too slow and it is quicker to follow the technique of normal long division.

The operation of division by computer is a complicated procedure and the study of the following explanation should be undertaken with care. In what follows we shall use the normal terminology

$$\frac{\text{DIVIDEND}}{\text{DIVISOR}} = \text{QUOTIENT}$$

Consider the division of 11 by 3 in binary, $\dfrac{1011}{11}$

```
           1 1·1  0 1 0 1 . . . etc.
     1 1 | 1 0 1 1
         |   1 1
          -------
             1 0 1  <--------------  next digit brought down
               1 1
             -----
               1 0 0  <------------  zero brought down
                 1 1
               -----
                   1 0 0  <--------  2 zeros brought down
                     1 1
                   -----
                       1 0 0  <--  2 zeros brought down
                         1 1
                       -----
                           1 . . . etc.
```

The answer is then 11·10101 . . . . or $3\frac{2}{3}$.

This requires the subtraction of the divisor from part of the dividend and the bringing down of the next dividend digit. To make the division simpler for the computer the numbers are first shifted in the registers to make the divisor greater than the dividend. This ensures that the digits brought down are all zeros. The answer must then be corrected by shifting the binary point to the right by the necessary number of places.

Note that bringing down a zero is simply a process of doubling in binary.
The first step in the above problem would be to change

$$\frac{1011}{11} \text{ to } \frac{1011}{1100}$$

remembering that the binary point in the answer must then be shifted two places to the right.

The division becomes:

```
                                                   0·1 1 1 0 1 0 1 0 1
                                          ______________________________
                                  1 1 0 0 | 1 0 1 1·0
Subtract divisor                              1 1 0 0
                                           _________
Double the remainder                         1 0 1 0 0
Subtract divisor                               1 1 0 0
                                             _________
Double the remainder                           1 0 0 0 0
Subtract divisor                                 1 1 0 0
Double the      { (next remainder will be }    _________
    remainder   { neg. so double it again) }       1 0 0 0 0
Subtract divisor                                     1 1 0 0
. . . etc.                                         _________
                                                       1 0 0 0 0
                                                         1 1 0 0
                                                       _________
                                                           1 0 0 0 0
                                                             1 1 0 0
                                                           _________
                                                               1 0 0
                                                            . . . etc.
```

and moving the binary point two places to the right, the answer is

$$11{\cdot}101010101\ldots$$

The division process may be shown as a flow chart (Fig. 7.8). A simplified logic circuit to perform division is shown in Fig. 7.9. The behaviour of the division circuit is described below with reference to Figs. 7.8 and 7.9.

> The sign digit store, G, and the quotient register are shifted only at the end of each complete word. G initially contains 0, which is inverted to 1 by D and opens gate E.
>
> A and B are shifted into the subtractor forming the first remainder A-B. A is also shifted into the store C, the extra 1-bit shifting it one place to the left (doubling it).
> B is also recycled back into its original position.
> The remainder A-B is fed back into the dividend register one place to the left (doubled).

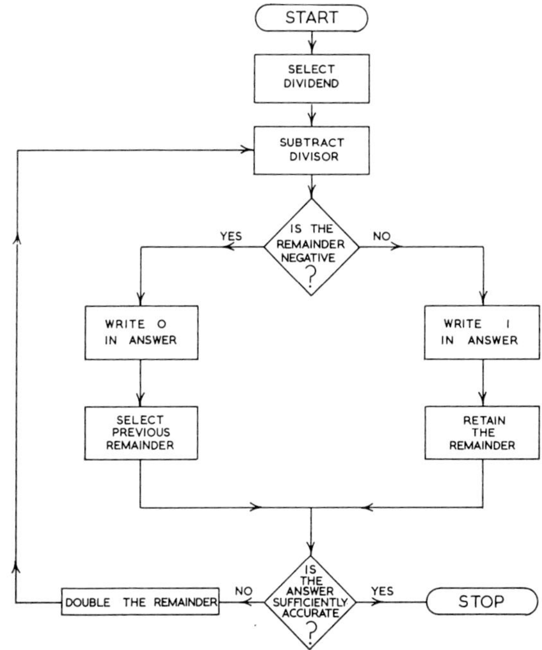

FIG. 7.8. THE DIVISION FLOW CHART

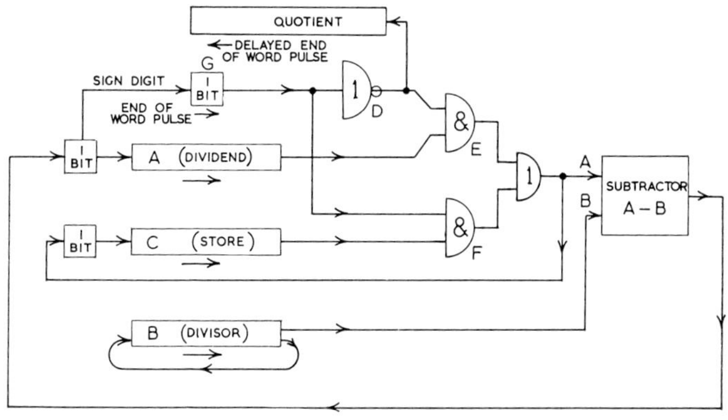

FIG. 7.9. DIVISION CIRCUIT

At the end of the word the sign digit is put into G, 0 if positive, 1 if negative. This is inverted by D and a 1 or 0 put in the quotient register.

(Note that the quotient register is fed in the **reverse** direction as the most significant digit of a quotient is produced first).

The quotient register shift pulse has a slight delay to allow time for G to accept the current sign digit.

The dividend register now contains the doubled remainder.
The store C contains the doubled previous remainder.
The divisor remains unchanged in B.

The first stage of the division is now complete.

If the remainder is positive, G contains 0 and gate E is open. The next subtraction takes the divisor B from the doubled remainder in the dividend register. The subtractor output is fed into the dividend register and doubled to form the next remainder.

If the remainder is negative, G contains 1 and gate F is open. The next subtraction takes the divisor B from the doubled **previous** remainder in the store. The contents of the store are recycled *via* gate F and doubled in case the next remainder is still negative. As before, the next remainder is doubled and put into the dividend register.

This sequence of subtraction continues until sufficient accuracy has been obtained or the quotient register is filled. If the content of the dividend register is positive it holds the remainder; if negative, the true remainder is in the store C.

Input and Output Functions

The computer processes data in binary form, and although the input tapes and cards could be prepared in binary this is a tedious and lengthy task. It is also a possible source of error as the binary numbers are difficult to read and check. It is far more convenient to the programmer and punch operator if the data is prepared in decimal form.

The task of converting the decimal input into binary, and similarly the binary output back into decimals, may be quickly and accurately performed by the computer itself. Circuits for 'encoding' from decimal to binary and 'decoding' from binary to decimal have been given in Chapter 5. However, it is generally more convenient to perform the input conversion as the tape or cards are being fed into the machine, and to perform output conversion in a form suitable for operating the printer.

Input

Consider a punched card input system. If the data is punched in decimal form each column on the card represents a certain place value, *e.g.* units, tens, hundreds, etc. A typical card layout has been illustrated in Chapter 1, where an account number of six decimal digits is punched in columns 74 to 79 (Fig. 1.5, page 7).

The account number shown is 092073. As the card is read in the number punched in each column must be multiplied by one of the constants

100,000; 10,000; 1,000; 100; 10; 1

which are stored in the computer in binary form. The holes in the card are read by electrical contacts or photoelectric cells, one for each column. The electrical pulse resulting from the detection of a hole is fed to an input store holding the appropriate constant for the column, Fig. 7.10.

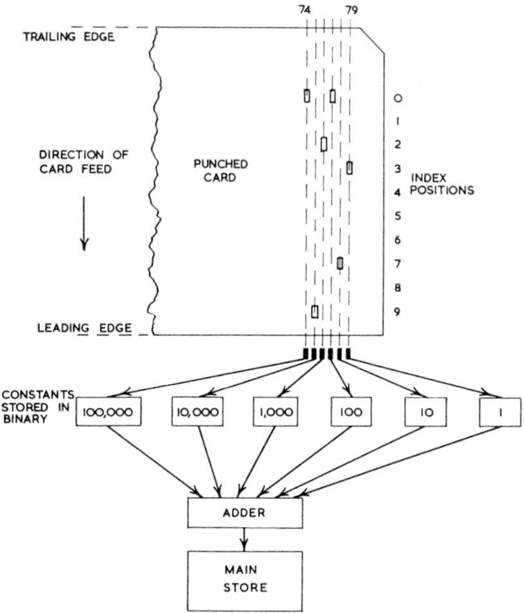

FIG. 7.10. INPUT CONVERSION

The card is fed into the reader with index position 9 leading. When a hole is detected the appropriate input store is triggered and its contents added into the main store **at each index position.** In the example the 9 in column 75 is first detected, putting 10,000 into the store at each of the 9 index positions. The 7 in column 78 puts 10 into the store 7 times, etc. The number on the card is built up in binary form by the adder and put into the main store.

Problem 2. Design a card layout representing inches, feet and miles, with a capacity of 10 miles. Give the constants required to convert to binary inches.

(Answer is on page 178)

The input of fractional quantities is possible by allocating card columns for the integers and decimal fractions, *i.e.*

1,000 100 10 1 0·1 0·01 0·001.

The conversion constants will be as shown above, but in binary form. It is unfortunate that the binary numbers for 0·1, 0·01, etc. are non-terminating and can only be represented approximately. These errors have been discussed in Chapter 3.

The system is different if paper tape is used. The input pulses are grouped into **characters,** each combination of holes or spaces across the tape representing one character (see Fig. 1.6, page 8). In some machines, particularly those for commercial data processing, the information is left in character form, *i.e.* groups of 4 to 8 digits. The registers and store locations may then each hold several characters. A 24-bit register may contain three 8-bit characters, four 6-bit characters or six 4-bit characters, etc.

Output

The output from the computer may be recorded on magnetic tape, paper tape or punched cards. In these cases little or no conversion is necessary as the data remains in binary form. However, if a decimal **print out** is required for visual inspection the binary output must be converted to a form suitable for operating a printer.

Printing is a slow process compared with electronic computing, and much operating time may be lost on this function unless the printer operates at as high a speed as possible. To do this it is arranged to assemble and print a complete line of characters at a time, rather than one character at a time as on a teleprinter or typewriter. It is then called a **line printer.**

One method of line printing is to mould the type face on **print-wheels,** one wheel for each character position on the paper. Each wheel holds the complete alphabet, numbers from 0 to 9, and any punctuation and mathematical symbols required (Fig. 7.11).

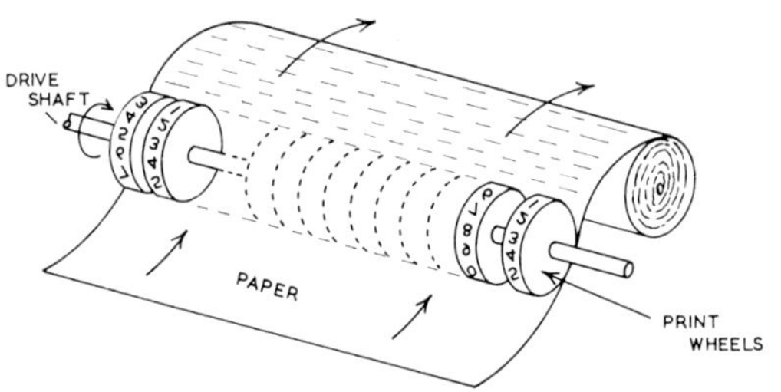

FIG. 7.11. A LINE PRINTER

A drive shaft rotates the wheels which are arrested in their required positions by brakes actuated by the computer output. The whole row of wheels is then moved forward to strike the paper through an inked ribbon. The paper is then moved up one line and the print wheels reset to a blank position ready to receive the impulses for the next line of type. An alternative scheme is to strike the back of the paper by small hammers at the instant the required character passes in front of it.

Each wheel can print from 0 to 9 and so four binary digits per wheel are required. The binary output from the computer is converted into groups of four digits or characters, each group operating one print-wheel. This converted output is called Binary-Coded Decimal (B.C.D.). For example, 3,128 would be produced by the computer as

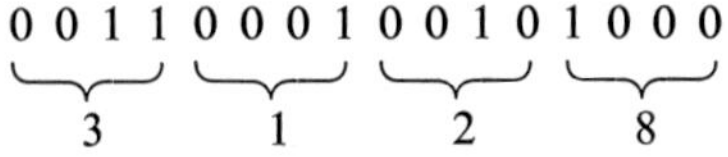

$$\underbrace{0\ 0\ 1\ 1}_{3}\ \underbrace{0\ 0\ 0\ 1}_{1}\ \underbrace{0\ 0\ 1\ 0}_{2}\ \underbrace{1\ 0\ 0\ 0}_{8}$$

Note that the binary-coded-decimal number is *not* the true binary number

for 3128. In machines using characters instead of complete words output conversion may not be necessary as the digits are already grouped, each group or character operating a print-wheel or print-hammer. The conversion from binary to B.C.D. may be done by a built-in program.

The values of the digit positions in B.C.D. are:

etc. . . . 800 400 200 100 (hundreds) 80 40 20 10 (tens) 8 4 2 1 (units)

and these constants are stored in the computer in binary form. To determine whether a 1 or 0 occurs in a particular position in the B.C.D. number, the binary number is tested to see if it contains the appropriate constants.

As an example consider a number less than 999.

800 is subtracted from it.

If the difference is **positive,** the number contains 800, a 1 is written in the answer and the difference is retained for testing by the next highest constant, 400.

If the answer is **negative,** the number does not contain 800, a 0 is written in the answer and the original number retained for subsequent testing by 400.

The process is continued until the lowest constant, 1, has been used.

Example. If the number to be converted is 562, the detailed operations would be:

	562	Sign of Difference	B.C.D.
Subtract 800	562	−	0
Subtract 400	162	+	1
Subtract 200	162	−	0
Subtract 100	62	+	1
Subtract 80	62	−	0
Subtract 40	22	+	1
Subtract 20	2	+	1
Subtract 10	2	−	0
Subtract 8	2	−	0
Subtract 4	2	−	0
Subtract 2	0	+	1
Subtract 1	0	−	0

Hence the result is

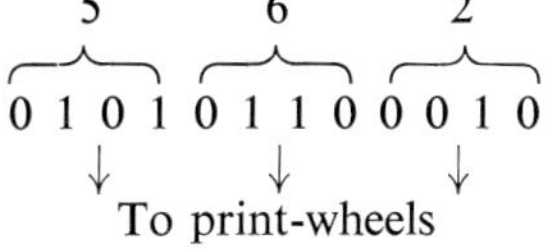

A flow diagram of this process is given in Fig. 7.12.

The comparison of Fig. 7.12 with Fig. 7.8 will show that the output conversion is essentially the same as division, and a similar circuit is used. The constants may be chosen to convert numbers to bases other than 10.

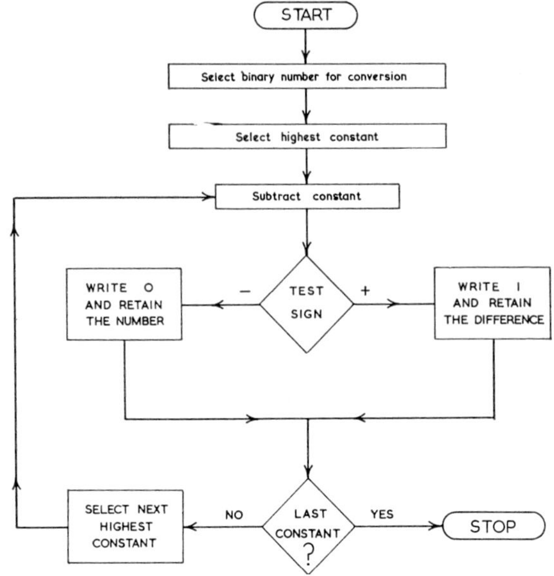

FIG. 7.12. OUTPUT CONVERSION, BINARY TO B.C.D.

Example. Convert 896 binary days to print out in years, weeks, and days. The constants required will be:

2920, 1460, 730, 365, 560, 280, 140, 70, 56, 28, 14, 7, 8, 4, 2, 1

(2920, 1460, 730, 365: years; 560, 280, 140, 70, 56, 28, 14, 7: weeks; 8, 4, 2, 1: days)

and the conversion will proceed as:

Constants	896	Sign of Difference	B.C.D.
2920	896	−	0
1460	896	−	0
730	166	+	1
365	166	−	0
560	166	−	0
280	166	−	0
140	26	+	1
70	26	−	0
56	26	−	0
28	26	−	0
14	12	+	1
7	5	+	1
8	5	−	0
4	1	+	1
2	1	−	0
1	0	+	1

and the converted output is

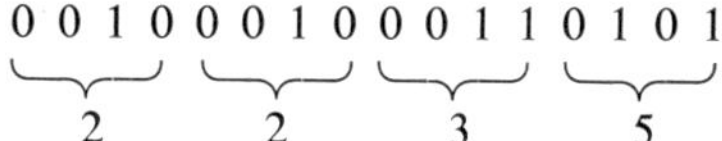

or 2 years, 23 weeks, 5 days.

In the above example the conversion constants 560 and 8 are actually redundant and are only included to space the answer correctly.

Redundancy and Parity Checking

Redundancy is the presence of information above that required for conveying the sense of the data. Redundancy is common in all forms of language: compare a letter with a telegram for example. Because of its redundancy a letter can be understood even if many of the words are unreadable, and some of the words may be understood when some of their individual letters are unreadable; but the sense of a telegram may be completely destroyed if only one word is omitted. Indeed, much of this paragraph is redundant and is only included as an aid to understanding rather than the conveyance of relevant facts.

If all the available digits in a binary word are required to represent the numerical information, there is no redundancy and a mistake in **one** digit may cause a serious and undetected error. However, if more digits are included the extra or **redundant** digits may be utilized for checking the information.

In data processing involving many thousands or millions of operations it is unwise to assume that no errors will occur and some redundant information must be included in an attempt to detect these errors. The most common source of error is in card or tape reading, but electrical interference has been known to cause trouble. Notice that tests on the computer itself would fail to indicate that anything was wrong.

The usual error is a single digit inversion, *i.e.* a 1 is read for a 0, or a 0 for a 1. One redundant digit per word is sufficient to detect this and is called a **Parity Check digit.** A parity digit is added at the end of each binary number to make the sum of the 1s either odd or even, depending upon whether odd or even parity has been chosen. The word 'parity' means 'pairing'. If a single error occurs in a binary word the parity is

(*continued overleaf*)

destroyed. The computer counts the 1s in each word and stops if the parity is incorrect, initiating a visual or audible alarm.

Suppose that even parity has been chosen as a test. The numbers 0 to 7 would be represented by **four** binary digits, three for the binary numbers up to 7, plus 1 redundant digit.

Decimal	Binary + Parity
0	0 0 0 0
1	0 0 1 1
2	0 1 0 1
3	0 1 1 0
4	1 0 0 1
5	1 0 1 0
6	1 1 0 0
7	1 1 1 1
	↑ parity digits

If the computer received the word 1011, it would detect an odd number of 1s and indicate that an error had occurred. A mistake in the parity digit itself is also detected by this system. Obviously, this does not detect **two** errors in one word, which would restore the correct parity. It is found in practice that parity checking is quite adequate for normal card and tape operations. The tape in Fig. 1.6 (page 8) has 'even parity', the bottom row of holes being the parity digits.

Error-Correcting Codes

With more redundancy it is not only possible for the computer to detect an error but also to correct it. This is useful where 'data links' are used to connect a remote terminal to a computer situated many miles away. All that has to be done is to locate the position of the faulty digit and invert it.

Consider a single binary digit, which can be either 0 or 1. Add an **even** parity digit:

	Binary	Parity
Zero	0	0
One	1	1

Now, an error could occur in either digit giving

0 1 or 1 0

But the position of the error is still unknown as either could be a mistake for 0 0 or 1 1. We need a second redundant digit to detect the position of the error, selected so that the lack of parity produces a binary number indicating this position.

There are now three digits, a b c, and we may identify their positions by the addresses (01), (10), and (11); or in general by (xy). An error in the first digit, a, or the third digit, c, must produce a digit y. An error in the second digit, b, or the third digit, c, must produce a digit x. If there is no error the output from the parity circuit is (00) and so the redundant digits are chosen to make x and y zero in the equations

$$(b) + (c) = x$$

$$(a) + (c) = y$$

That is

	a	b	c
Zero	0	0	0
One	1	1	1

Suppose that the computer is fed with the number 001. Here $b + c = 1$ and $a + c = 1$, the parity output is (11) indicating that the error is in the third digit; inverting this gives the corrected number 000.

Again, 101 gives $b + c = 1$ and $a + c = 0$, the parity output is (10) indicating position 2, and the corrected number is 111.

We do not always require three times as many digits to achieve error correcting. As the number of binary digits is increased the proportion of redundant digits needed falls rapidly. The following table gives the binary and redundant digits required for various word lengths.

No. of digits in binary number	**No. of redundant digits required**	**Highest number that can be represented**
1	2	$2^1 - 1 = 1$
4	3	$2^4 - 1 = 7$
11	4	$2^{11} - 1 = 2047$
26	5	$2^{26} - 1 = 67108863$
57	6	$2^{57} - 1$
$2^N - N - 1$	N	$2^{2^N - N - 1} - 1$

Most computers have a word length less than 63, so a practical limit is a 31-digit word including 5 redundant digits with a range of 0 to 67, 108, 863.

An example of a 15-bit error correcting code is given in Appendix B.

Examples (Chapter 7)

(1) Design a card layout for years, days, hours and minutes with a maximum capacity of 30 years. Give the constants required to convert to binary minutes.

(2) Derive a 7-digit error-correcting code having a range of 0 to 15. Write out the numbers 0 to 9 in this code.

(Answers are on page 178)

8

DATA FLOW AND COMPUTER OPERATION

Data Flow

To see how the computer performs the sequence of operations forming a complete program, we must trace the flow of data through the machine. In the simplified diagram of Fig. 8.1 the main components are shown interconnected by possible data flow paths.

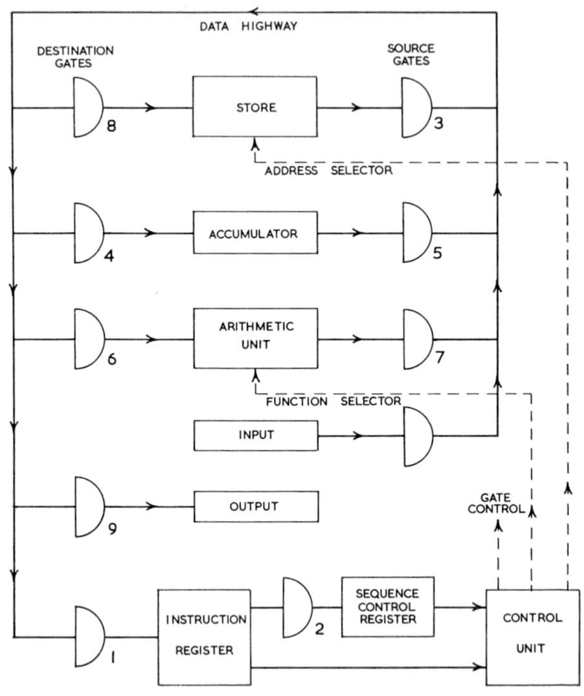

FIG. 8.1. DATA FLOW PATHS IN A SEQUENTIALLY OPERATED COMPUTER

The outputs from the various items of equipment are taken through the **source gates** to the main data highway, and are connected to the required inputs by **destination gates.** In a sequentially controlled computer the instructions are selected in numerical order, the address of the instruction to be obeyed next being held in the sequence control register. This register initially holds the address of the first instruction.

Consider, as an example, the addition of two numbers. We will assume that the program has been written and that the instructions and data have been loaded into the store. The sequence control register holds the address of the first instruction, 1. This instruction must be passed to the instruction register and the sequence control register then increased by one. The gates to be opened are

3, 1 and 2.

The first instruction passes its message to the control unit, which decodes it, selecting the address of the first binary number required from the stored data, and opening gates

3 and 4.

The selected number is now in the accumulator and the sequence control register contains 2. The next instruction, address 2, is required by the control unit and so gates

3, 1 and 2

are opened again.

The second instruction selects the second number from the data and adds it to the first by opening gates

3, 5 and 6, followed by 7 and 4.

The sum is now in the accumulator and the sequence control register contains 3. The third instruction is located and brought into the instruction register by opening again

3, 1 and 2.

This instruction puts the sum back into the store by opening gates

5 and 8.

The fourth instruction is located and put into the register by again opening

3, 1 and 2

and this prints the answer by instructing the control unit to open gates

3 and 9.

If we examine this sequence of activities we see that the computer has a **two-beat** operation. The gates opened in this program are:

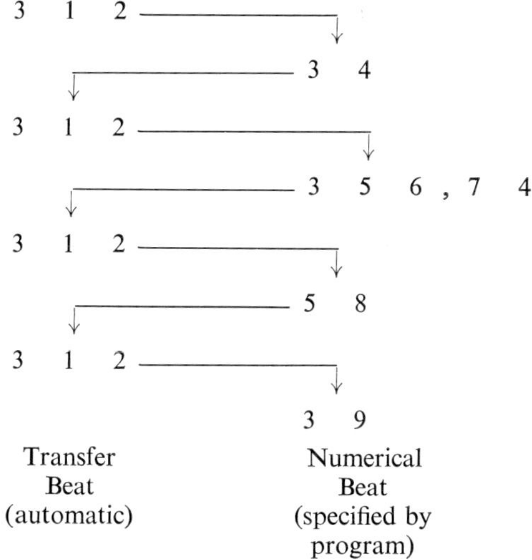

The operation of locating the next instruction is the **transfer beat,** and the data handling operation is the **numerical beat.** Most computers work on this two-beat cycle, although in practice it may be possible to save time by overlapping them so that the numerical operation and the selection of the next instruction are taking place simultaneously.

The above description is limited to single-address instructions and sequential operations in which **jumps** do not occur. This is not sufficiently sophisticated for modern requirements, and we now consider multiple-address instructions which may be selected in any order. Fig. 8.2 shows the layout of a 1+1 address computer with an instruction format

Function	Address of Operand	Next Instruction		Location

The 'location' is not part of the instruction; it informs the computer where to store the incoming word. The 'next instruction' address may be specified by the programmer as **any** store location and need not follow sequentially as in Fig. 8.1.

The data and instructions are initially fed into the store by opening gate 2, putting the input into register B. Gate 12 allows the location to set the address register, and the contents of B are then passed to the correct store location. When all the instructions and data are stored, the end of the tape (or the last punched card) sets the address of the first instruction in the sequence control register and starts the two-beat sequence of operations.

The first instruction is put into register B by opening gates 1 and 11.

Now the function, address and next instruction parts of the word in B are taken to the instruction register, address register and sequence control register respectively *via* gate 9. The function pulses are decoded and determine which gates are to be opened to perform the specified function. The times at which these gates are opened are controlled by the outputs from the clock circuit.

After completion of the numerical beat the sequence control register contains the address of the next instruction, which is selected and put into register B by again opening gates 1 and 11.

A typical addition operation would require the gates to open in the following sequence:

1, 11, 9	Select 1st instruction
1, 6, 7, 4	1st number is now in accumulator
1, 11, 9	Select 2nd instruction
1, 6, 5, 7, then 4	Sum now in accumulator
1, 11, 9	Select 3rd instruction
3	Sum transferred to store.

Note that the arithmetic register is required as a 'buffer' store to hold the sum whilst the accumulator still holds one of the numbers being added. After the sum has been completely formed it can be passed to the accumulator. This explains why the opening of gate 4 has to be delayed.

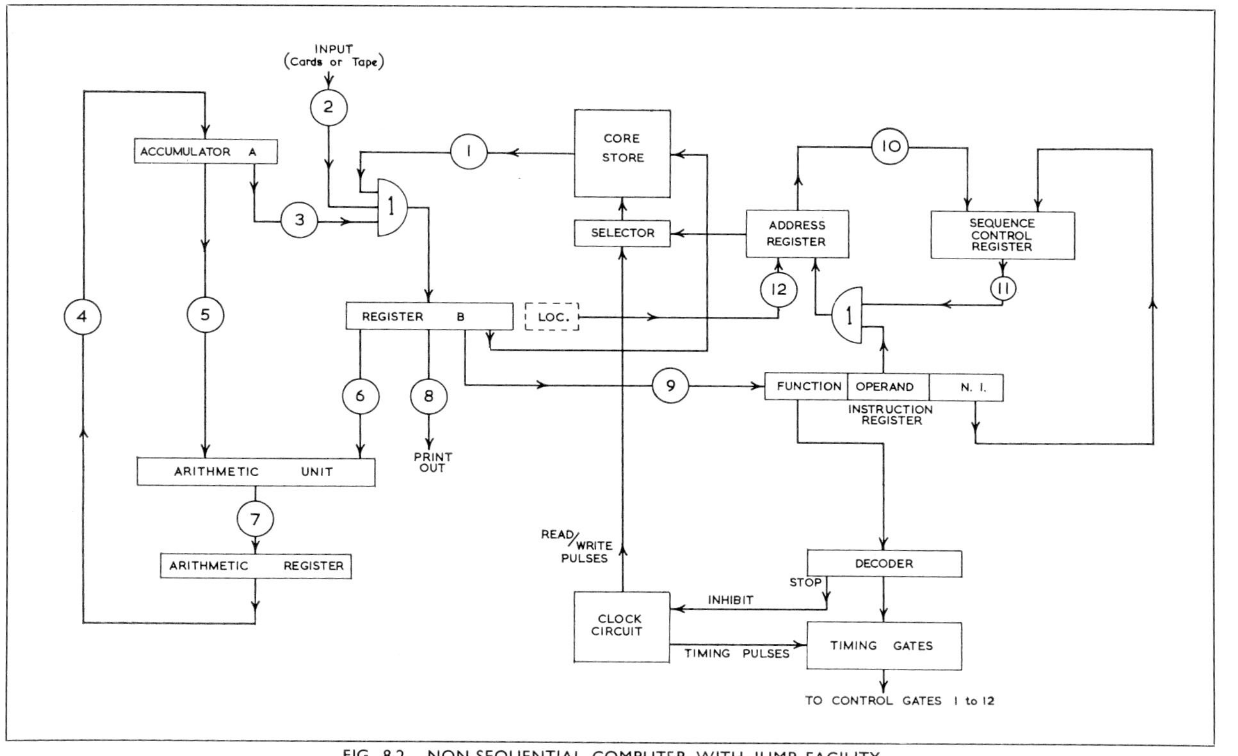

FIG. 8.2. NON-SEQUENTIAL COMPUTER WITH JUMP FACILITY

Address Modification

The ability of a computer to modify the programmer's instructions was briefly referred to in Chapter 1. This is required in order that a closed loop of repeated instructions may be obeyed. Suppose that we are adding together the contents of the first hundred store locations. The instructions could be:

Inst. No.	Function	Operand	Next Instruction
1	Add to Acc.	0	2
2	Add to Acc.	1	3
3	Add to Acc.	2	4
4	Add to Acc.	3	5
5			

. . . etc. One Hundred Times!

This may be executed by performing the **same** instruction over and over again 100 times, provided that the operand is increased by **one** every time, *e.g.*

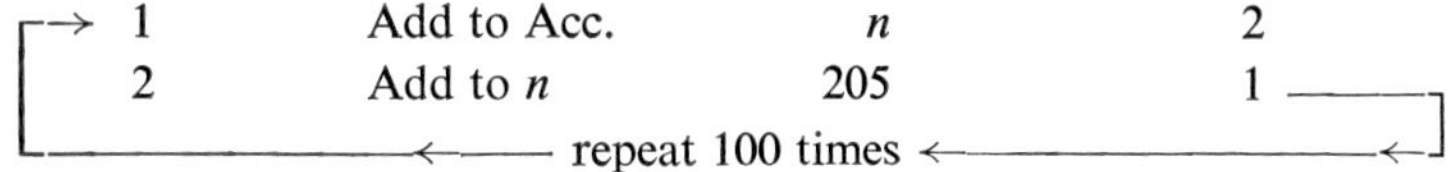

1 Add to Acc. n 2
2 Add to n 205 1
repeat 100 times

If we now put **one** in store location 205 and if the address of the first number to be added is n, we see that the operand is increased by 1 after each addition.

Instruction 2 is the **address modification** of instruction 1.

The computer of Fig. 8.2 is capable of doing this by specifying the address of an **instruction** in place of the usual binary number. This brings the instruction into register B ready for arithmetic modification on the numerical beat.

The program may **exit** from a loop when either

(a) the loop has been performed a given number of times; or

(b) the number held in some stated location is above or below a given value.

To **count** a given number of operations, a 1 in the store is added to a particular location at the completion of every loop. The summation may be extracted from the store at any time and tested to see if it has attained the required value. The details of the **test** or **jump** function are explained in the next section.

The Jump or Test Function

This is one of the most powerful functions of the computer, enabling it to make decisions as to which instruction it shall obey next. In its simplest form it consists of testing the number in the accumulator to see if it is positive or negative. If it is positive the computer obeys the **next**

instruction; if it is negative it obeys the instruction whose address is specified in the **operand.**

If, say, function 35 is the **jump** function, an instruction such as

Function	Operand	Next Instruction
35	21	17

means:

Test the accumulator.

If it is positive go to the instruction in location 17.

If it is negative jump to the instruction in location 21.

It has been shown in Chapter 3 that we only need to examine the most significant digit in the accumulator to see if its contents are positive or negative. If it is a 0 the contents are positive; if 1 the contents are negative. This digit, together with a pulse provided by the decoder when the jump function has been specified, are applied to an **and** gate as in Fig. 8.3.

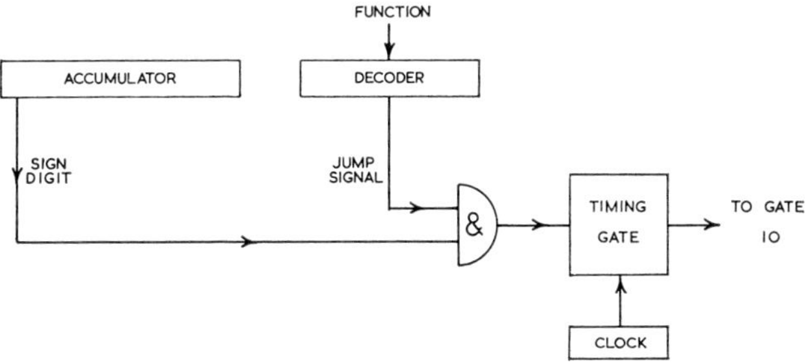

FIG. 8.3. TESTING THE SIGN OF THE ACCUMULATOR CONTENTS

If both pulses are present an output is obtained which closes gate 10 (Fig. 8.2) and puts the number from the **address** register (the operand) into the sequence control register. This number is then taken as the address of the next instruction.

If the number in the accumulator is positive, gate 10 is not opened and the sequence control register is left unaffected with the 'next instruction' address in it. Remember that **zero** is classed as a **positive** number in the complementary negative system.

Computer Operation

To use our computer we switch on and set the 'feed' instruction into the instruction register. (Sometimes the feed function is given the symbol **zero** in the instruction code, so that if the computer is clear of any other instructions it automatically feeds in the data). The punched cards are placed in the hopper and the paper or magnetic tapes threaded into the tape reader.

The start switch is pressed to initiate the motor-driven feed mechanism which then runs continuously until either

(a) an input signal halts the feed; or

(b) the last card or end of the tape is reached.

The data and instructions on the input cards or tape are loaded into the store by the read-write pulses generated by the clock circuit. Remember that if a drum store is used the clock pulses are derived from the drum itself. The clock also provides the shift pulses for moving the data from register to register and the timed gating pulses for selecting the path along which the data flows.

When the **feed** operation is stopped the clock produces the two-beat sequence of pulses, starting the program by transferring the first instruction into the instruction register.

At the end of the program the stored results of the computation are printed or punched out, and the program calls for a **stop** instruction. When this is received by the instruction register it is decoded to produce an inhibit pulse which stops the clock. The computer then ceases all operations until this inhibit is removed by the operator or by an external signal fed into the machine.

9

PROGRAMMING

PROGRAMMING is the preparation of the instructions for the computer. The subject is a vast one and this chapter can serve only as an introduction. When presented with a problem the programmer first prepares a **flow chart** showing each step of the computation in block form. The operations are represented by **boxes** which are numbered for reference.

For example, suppose that the function $x^2 + x + 41$ is required for all integer values of x from 1 to 1,000. The computation of the function must be repeated 1,000 times, each for a different value of x. Fig. 9.1 shows the flow chart.

Here $x + 1 \rightarrow x$ means that $x + 1$ becomes the new value of x, *i.e.* 1 has been added to the location of x. The accumulator is referred to as A.

To repeat the computation a **loop** has been included together with **decision** or **test** operation. This provides an exit from the loop after 1,000 values have been computed.

Following the flow chart through step by step, we have:

(1) x is initially set to zero.

(2) Add 1 to x. This then becomes the new value of x.
This operation is required so that x can be increased by 1 after each complete loop.

(3) The value of x is needed again in operation (5), so it is temporarily held in store.

(4) Square x.

(5) Add x [see operation (3)].

(6) Add 41, this gives the required answer.

(7) Print the answer.

(8) Put x in accumulator and subtract 1,000.

(9) Test. If x is less than 1,000, go back to operation (2).
x is increased by 1 and the loop is repeated.
If $x = 1{,}000$, $x - 1{,}000$ is zero and the computation stops.

The Instruction Code

Having prepared the flow chart, the programmer must write the operations in a form acceptable to the computer. The instruction code is a set of functions which the computer can perform, coded so that each function is represented by a number. If the programmer uses only these basic instructions and specifies the movement of each number, together with the store addresses, the program is said to be written in **machine code.**

If, however, previously prepared sub-routines are used by the programmer (such that one of his instructions initiates a program executing a section of his computation) much time and labour are saved in writing the program. He is no longer restricted to the basic instruction set and is using an **autocode.** (Autocodes will be discussed more fully later).

In the examples which follow we shall use the following instruction code, which is a part of the City and Guilds Code given in Appendix C.

0 0	Clear accumulator and load operand	$(n) \rightarrow A$
0 1	Add operand to accumulator	$(A) + (n) \rightarrow A$
0 2	Subtract operand from accumulator	$(A) - (n) \rightarrow A$
0 3	Multiply contents of accumulator by operand	$(A) \times (n) \rightarrow A$
0 4	Divide contents of accumulator by operand	$(A) \div (n) \rightarrow A$
2 0	Store contents of accumulator in location n	$(A) \rightarrow n$
3 5	Jump to instruction in n if accumulator is negative.	
5 3	Print contents of accumulator.	
9 9	Stop.	

The **print** function will be assumed to include the **conversion** process as a sub-routine. The conversion function and the necessary constants will be omitted.

Instruction Format

In Chapter 1 we saw that the instruction word could take several forms, classed as either single address or multiple address. We shall consider several instruction forms and use them later to prepare programs for simple calculations.

(a) Single Address Instructions.

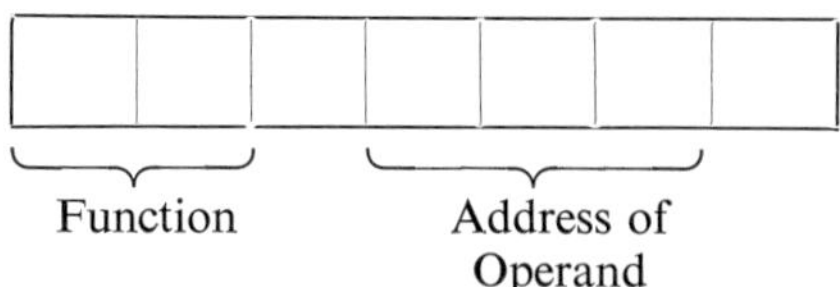

The instruction consists of two parts, the function and the address of the operand. For a computer to be of practical value we need at least 7 decimal digits per word, which will be converted to 24 binary digits. Let the store capacity be 1,000 words, the addresses ranging from 000 to 999 inclusive.

Address 000 will be assumed to contain zero at all times, and address 001 will be used as the accumulator A. The 3rd and 7th digits are not required in an instruction but may be used in a 7-digit number. As no 'next instruction' can be specified the computer must obey the instructions sequentially, in the order in which they appear in the store, unless function 35 is specified. In this case the program may jump out of sequence to the instruction held in the operand address, n.

(b) One-plus-one Address Instructions.

The computer discussed in Chapter 8 used instructions of the form

Function	Operand	Next Instruction

This form of instruction allows more freedom and versatility as the instructions need not be obeyed sequentially. The program may jump to any desired instruction without specifying a separate jump function.

(c) Three-plus-one Address Instructions.

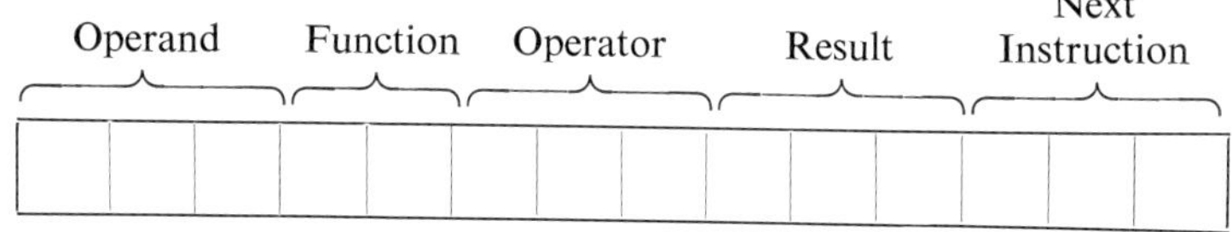

This is perhaps the most comprehensive type of instruction in machine coding. Notice that the word length required is now 14 decimal digits, with addresses limited to 999. For a larger store, higher address numbers would be required with a consequent increase in word length. This is one disadvantage of the multiple address instruction.

The Program

We now have sufficient information to write a program.

Example 1. Compute $x^2 + x + 41$ for integer values of x from 1 to 1,000.

The flow chart is given in Fig. 9.1.

This example will use single address instructions and sequential operation.

The constants 1, 41, and 1,000 are required and will be stored in locations 22, 23 and 24 respectively.

The variable x will be allocated to location 21, and initially will be zero.

Two **directives** are required:

(i) Store program sequentially from location n onwards.

(ii) Execute program beginning at instruction in location n.

These directives are placed at the beginning and end of the input tape (or card pack) respectively.

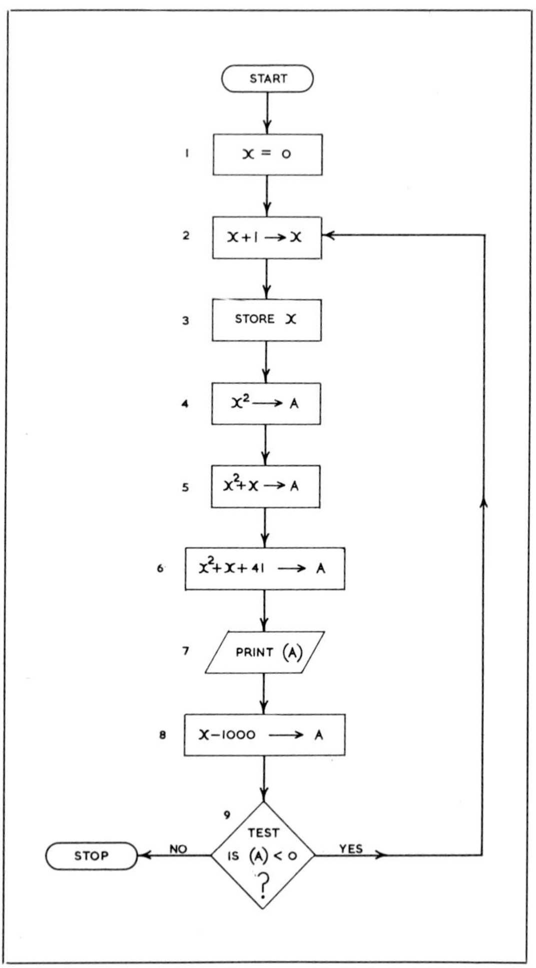

FIG. 9.1. COMPUTATION OF $x^2 + x + 41$, x FROM 1 TO 1000

The Program may be written:

NARRATIVE	FUNCTION	OPERAND	LOCATION OF INSTRUCTION OR DATA
(Store program from location 10)			
Instructions:			
$x \to$ A ←	0 0	0 2 1	0 1 0
$x + 1 \to$ A	0 1	0 2 2	0 1 1
(A) → Store Loc. 21	2 0	0 2 1	0 1 2
$x^2 \to$ A	0 3	0 2 1	0 1 3
$x^2 + x \to$ A	0 1	0 2 1	0 1 4
$x^2 + x + 41 \to$ A	0 1	0 2 3	0 1 5
Print (A)	5 3	0 0 0	0 1 6
$x \to$ A	0 0	0 2 1	0 1 7
$x - 1000 \to$ A	0 2	0 2 4	0 1 8
Test A. If −ve, go to 10 If zero, go to 20	3 5	0 1 0	0 1 9
Stop ←	9 9	0 0 0	0 2 0
Data:	← 7-bit word length →		
0	0 0 0	0 0 0 0	0 2 1
1	0 0 0	0 0 0 1	0 2 2
41	0 0 0	0 0 4 1	0 2 3
1000	0 0 0	1 0 0 0	0 2 4

(Execute program beginning at instruction in location 10)

Several important points are illustrated by this program.

(a) It must **never** be assumed that a location is empty, unless it is specified as such. A previous user may have left his program and data in the store. Zero was put into location 21 as the initial value of x.

(b) All the digits in the words must be in their correct positions, even the zeros.

(c) A store location cannot contain more than one instruction or number at a time. Care must be taken not to allocate two words to the same address. If a location is **overwritten** by a second word, the original information will be erased and lost.

(d) The use of a number from the store does not erase it. It remains for further use until cleared or overwritten.

It would be desirable to extend the use of this program by making it suitable for evaluating **any** quadratic expression of the form

$$ax^2 + bx + c$$

The constants a, b and c, together with the range of x required, could then be inserted as data by anyone wishing to use the program.

For a computer using one-plus-one address instructions the program would have an additional column giving the 'next instructions'. The program would begin:

FUNCTION	OPERAND	NEXT INSTRUCTION	LOCATION
0 0	0 2 1	0 1 1	0 1 0
0 1	0 2 2	0 1 2	0 1 1
2 0	0 2 1	0 1 3	0 1 2

. . . etc.

In this case the instructions need not be stored sequentially as we can jump to any 'next instruction'.

Example 2. Compute the squares of the integers 1, 2, 3, . . . etc.

This does not require the use of the **multiply** function, for given N and N^2 we produce $(N + 1)^2$ by computing

$$N^2 + 2N + 1.$$

Remember that multiplication is a lengthy process compared with addition. The calculation is then repeated using $(N + 1)$ and $(N + 1)^2$ in place of N and N^2. If N is initially zero we can thus find the squares of 1, 2, 3, . . . etc.

We shall first use a one-plus-one address instruction from. The flow chart is given in Fig. 9.2, where (n) means the **contents** of location n.

The complete program is then:

NARRATIVE	FUNCTION	OPERAND	NEXT INST.	LOCATION
Instructions:				
$1 \rightarrow$ A	0 0	0 1 9	0 1 1	0 1 0
$1 + N \rightarrow$ A	0 1	0 2 0	0 1 2	0 1 1
$1 + N \rightarrow$ Store (022)	2 0	0 2 2	0 1 3	0 1 2
$1 + 2N \rightarrow$ A	0 1	0 2 0	0 1 4	0 1 3
$1 + 2N + N^2 \rightarrow$ A	0 1	0 2 1	0 1 5	0 1 4
(A) $\rightarrow$ Store (021)	2 0	0 2 1	0 1 6	0 1 5
Print (A)	5 3	0 0 0	0 1 7	0 1 6
$N + 1 \rightarrow$ A	0 0	0 2 2	0 1 8	0 1 7
(A) $\rightarrow$ Store (020)	2 0	0 2 0	0 1 0	0 1 8
Data:				
1	0 0	0 0 0	0 0 1	0 1 9
N (Initially zero)	0 0	0 0 0	0 0 0	0 2 0
N^2 (Initially zero)	0 0	0 0 0	0 0 0	0 2 1
($1 + N$	Working Space, no input required.			0 2 2)

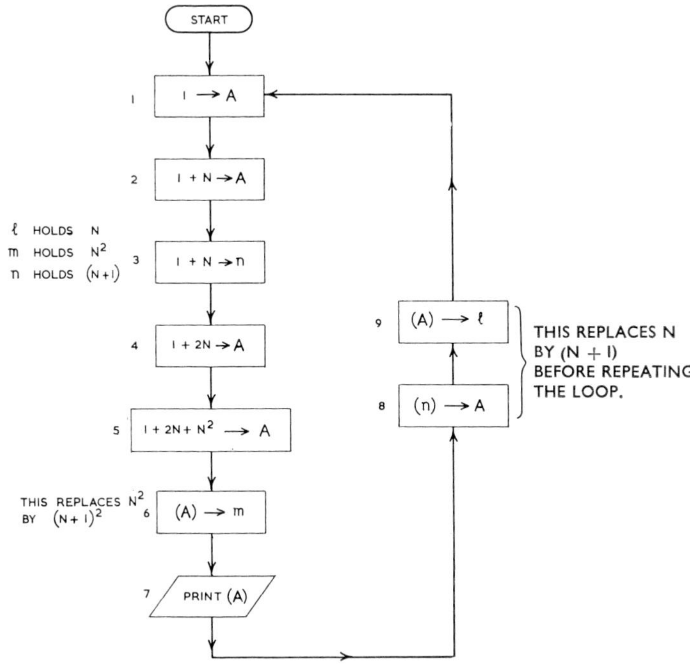

FIG. 9.2. FLOW CHART FOR THE SQUARES OF INTEGERS

As no stop instruction has been included this program is non-terminating. It is obviously undesirable to leave the program like this in practice.

Problem 1. Explain the behaviour of the computer and its printed output if the program is allowed to run on indefinitely.

(Answer is on page 178)

(*continued overleaf*)

The number of output conversion constants required will depend on the largest number that has to be printed. In the above program 8 decimal digits are used, the highest conversion constant being 80,000,000. The one above this would be 100,000,000 which is too large for the computer. Tabulating the constants from 80,000,000 down to 1, according to the pattern established in Chapter 7, we find that 32 constants are required.

This same program in 3 + 1 address instruction form is:

NARRATIVE	OPD.	FUNC.	OPR.	RES.	N.I.	LOC.
Instructions:						
$1 + N \rightarrow$ Store (019)	0 1 6	0 1	0 1 7	0 1 9	0 1 1	0 1 0
$1 + N + N^2 \rightarrow$ Store (018)	0 1 9	0 1	0 1 8	0 1 8	0 1 2	0 1 1
$1 + 2N + N^2 \rightarrow$ Store (018)	0 1 8	0 1	0 1 7	0 1 8	0 1 3	0 1 2
$(N + 1)^2 \rightarrow$ A	0 1 8	0 0			0 1 4	0 1 3
Print (A)		5 3			0 1 5	0 1 4
(019) → 017	0 1 9	0 1	0 0 0	0 1 7	0 1 0	0 1 5
Data:						
1					1	0 1 6
N (Initially zero)						0 1 7
N^2 (Initially zero)						0 1 8
($1 + N$ Working space, no input required.						0 1 9)

Example 3. Address Modification.

By performing arithmetic operations on an instruction the **address** of the operand may be varied to perform a function on more than one number held in the store. Suppose we wish to find the average value of the numbers held in the 200 consecutive locations 30 to 229 inclusive. The flow chart would be as in Fig. 9.3, where the first number to be used is in location n, and the sum formed in location m. Remember that the **contents** of a store location are written as (n), whereas n is its **address.**

The instruction in box 2, 'clear accumulator and load the contents of location n', is being modified in box 6 after being put in the accumulator in box 5. After each summation n is increased to $n + 1$ and the modified instruction returned to its original location by box 7. The required numbers are thus extracted from the store in sequence.

The constants required for the program will be 0, 1, 230 and 200. The cumulative sum of the numbers will be formed in location 22.

(*continued on page* 124)

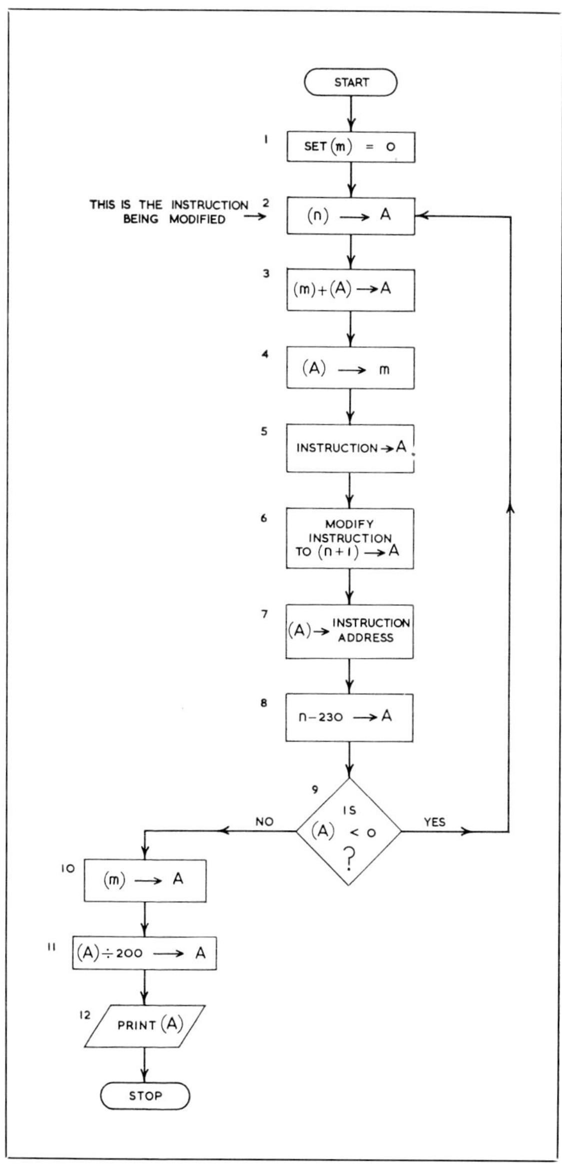

FIG. 9.3. FLOW CHART FOR THE AVERAGE OF 200 NUMBERS USING ADDRESS MODIFICATION

Using single address instructions the program is:

NARRATIVE	FUNCTION	OPERAND	LOCATION
(Store program sequentially from location 10)			
Instructions:			
$(n) \to A$	0 0	0 3 0	0 1 0
$(m) + (A) \to A$	0 1	0 2 2	0 1 1
$(A) \to m$	2 0	0 2 2	0 1 2
$(10) \to A$	0 0	0 1 0	0 1 3
Modify Inst.	0 1	0 2 3	0 1 4
$(A) \to 10$	2 0	0 1 0	0 1 5
$(A) - 230 \to A$	0 2	0 2 4	0 1 6
Test. $n - 230 < 0$? Yes / No	3 5	0 1 0	0 1 7
$(m) \to A$	0 0	0 2 2	0 1 8
$(A) \div 200 \to A$	0 4	0 2 5	0 1 9
Print (A)	5 3	0 0 0	0 2 0
Stop	9 9	0 0 0	0 2 1
Data:			
Sum in m	0 0 0	0 0 0 0	0 2 2
1	0 0 0	0 0 1 0	0 2 3
230	0 0 0	2 3 0 0	0 2 4
200	0 0 0	0 2 0 0	0 2 5
(Store data sequentially from location 30)			
(Execute program beginning at instruction in location 10)			

Notice again that care has been taken not to overwrite any instructions or data.

The program is stored in locations 10 to 21.

The constants and working space are allocated to locations 22 to 25.

The numerical data is stored in locations 30 to 229.

The constants 1 and 230 have been written as 10 and 2300 so that they correspond to the digit positions in the address of the operand.

Autocodes

Programs using only the basic instruction code of the computer are said to be written in **machine code.** These are difficult and lengthy to write but may be used in specialized data processing. For mathematical and technical computations machine programming requires great skill and experience. To simplify the programming **autocodes** are used. These enable simplified instructions to be given to the machine which are **interpreted** or **translated** into machine code by the computer itself.

Two methods are available:

(a)

in which each autocode instruction is separately interpreted as a machine code sub-routine already stored in the computer.

(b)

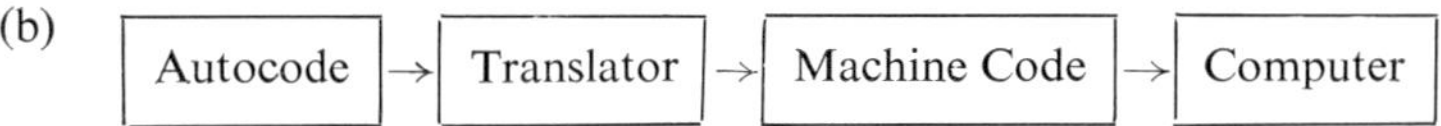

Here the complete program is translated or **compiled** into machine code which is then executed by the computer. The interpreter, translator or compiler must first be written in machine code and may take many man-years to perfect. However, once written they form part of the computer equipment; autocode compilers are supplied by the manufacturers as 'software' (the machine itself is the 'hardware').

A **mnemonic** code is one in which the numerical instructions are referred to in words or abbreviated groups of letters; part of the City and Guilds mnemonic code is given in Appendix C. The mnemonics are chosen so that the programmer finds them easy to learn and remember by their similarity to normal language.

For example:

ADD	means add
SUB	means subtract
MLT	means multiply
DIV	means divide
. . . etc.	

By including such functions as square roots, logarithms, trigonometrical functions and automatic address modification (see Appendix C) as sub-routines, we are not restricting ourselves to the basic instruction set of the machine. Sub-routines may be included in the autocode to perform all the arithmetic in floating point form (see Chapter 3).

Autocodes whose programs differ only slightly from machine code are called **low-level** or machine oriented languages. Those whose programs are written more like normal English are called **high-level** or problem oriented languages. The City and Guilds code is a low-level language, whereas **Algol, Fortran** and **Cobol** are high-level languages.

We shall consider two programs using the mnemonic code given in Appendix C.

Example 4. Find the largest of 800 numbers in the computer store.

Let the largest number encountered during a sequential search through the store be held in location L.

Let n be the location of the current number being examined.

The program then consists of comparing (n) with (L).

If (n) < (L) no action is taken and n is increased to $n + 1$, but if (n) $\geqslant$ (L) then (L) is replaced by (n).

The number of tests is counted and after the 800th the largest number, now in location L, is printed.

The flow chart is shown in Fig. 9.4.

The complete program will be:

	INSTRUCTION	m, n	LOCATION	BOX NO.
(Store program sequentially from location 10)				
	LDA	23	10	1
	STA	02	11	1
	LDA	29	12	1
	STA	05	13	1
→	LDA	29, 2	14	2
	SUB	27	15	3
	JLT	19	16	4
if	LDA	29, 2	17	5
(n) − (L) < 0	STA	27	18	5
→	LOP	23	19	6
	LDA	27	20	7
if	WNB	00 (floating point)	21	8
(c) < 800	STOP		22	
→	LDA	02	23	9
	ADD	28	24	9
	STA	02	25	9
	JUN	14	26	9
Constants:	L (initially zero)		27	
	1		28	
	800		29	
Data: (800 numbers)			30 to 829 inclusive.	

(Execute program beginning at instruction in location 10).

The index register 2 is used to modify the address of the number being compared with (L) in location 27. For easy reference the flow chart box numbers have been included alongside the program. Location 5 holds the number in the counter which is automatically reduced by 1 prior to the LOP test.

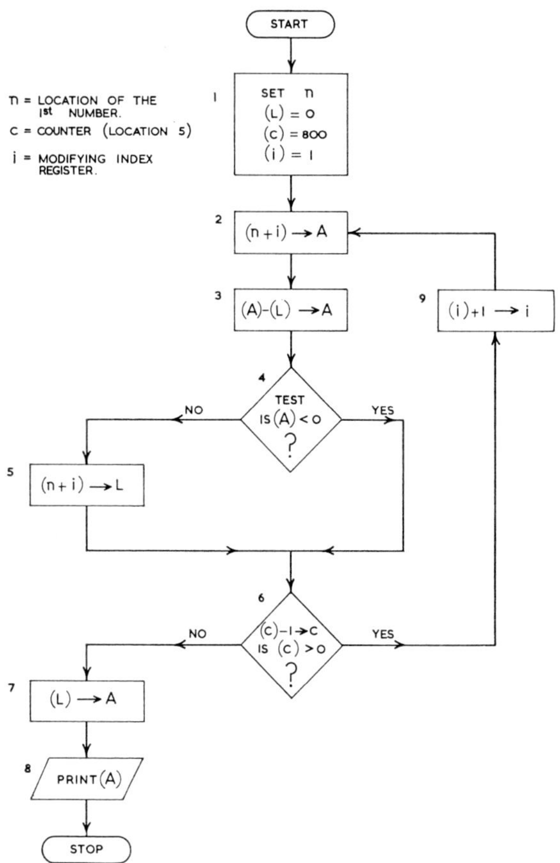

FIG. 9.4. FLOW CHART FOR FINDING THE LARGEST NUMBER

Example 5. Evaluate $K \sin e^x$, for K from 1 to 10
in increments of 1,
and x from 0·1 to 5
in increments of 0·1.

The print out is to be arranged in 10 blocks, one for each value of K. Each block will have 50 numbers corresponding to the values of x. A space of two lines is to separate each block, that is

$K = 1$

$x = 0{\cdot}1$
$x = 0{\cdot}2$
.....
.....
$x = 5{\cdot}0$

Space

$K = 2$

$x = 0{\cdot}1$
$x = 0{\cdot}2$
.....
.....
$x = 5{\cdot}0$

Space

. . . etc.

Fig. 9.5 shows the flow chart.

This is not the quickest way of calculating $K \sin e^x$. It would be quicker to calculate $\sin e^x$ for each value of x and multiply by $K = 1$, $K = 2$, etc., thus reducing the number of times that the exponential and sine functions have to be evaluated. However, for the print-out form required the system shown is easier to follow.

(*continued on page* 130)

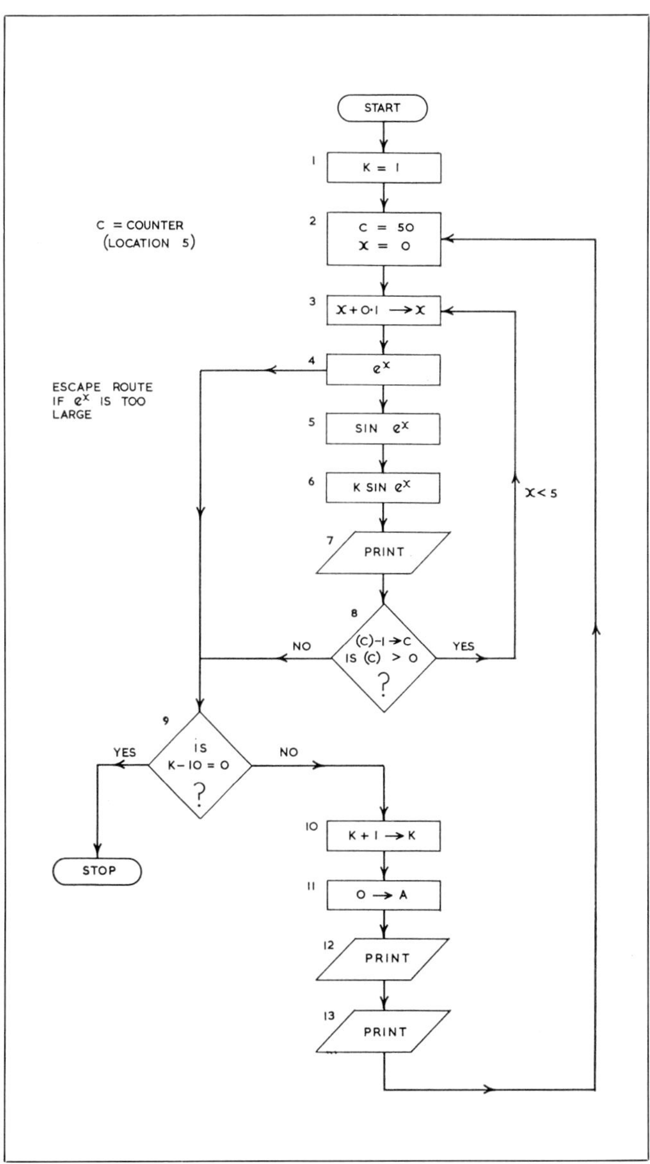

FIG. 9.5. FLOW CHART FOR THE EVALUATION OF $K \sin e^x$

The program for this example is:

(Store program sequentially from location 10)

	INSTRUCTION	m, n	LOCATION	BOX NO.
	LDA	34	10	2
	STA	05	11	
	LDA	00	12	
	STA	38	13	
	LDA	38	14	3
	ADD	35	15	
	STA	38	16	
$x < 5$	EXP	22	17	4
	SIN		18	5
	MLT	33	19	6
	WNA	00	20	7
	LOP	14	21	8
	LDA	33	22	9
	SUB	36	23	
	JEQ	32	24	
	LDA	33	25	10
	ADD	37	26	
	STA	33	27	
$K = 10$	LDA	00	28	11
	WNA	00	29	12
	WNA	00	30	13
	JUN	10	31	
	STOP		32	
Constants:	K (initially 1)		33	1
	50		34	
	0·1		35	
	10		36	
	1		37	

(Execute program beginning at instruction in location 10).

Saving in labour and computing time can sometimes be achieved by rearranging the function to be evaluated.

Consider

$$y = x^4 + 3x^3 + x^2 + 2x + 4$$

Rearrange the function as

$$y = x\left\{x^3 + 3x^2 + x + 2\right\} + 4$$

$$\text{hence } y = x\left\{x[x^2 + 3x + 1] + 2\right\} + 4$$

$$\text{and finally } y = x\left\{x[x(x + 3) + 1] + 2\right\} + 4$$

START HERE

Now the function can be evaluated as in Fig. 9.6.

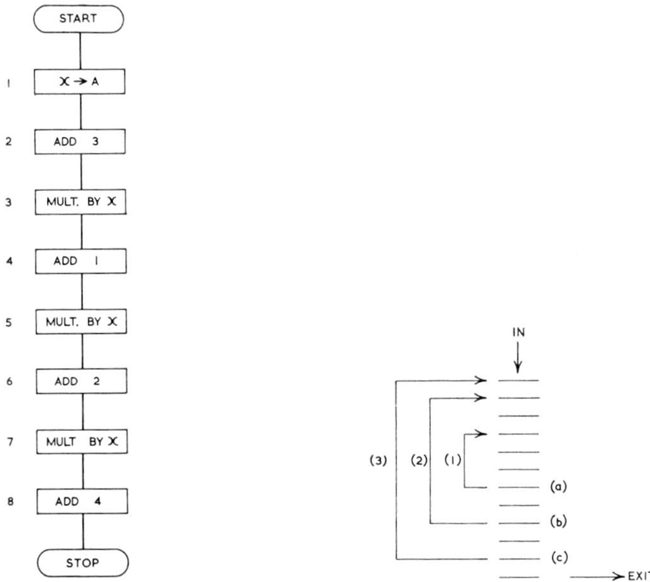

FIG. 9.6. EVALUATION OF $y = x^4 + 3x^3 + x^2 + 2x + 4$

FIG. 9.7. NESTED INSTRUCTIONS

Nesting may be considered as providing loops within other loops. A formal definition is ‘a structure which contains as part of itself a structure of similar form’. Fig. 9.7 represents a list of instructions with decisions and jumps. The instructions are obeyed sequentially down to (a) when loop (1) is entered. After cycling round loop (1) for the requisite number of times the program moves down the list of instructions to (b) when loop (2) is entered. After leaving loop (2), which may involve further excursions round loop (1), the program moves down to (c) and enters loop (3). The loops in Fig. 9.7 are said to be nested ‘3 deep’.

10

ANALOGUE COMPUTING

If we are presented with a mathematical equation we may find that the pencil and paper method of solution is difficult or even impossible. It should be emphasized that in science and technology the likelihood of this is very high. Examples of equations in text books are chosen so that they lead to known solutions, but in real life nature is not so considerate and many equations resulting from scientific investigation are not easily solved.

If, however, we know a simple mechanism or electrical circuit which behaves in accordance with the equation, it may be easier to construct the mechanism or circuit, plot its behaviour, and use this as the solution to the equation. We then say that the 'model' we have made is the **analogue** of the system under investigation.

Figs. 10.1 and 10.2 show simple examples of mechanical and electrical systems that have been used as analogues to perform addition, multiplication, division, etc.

In most modern computers **mechanical rotation** or **voltage** is used to represent the numerical quantity.

Multiplication by a Constant

In any equation there are constant coefficients which must be set into the computer. For example, in

$$4x^2 - 6x + 1 = 0$$

x^2 must be multiplied by 4

x must be multiplied by -6

and the constant 1 added.

The 4, -6, and 1 are the coefficients.

If mechanical rotation is being used as the analogue the coefficients are set by selecting gear ratios, and if voltage is used the coefficients are set by potentiometers, Fig. 10.3. The advantage of using electrical analogues is obvious in this instance; it is easier to turn a knob than to select and change gear wheels.* Notice that the potentiometer can only be set to a value less than one, for coefficients greater than one an amplifier must be incorporated into the circuit.

If current is taken from the output of a potentiometer **loading errors** will occur. Suppose we have a 20 kilohm potentiometer set to a ratio of 0·4. If the input is 100 volts the output will be 40 volts as expected, but if a 100 kilohm load resistor is connected across the output the voltage falls to 38·1 giving an error of approximately 4%.

Potentiometers must be set by measuring the output voltages with the loads connected and *not* by setting the shaft position. The calibrated

* In 1881 the Astronomer Royal, Sir G. B. Airy, produced a table of 3040 gear ratios for use with wheels having up to 100 teeth.

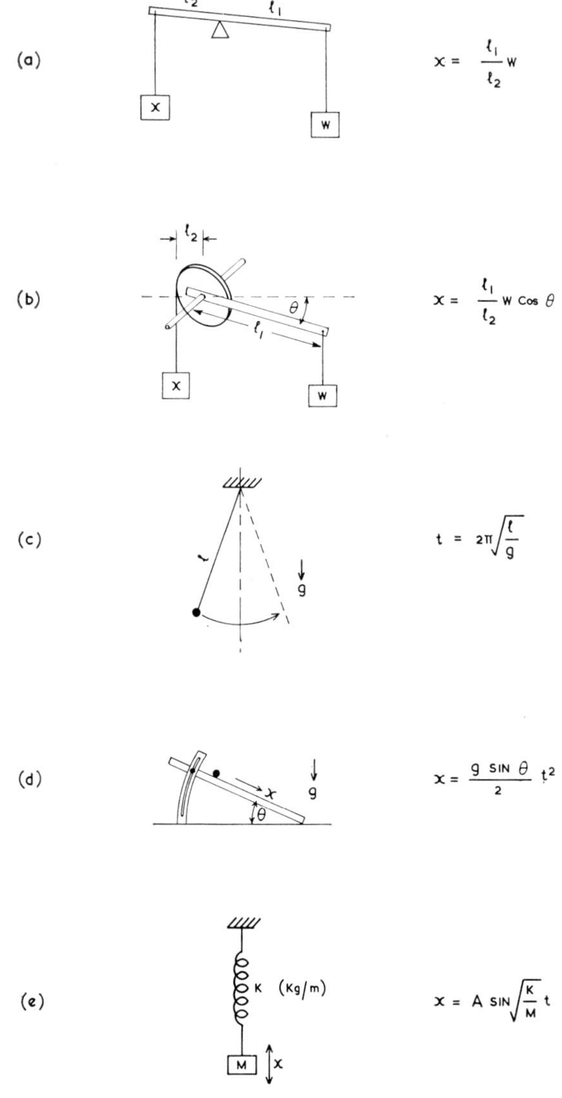

FIG. 10.1. SIMPLE MECHANICAL ANALOGUES

dials that are so often provided are of limited use. It is difficult to set a potentiometer to a very low coefficient, say 0·017, with accuracy. In this case two potentiometers would be used in cascade, as in Fig. 10.4, one set to 0·1 and the other to 0·17.

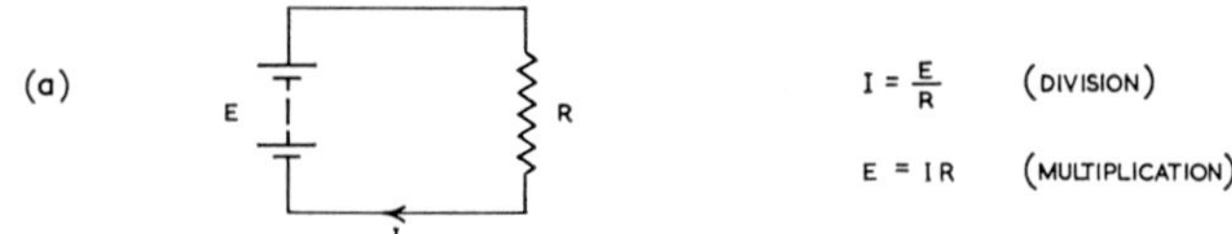

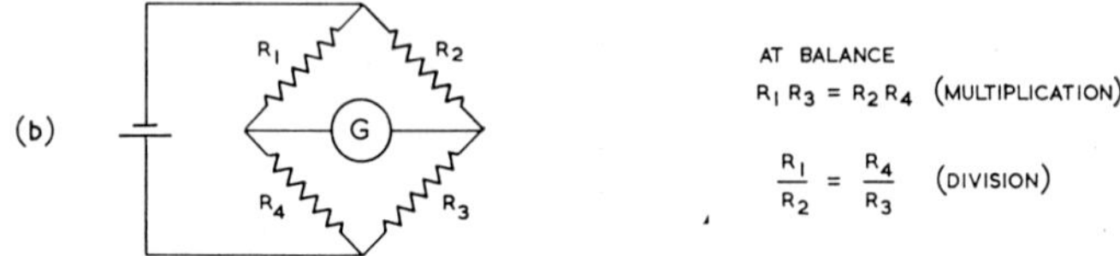

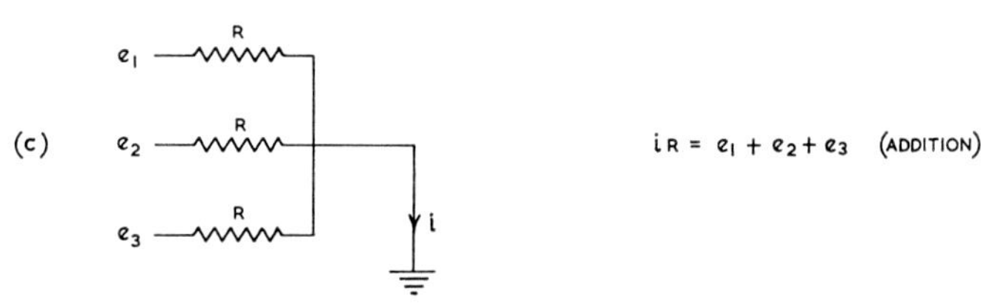

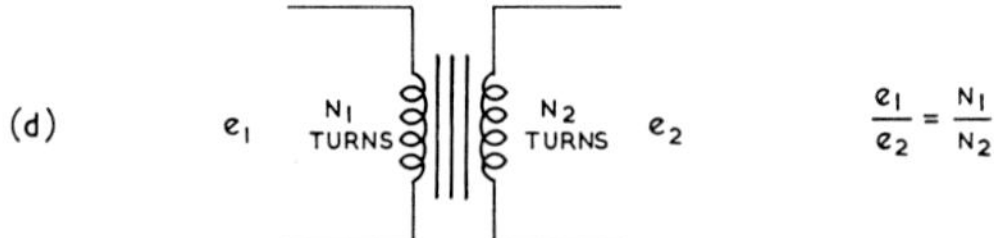

FIG. 10.2. SIMPLE ELECTRICAL ANALOGUES

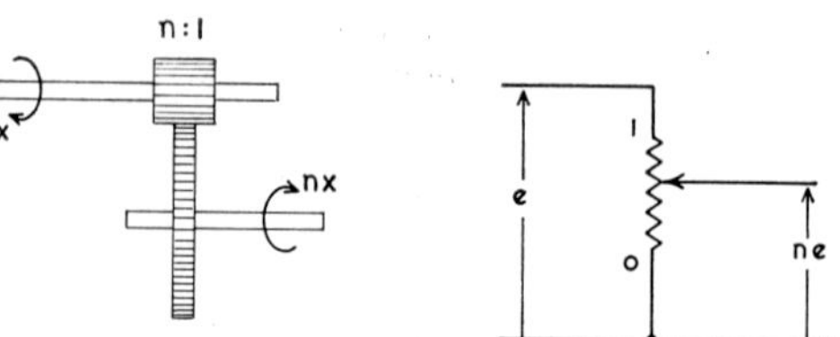

FIG. 10.3. SETTING A COEFFICIENT, n, IN MECHANICAL AND ELECTRICAL ANALOGUES

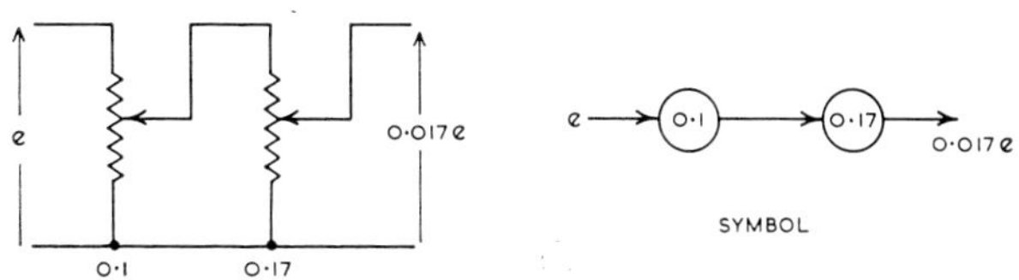

FIG. 10.4. POTENTIOMETERS IN CASCADE

Addition (Summation)

The simple circuit of Fig. 10.2(c) is not satisfactory as a practical adder in an electrical computer. If voltage is used as the analogue the output must also be a voltage, not a current as in this case. To provide this output voltage an **operational amplifier** is used as in Fig. 10.5.

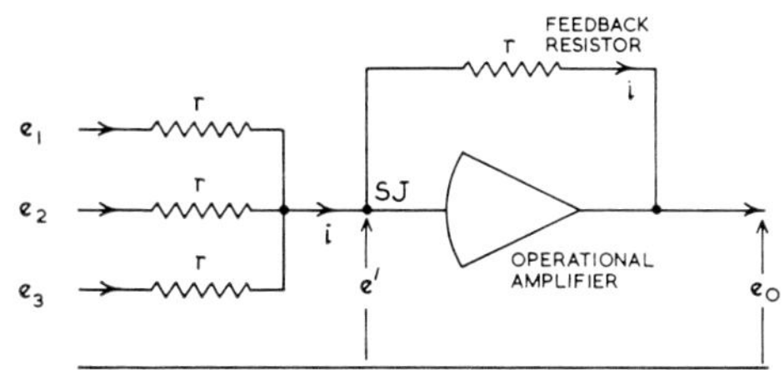

FIG. 10.5. A PRACTICAL ADDER CIRCUIT

This d.c. amplifier has a very high gain ($> 10^6$), a very high input impedance and is sign-reversing, a positive input giving a negative output. As the gain is high e' will be negligible for reasonable values of e_o (± 100 V), and the summing junction, SJ, is called a **virtual earth.** A feedback resistor is connected across the amplifier as shown.

As e' is negligible, the current i is accurately given by

$$i = \frac{e_1}{r} + \frac{e_2}{r} + \frac{e_3}{r}$$

As the amplifier input impedance is high this current can only flow in the feedback resistor. The voltage across the feedback resistor is $-e_o$ (the amplifier changes the sign) and its current will therefore be

$$\frac{-e_o}{r}$$

Equating these currents gives

$$\frac{e_1}{r} + \frac{e_2}{r} + \frac{e_3}{r} = -\frac{e_o}{r}$$

and hence $e_o = -(e_1 + e_2 + e_3)$.

The output voltage is the sum of the inputs, with a change of sign.

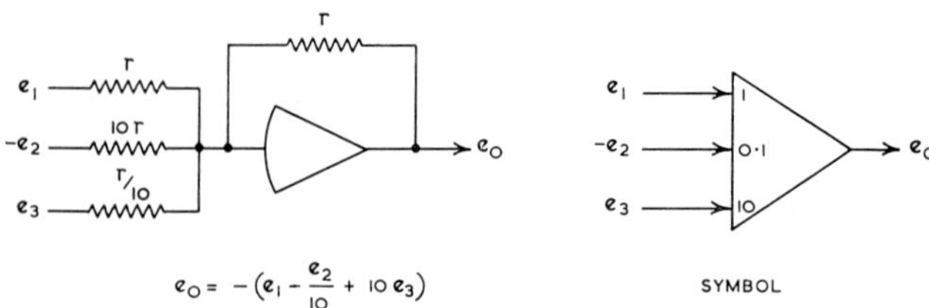

FIG. 10.6. THE ADDITION CIRCUIT AND ITS SYMBOL

The resistors may be of different values to 'weight' the inputs, usually by factors of 10 as in Fig. 10.6.

If some of the inputs are negative the circuit behaves equally well as a subtractor, and of course the number of inputs is not restricted to three as shown in the diagrams. Input and feedback resistors of 1 MΩ, 100 kΩ and 10 kΩ are plugged or 'patched' into the amplifiers as required. Constant input voltages are obtained from a stabilized d.c. supply *via* coefficient potentiometers. The output may be read by a voltmeter if it is a constant (a digital instrument for high accuracy), or displayed on an oscilloscope or x/y graph plotter if it varies with time.

Example 1. An analogue is required to give

$$-47{\cdot}2 + 9{\cdot}8 + 123.$$

Figs. 10.7(a) and (b) show the circuit and its symbol.

In practical computing not all the inputs will be constants but may

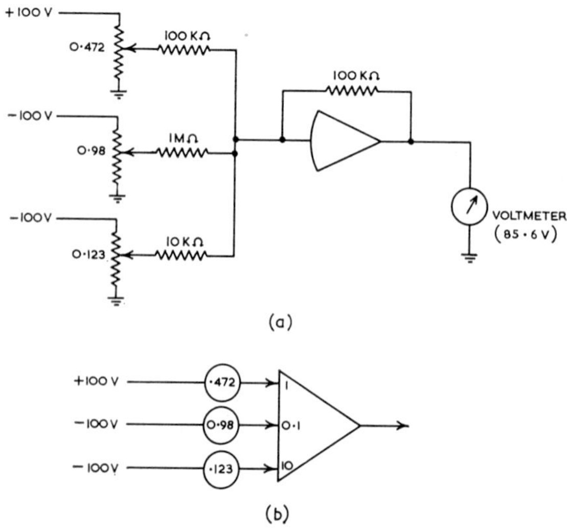

FIG. 10.7. SUMMATION OF $-47{\cdot}2 + 9{\cdot}8 + 123$

represent some time varying functions such as sine waves, exponentials, algebraic functions, etc.

Problem 1. Sketch an electrical analogue to compute

$$2 + 12 - 110.$$

(Answer is on page 179)

Integration

An elementary knowledge of calculus is necessary to understand this section.

To use the operational amplifier as an integrator we replace the feedback resistor of the previous section by a capacitor, Fig. 10.8.

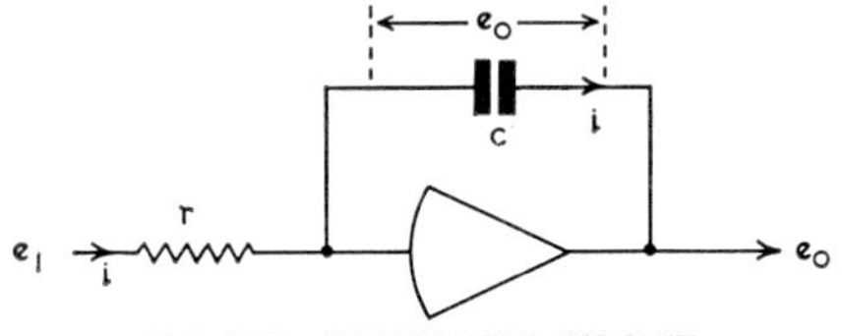

FIG. 10.8. INTEGRATOR CIRCUIT

The current through a capacitor is equal to its capacitance (in Farads) multiplied by the rate of change of voltage across it, and so the capacitor current is

$$C\frac{d(-e_o)}{dt}$$

Equating this to the input current

$$\frac{e_1}{r} = C\frac{d(-e_o)}{dt}$$

and therefore $$d(e_o) = -\frac{e_1}{rC}\,dt$$

Integrating both sides gives

$$e_o = -\frac{1}{rC}\int e_1\,dt$$

and the output is the integral of the input, e_1, again with a change of sign. The constant

$$\frac{1}{rC}$$

is the **integrator constant** and may be made equal to unity by choosing r as 1 MΩ and C as 1 μF.

Problem 2. Show that if the resistor and capacitor are interchanged, the output is proportional to the differential of the input.

(Answer is on page 179)

Summing and integrating may be performed using only one amplifier, Fig. 10.9.

As the integration is performed with respect to time, t, the variable in any equation must be considered as a function of time $f(t)$. When

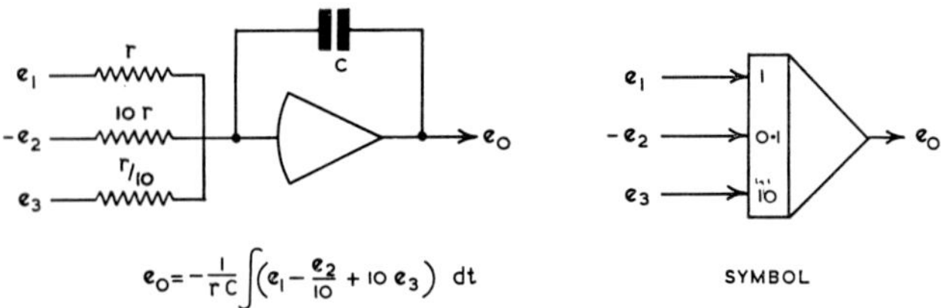

FIG. 10.9. SUMMING AND INTEGRATING

computing starts, the voltage across the capacitor, $-e_o$, must represent the **initial condition,** *i.e.* the value of the output at $t = 0$. This value, in volts, is given in a rectangle alongside the integrator symbol. A terminal is provided on the amplifier for inserting this initial voltage, which is taken from a coefficient potentiometer. If no initial condition is applied the integration commences with the capacitor discharged ($e_o = 0$). The computer control switch is initially in the 'reset' position, and to start integrating it is switched to 'compute' at a time corresponding to $t = 0$.

Example 2. To compute $y = 3x + 4$.

Let x represent time in seconds.

The initial condition ($x = 0$) gives $y = 4$.

The output y must be the result of integrating

$$-\frac{dy}{dx}$$

(note the sign change because of the integrator).

But

$$\frac{dy}{dx} = 3$$

hence the analogue will be as in Fig. 10.10.

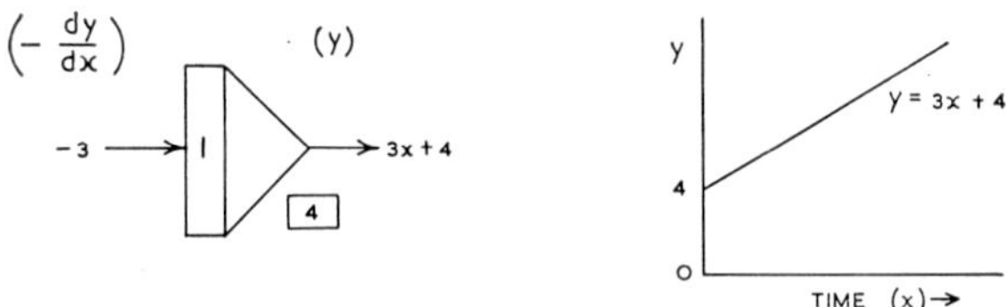

FIG. 10.10. COMPUTATION OF $y = 3x + 4$

To generate algebraic functions of a higher order, quadratics, cubics, etc., more integrators are used.

Example 3. To compute $f(t) = t^2 - 5t + 6$

This is the result of integrating $-(2t - 5)$ which is itself the result of integrating 2.

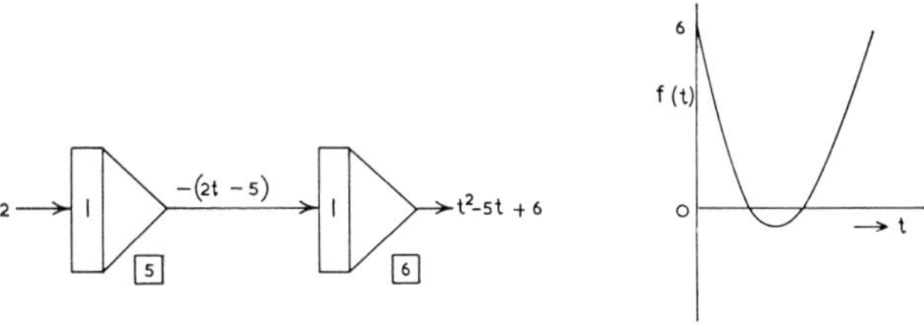

FIG. 10.11. COMPUTATION OF $f(t) = t^2 - 5t + 6$

Fig. 10.11 shows the analogue arrangement with the required initial conditions.

If the output voltage is fed into an oscilloscope or x/y plotter the graph of the function will be produced. Note that negative values of the variable are not permitted as this would require 'negative time'. If the computation is not stopped the output voltage will continue to rise until the amplifier **saturates.** Above this value the output is meaningless. The saturation voltage is usually 100 V for a valve computer and 10 V for one using transistors.

Some Uses of the Computer in Dynamics

The motion of a body under constant acceleration is given by

$$v = u + at$$

$$v^2 = u^2 + 2as$$

$$s = ut + \tfrac{1}{2}at^2$$

where v = velocity at time t

u = initial velocity at $t = 0$

a = acceleration

s = distance travelled.

Note that as

$$v = \frac{ds}{dt} \quad \text{and} \quad a = \frac{dv}{dt}$$

s is the integral of v and v is the integral of a.

An analogue for the distance, s, is shown in Fig. 10.12.

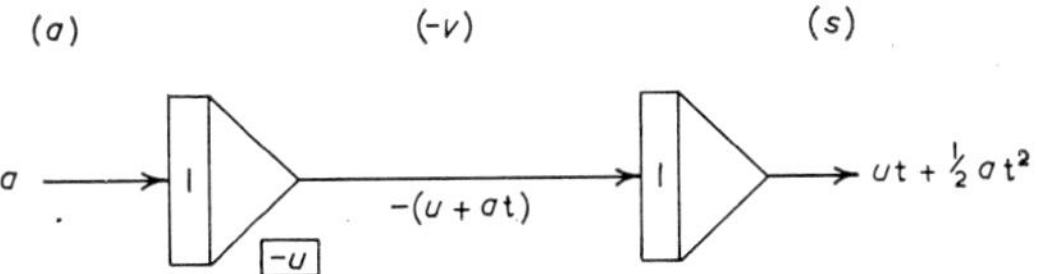

FIG. 10.12. ANALOGUE FOR THE POSITION OF A BODY UNDER CONSTANT ACCELERATION

To obtain numerical results the relationship between the mechanical units and the computer voltages must be determined. This is called

amplitude scaling, and is illustrated by the following example.

Example 4. A body of mass 10 kg is released from a height of 70 m. Construct an analogue giving the position of the body after release at $t = 0$.

In order that the amplifiers do not saturate we must ensure that the integrator outputs do not exceed, say, 100 V. The maximum values of velocity, v, and distance, s, must be estimated.

s_{max} will be 70 m as given in the problem.

The maximum velocity is calculated from

$$v^2 = u^2 + 2gs$$

and will occur when $s = 70$ m.

$u = 0$, initially at rest.

$g =$ acceleration due to gravity, 9·81 m/s².

$$\therefore \; v_{max} = \sqrt{2gs} = \sqrt{2 \times 9{\cdot}81 \times 70} \simeq 38 \text{ m/s}.$$

We now choose a scale such that the voltages do not exceed 100, but are not too small. For best accuracy the voltages should be as large as possible within the permitted range.

Let 1 volt represent 1 metre, giving a maximum of 70 V.

Let 1 volt represent 0·5 m/s, giving a maximum of 76 V.

The scaled analogue is then as in Fig. 10.13.

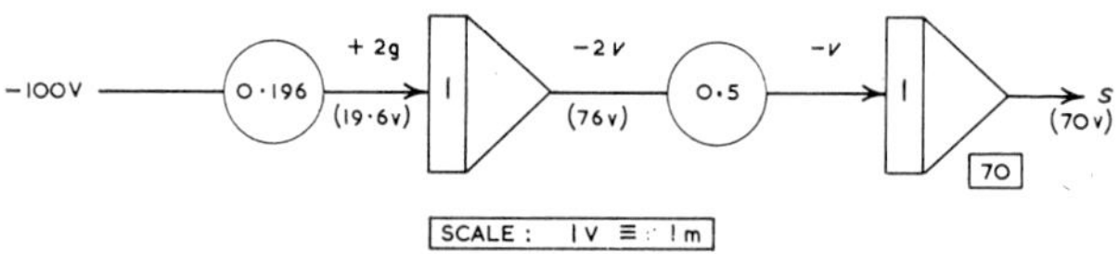

FIG. 10.13. SCALED EXAMPLE FOR A FALLING BODY

As the acceleration is acting **downwards** it is represented by a **negative** voltage. To obtain a velocity scale of 1 V = 0·5 m/s, $-2v$ is required as the output from the first integrator and is obtained by integrating $2g$, ($2 \times 9{\cdot}81 = 19{\cdot}62$). This must be reduced by the potentiometer to v before integrating to obtain s. The initial condition of $s = 70$ m is represented by applying 70 V to the second integrator.

In practice most moving bodies will be subjected to some form of damping or air resistance. Assuming this to be proportional to the velocity, say Kv,

$$\text{Force} = \text{Mass} \times \text{Acceleration}$$

therefore the deceleration, a_r, due to the resistive force Kv, is given by

$$Kv = Ma_r \quad \text{where } M \text{ is the mass,}$$

or

$$a_r = \frac{Kv}{M}$$

The total acceleration on the body will be $a - a_r$

$$\text{or} \qquad a - \frac{Kv}{M}$$

The analogue must now be modified to that shown in Fig. 10.14.

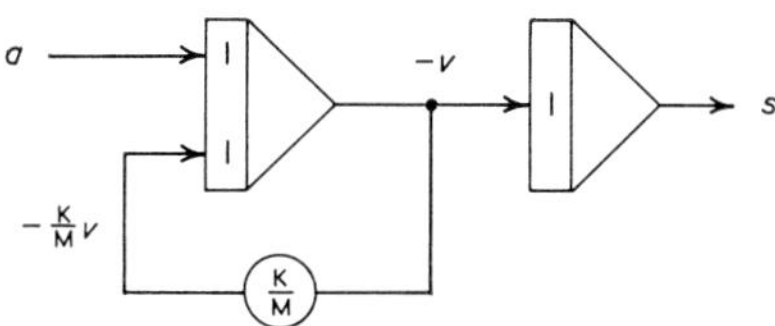

FIG. 10.14. MOTION WITH RESISTANCE PROPORTIONAL TO VELOCITY

Let the resistive force be 0·1 newton/metre/second in the previous scaled example.

$$\text{Then} \qquad \frac{K}{M} = \frac{0{\cdot}1}{10} = 0{\cdot}01$$

and the analogue is as Fig. 10.15.

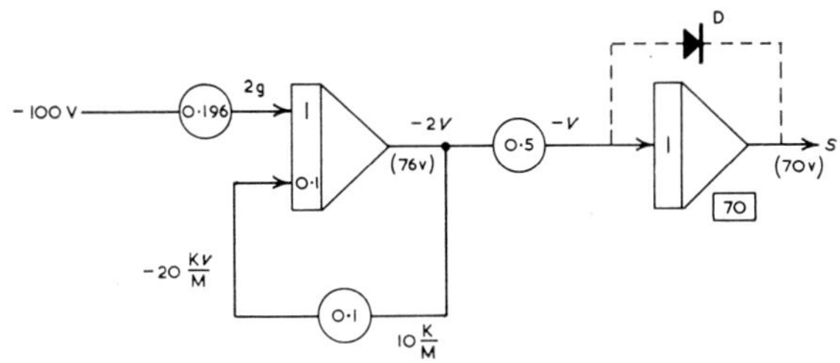

FIG. 10.15. SCALED EXAMPLE OF A FALLING BODY WITH AIR DAMPING

As the setting of the

$$\frac{K}{M}$$

potentiometer is difficult, 0·1 is used together with a factor of 0·1 at the integrator input. The diode D prevents the output from going negative and hence simulates the body falling to rest at ground level.

Example 5. To compute the path of a body projected with an initial velocity v at an elevation of $\theta°$ to the horizontal.

The horizontal and vertical components of the initial velocity are $v \cos \theta$ and $v \sin \theta$ respectively, Fig. 10.16. The equations of motion are

$$\frac{dx}{dt} = v \cos \theta \quad ; \quad \frac{dy}{dt} = v \sin \theta - gt \quad ; \quad \text{and} \quad \frac{d^2y}{dt^2} = -g$$

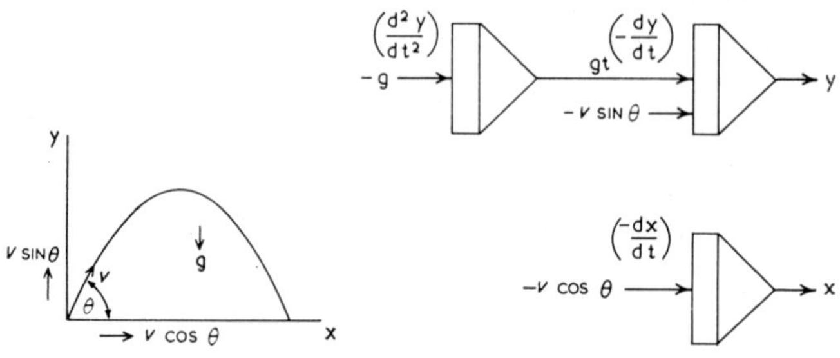

FIG. 10.16. THE PATH OF A PROJECTILE

If the x and y voltages are applied to an oscilloscope or x/y plotter the path of the body in space will be displayed.

Problem 3. Scale an analogue to compute the path of a body projected with a velocity of 30 m/s at an elevation of 60°. (g = 9·81 m/s^2).

(Answer is on page 179)

Time-Scaling

We have seen that the **amplitudes** of the quantities may be scaled by choosing the voltage levels and multiplying factors. In certain circumstances it is necessary to change the **time-scale** and produce the computed output either faster or slower than the real event. Take for example the heating and cooling curve of a large machine or building; a 24-hour period must be compressed into a few seconds in order that the temperature may be plotted or displayed on an oscilloscope. By contrast, the projectile in Example 5 may be a charged particle in an electrostatic field, the total time of flight of which is only a few microseconds. To display this result we must expand the time into several seconds.

Time-scaling is effected by changing **all** the integrator resistors (or capacitors) by the same factor. Fig. 10.17 shows an integrator with a

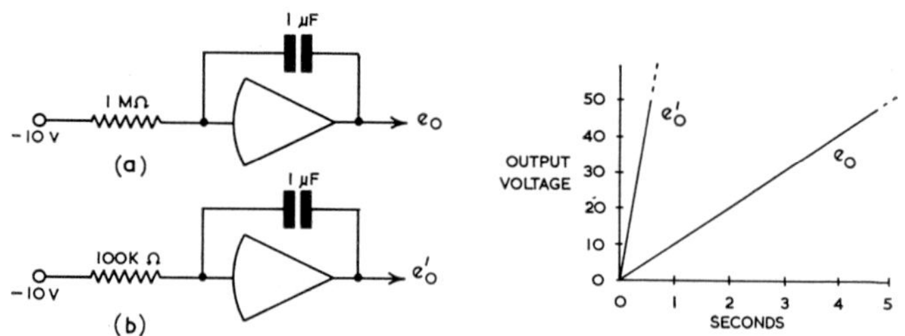

FIG. 10.17. TIME-SCALING AN INTEGRATOR

1 MΩ resistor (a), and a 100 kΩ resistor (b). The output in both cases is of the same form, a straight line if the input is a constant, but the time-scale differs by a factor of 10.

To **slow down** a computation the input resistors must be **increased,** and *vice versa.* The amplitude scaling remains unaffected as **all** the integrator resistors are changed by the same factor. Changing the capacitors is a possible method of time-scaling but a wider range of resistors is more often available.

Example 6. The path of an electron in an electric field.
Fig. 10.18(a) shows two metal plates 0·8 cm apart with a potential difference of 50 V between them. An electron e is fired between them with a velocity of 10^7 m/s at an angle of $\theta°$ to a plane parallel to the plates.

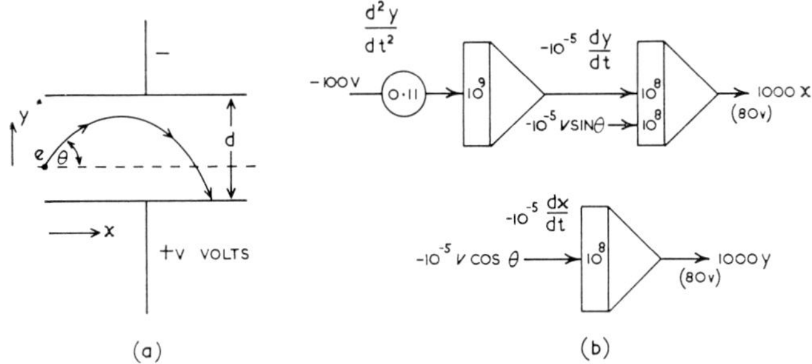

FIG. 10.18. PATH OF AN ELECTRON IN AN ELECTROSTATIC FIELD

The acceleration of the electron is given by

$$\frac{d^2y}{dt^2} = \frac{e}{m} \cdot \frac{V}{d}$$

where $\frac{e}{m} = 1{\cdot}76 \times 10^{11}$ coulombs/kg.

$V = 50$ V

and $d = 0{\cdot}008$ m.

Therefore $\frac{d^2y}{dt^2} = 1{\cdot}1 \times 10^{15}$

The basic analogue will be the same as Fig. 10.16, and a scaled diagram is given in Fig. 10.18(b).

For practical purposes the integrator multiplying factors are absurdly large, but if we reduce them **all** by 10^8 we have reasonable values, and the time-scale has been slowed down by 10^8. The final scaling is therefore

1 Second Computer Time $= 10^{-8}$ Seconds Real Time.

(continued overleaf)

Problem 4. Design an analogue to give the temperature within a building, θ_2, if the rate of change of θ_2 is given by

$$\frac{d\theta_2}{dt} = \frac{P}{H} - \frac{\phi}{H}(\theta_2 - \theta_1)$$

where

$P = 50$ kW (Heater)
$H = 840$ kJ/°C (Thermal Capacity)
$\phi = 6$ kW/°C (Rate of Heat Loss)
θ_1 = is the outside ambient temperature, and is the variable input.

Scale the computer so that 1 second computer time is equivalent to 10,000 seconds real time (8 seconds $\simeq$ 24 hours).

(Answer is on page 180)

Differential Equations

The previous examples are all solutions of differential equations of the types

$$A\frac{dy}{dx} + By + C = 0 \quad \text{.......................(1)}$$

and
$$A\frac{d^2y}{dx^2} + B\frac{dy}{dx} + Cy + D = 0 \quad \text{...........(2)}$$

We may generalize the results and give electrical analogues for both equations.

Rearranging the equations,

$$-\frac{dy}{dx} = \frac{B}{A}y + \frac{C}{A} \qquad \text{from (1)}$$

and
$$\frac{d^2y}{dx^2} = -\frac{B}{A}\frac{dy}{dx} - \frac{C}{A}y - \frac{D}{A} \qquad \text{from (2).}$$

Fig. 10.19 shows the analogues for these equations. Remember that the appropriate initial conditions must be applied to the integrators.

Function Generators

In solving problems it is often required to introduce algebraic functions, sines, cosines, exponentials, etc. These must be generated by the computer.

Algebraic functions of the form

$$Ax^n + Bx^{n-1} + Cx^{n-2} + \ldots$$

are generated by repeated integration, as in Examples 2 and 3. If the required function is repeatedly differentiated a constant will be produced eventually. This constant is fed into the first of a series of integrators with appropriate initial conditions.

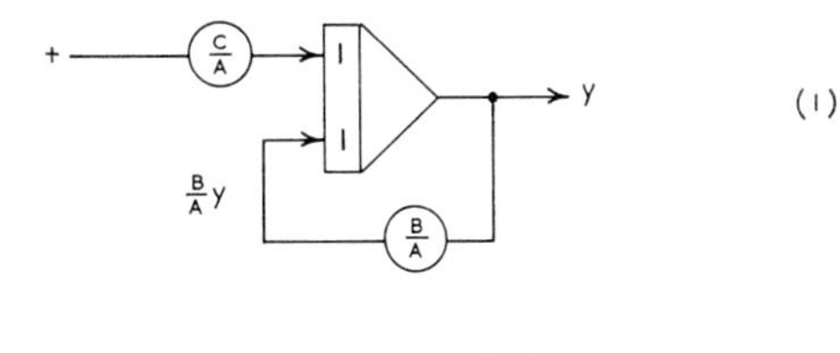

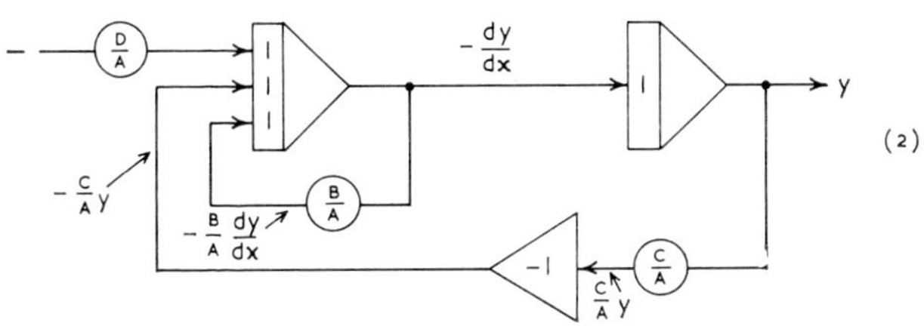

FIG. 10.19. GENERAL SOLUTIONS OF 1st AND 2nd ORDER DIFFERENTIAL EQUATIONS

Example 7.

$$y = x^4 + 4x^3 - 3x + 6$$

$$\therefore \frac{dy}{dx} = 4x^3 + 12x^2 - 3$$

and $$\frac{d^2y}{dx^2} = 12x^2 + 24x$$

and $$\frac{d^3y}{dx^3} = 24x + 24$$

and $$\frac{d^4y}{dx^4} = 24 \qquad \text{(the required constant).}$$

Reversing the process, y will be the result of integrating 24 four times, as in Fig. 10.20.

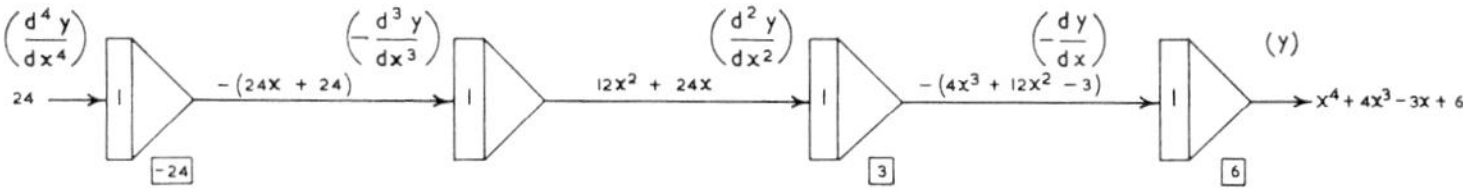

FIG. 10.20. GENERATION OF THE ALGEBRAIC FUNCTION $y = x^4 + 4x^3 - 3x + 6$

Several useful functions may be generated as known solutions of differential equations.

The solution of $$\frac{d^2x}{dt^2} = -x$$

will be either $x = A \sin t$

or $x = A \cos t$

depending on whether the initial condition is zero or A. Introducing a constant, ω, it is possible to generate the **trigonometrical functions** $A \sin \omega t$ and $A \cos \omega t$ from one circuit, as in Fig. 10.21.

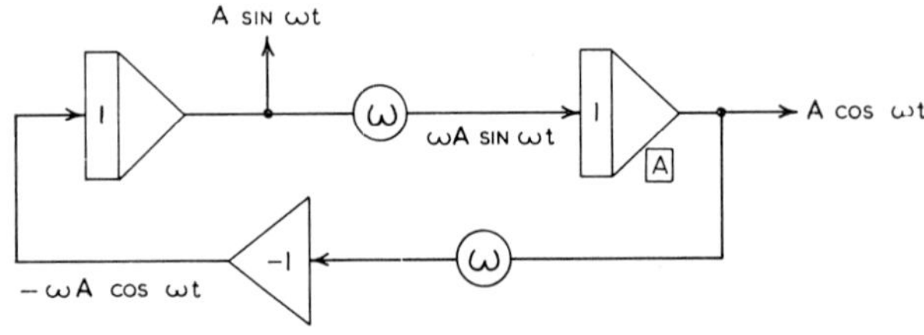

FIG. 10.21. GENERATION OF SINES AND COSINES

Solutions of $\dfrac{dx}{dt} = \pm Kx$ will be **exponentials** of the form $x = Ae^{\pm kt}$, and the circuits are shown in Fig. 10.22.

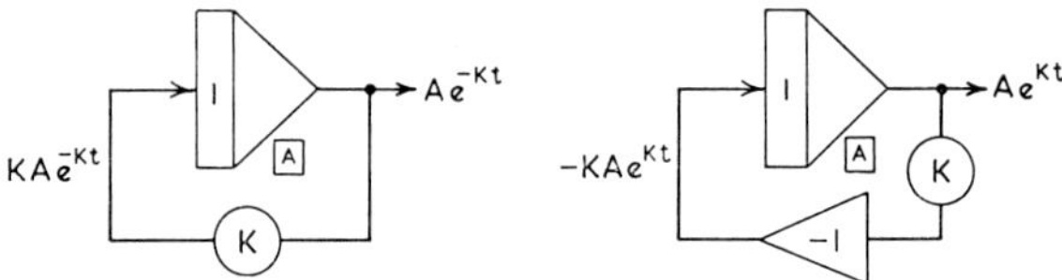

FIG. 10.22. GENERATION OF EXPONENTIAL FUNCTIONS

Transformer Analogues

Simultaneous equations may be solved by using the principle of Fig. 10.2(d), where the r.m.s. value of an a.c. voltage is the analogue quantity. This relies on the property of a transformer that the primary and secondary ampere-turns are equal (neglecting the magnetizing current).

To solve simultaneous equations of the type

$$ax + by + c = 0 \quad \ldots\ldots\ldots\ldots\ldots\ldots \quad (1)$$

$$dx + ey + f = 0 \quad \ldots\ldots\ldots\ldots\ldots\ldots \quad (2)$$

three transformers are used, the ratios being set to the coefficients *a*, *b*, *c*, *d*, *e* and *f*, as in Fig. 10.23.

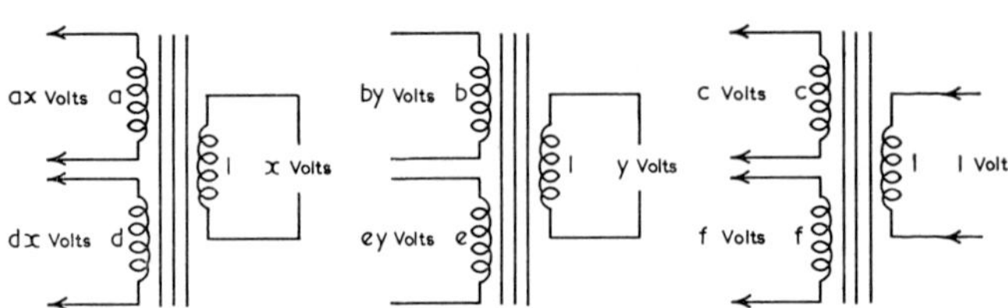

FIG. 10.23. TRANSFORMER ANALOGUE RATIOS

If we assume that the answers, x and y, are to appear at the secondaries of the first and second transformers, the primary voltages will be ax, dx, *by* and *ey*. Applying 1 volt to the third transformer secondary gives primary voltages of *c* and *f* volts.

Using equation (**1**), these three voltages may be connected in series and short circuited, as their sum is zero. The second equation is incorporated in a similar manner, giving the complete analogue, Fig. 10.24.

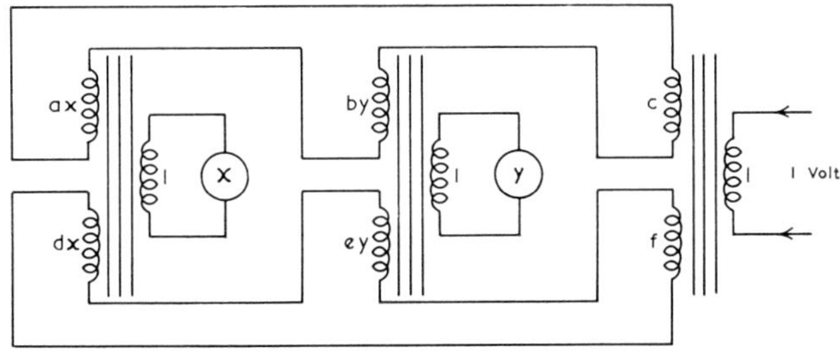

FIG. 10.24. TRANSFORMER ANALOGUE FOR TWO SIMULTANEOUS EQUATIONS

If 1 volt is applied to the third transformer, voltmeters connected to *x* and *y* will indicate the magnitude of the solutions.

The principle may be extended to any number of equations. The ratios are set by decade tappings on the windings and selected by switches. Transformer analogues are used in the solution of linear network problems, *e.g.* electricity supply grids covering an area of the country, where several hundred transformers may be used in the computer.*

Field Plotting Analogues

Analogues have been used for many years to determine the shape of **two-dimensional fields** such as magnetic or electrostatic fields, isothermals, fluid flow lines, contours, etc. These fields are difficult to calculate for all but the simplest geometrical boundary shapes.

It is possible to plot an electromagnetic field by the rather crude method of sprinkling iron filings on to a surface in the field, although this is difficult (if not impossible) to calibrate. Fortunately, all these fields are the solution of the same mathematical equation (Laplace's equation) and we may use the same analogue to solve them all.

Fig. 10.25 shows a typical field pattern where A and B represent the boundaries, *e.g.* magnetic pole-pieces, electrodes at different potentials,

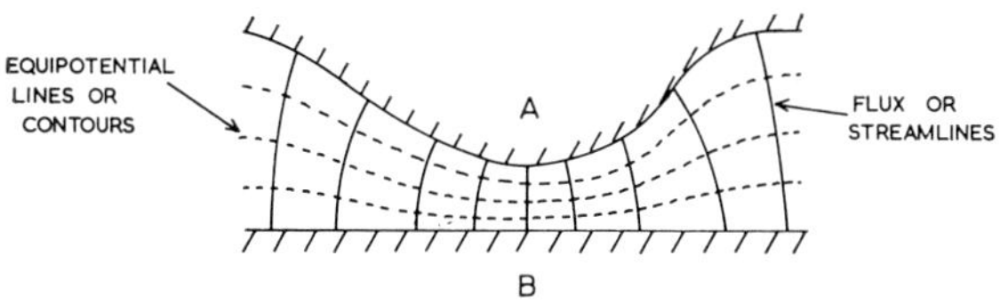

FIG. 10.25. TYPICAL TWO-DIMENSIONAL FIELD

surfaces at different temperatures, etc. The diagram will also represent the flow of a liquid or gas past a constriction in a pipe if the contours and stream-lines are interchanged.

* Humphrey Davies, M.W.; Slemon, G. R.; "Transformer–Analogue Network Analysers", *Proc.I.E.E.*, Vol. 100, Pt. II pp 469–486.

Resistance-Paper Analogues—Metal electrodes shaped to represent the boundaries of the field are attached or painted on to a sheet of paper coated with a thin layer of conducting material (usually graphite). When potentials are applied to these electrodes the voltage distribution across the paper represents a map of the field. The strength of the field at any point is determined by a metal probe connected to a voltage detector, Fig. 10.26. The probe current must be small in order not to affect the shape of the voltage distribution.

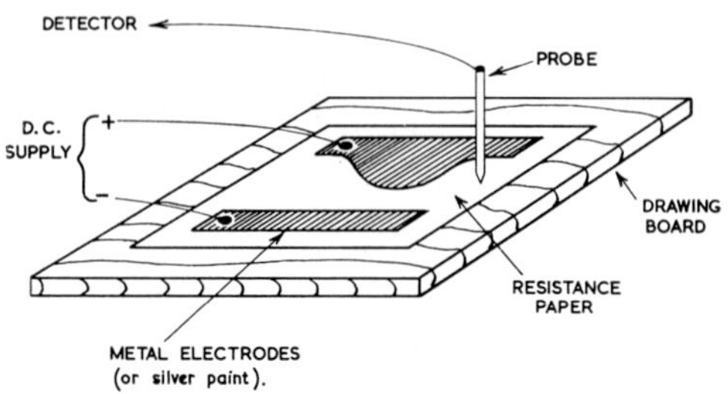

FIG. 10.26. RESISTANCE-PAPER ANALOGUE

To ensure this, it is preferable to balance the probe potential against a fixed reference voltage by means of a null-detecting galvanometer. In this way the equipotential lines may be plotted directly on to graph paper placed under the resistance paper by pricking points through with a needle point, or by using carbon paper. Pencil lines should not be drawn on the resistance paper.

Electrolytic Tank Analogue—An improvement on this form of field plotting is to replace the resistance paper by a shallow tank of liquid (the **electrolyte**), metal electrodes being placed in the tank to represent the field boundaries, Fig. 10.27. To avoid errors due to polarization a.c. is used as the supply. Salt water is a convenient electrolyte.

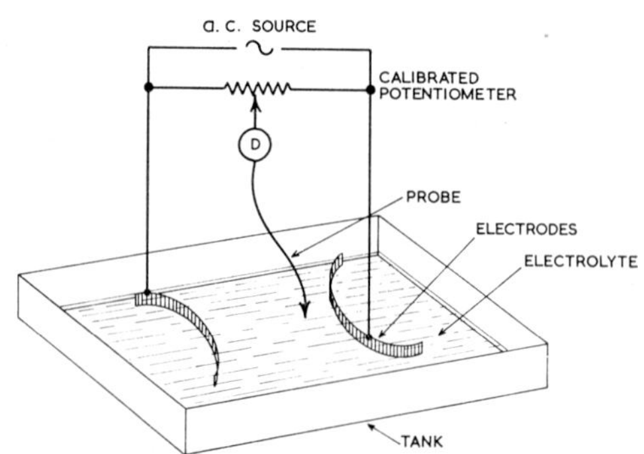

FIG. 10.27. THE ELECTROLYTIC TANK

If the probe voltage is fed into an x/y plotter, the pen carriage of which is mechanically connected to the probe, the field plot is drawn

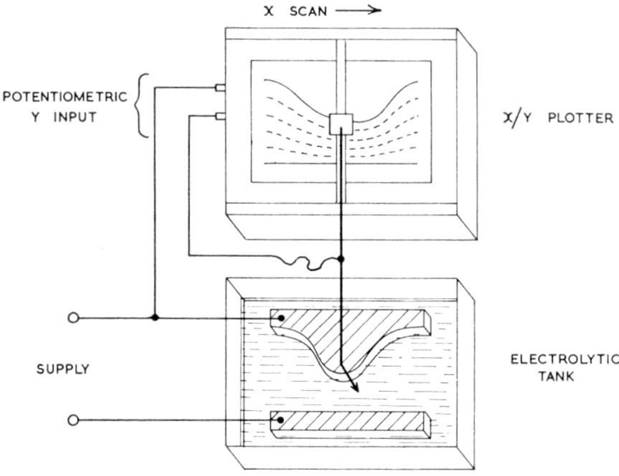

FIG. 10.28. AUTOMATIC FIELD PLOTTER

automatically as the pen is traversed across the paper, Fig. 10.28.

The lines plotted will be the equipotential lines of Fig. 10.25.

Rubber Sheet Analogues—If a rubber sheet is stretched tightly over models of the electrodes, where the relative physical heights of the models represent their potentials, the contours of the rubber sheet represent the potential contours of the field, Fig. 10.29.

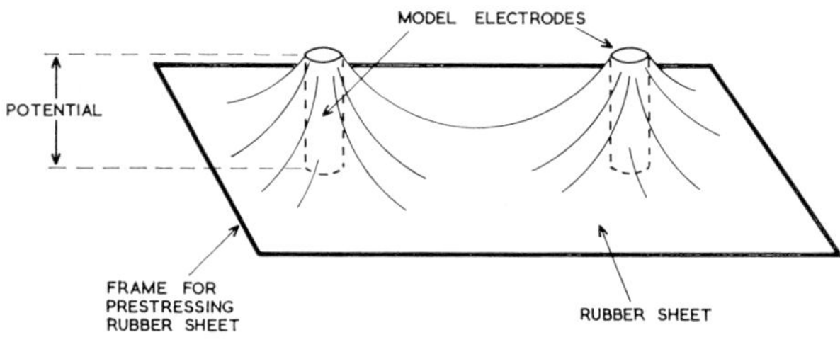

FIG. 10.29. RUBBER SHEET ANALOGUE

The advantage of this method is that the whole field contours are visible together. The rubber sheet analogue may be used for plotting electron paths in a field, as a small sphere (*e.g.* ball-bearing) released from a point on the sheet will trace out the same path under gravity as the electron would follow under the influence of the electric field. The flow lines may be recorded by exposing a camera plate or film above the sheet and illuminating the sphere by a flashing light. This produces a dotted trace on the plate, Fig. 10.30 (overleaf.)

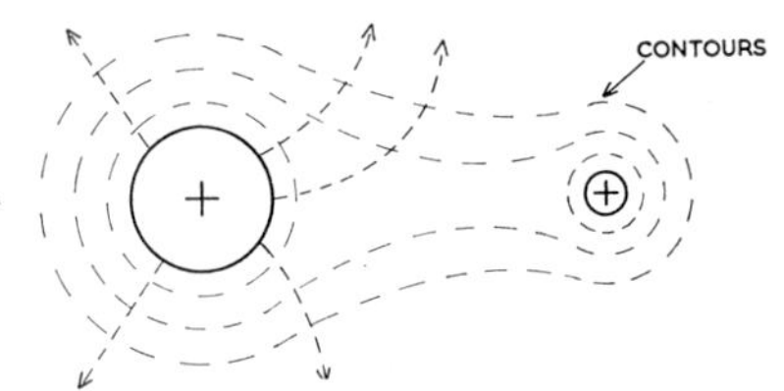

FIG. 10.30. ELECTRON PATHS IN AN ELECTRIC FIELD

Examples (Chapter 10)

(1) Give an electrical and a mechanical analogue to solve

$$4 + 6x + 2y = 0$$

for y, where x is a variable input.

(2) Design mechanical or electrical analogues to produce the following functions:

(a) $y = x^2 - 3x + 1$

(b) $y = 3 \sin x.$

(3) Sketch electrical analogues to solve

(a) $4y + 7x = 0$

$y + x = 0$ as simultaneous equations,

and (b) $4x = \dfrac{y}{9}$ assuming that either x or y is given.

(Answers are on pages 180/181)

11

COMPUTERS IN USE

Commercial Applications

Although computers are often thought of as mathematical tools it must be remembered that they developed from business machines and that the majority are used today in commercial applications. By comparison, the computing time devoted to mathematical research, technology and design, is small. This does not imply that such uses are less important, but that the day-to-day processing of payrolls, insurance contributions, bank transactions, invoices, etc., presents a greater work-load for the computer than does research and design in most organizations. The number of computers used in process control is, however, increasing, and with installations in machine shops, power stations, chemical and steel plants, navigation and traffic control, the commercial usage may not be so predominant in the future.

Data processing in commerce requires only elementary arithmetic functions such as addition, subtraction, multiplication, together with a vast storage capability and facilities for sorting, masking and shifting data. As magnetic tapes can store large amounts of information they are convenient for filing payments, accounts, inventories and records of all kinds. The 'files' are updated by feeding in daily or other periodic changes (the transactions) on punched cards or paper tape. These transactions may also be fed from on-line terminals operated remotely from the computer and connected by Post Office lines.

A simplified system is shown in Fig. 11.1.

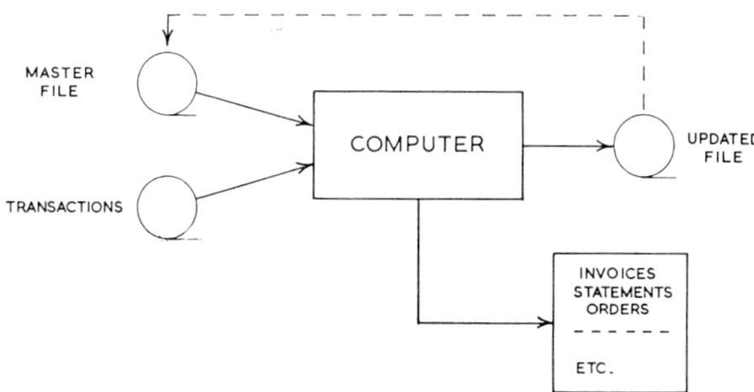

FIG. 11.1. UPDATING A TAPE FILE

At the end of one **run** the updated file becomes the new master file for the next run. In practice it is often more convenient to prepare the transactions on the cards or paper tape by a preliminary run on the computer which sorts the data and records it on magnetic tape. Several such tapes may be prepared from different sources and combined in a final run to update the master files. Fig. 11.2 shows this system in use for a banking application.

In stock control the recorded data may consist of part numbers, quantity in stock, reordering levels, delivery times and names and

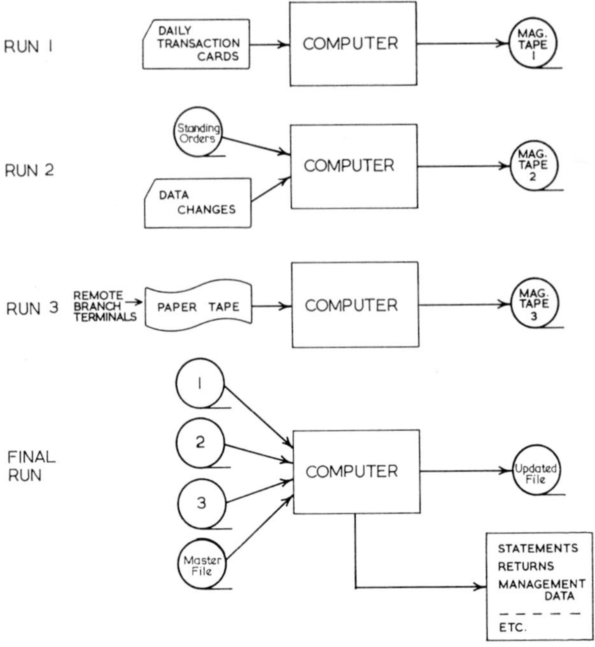

FIG. 11.2. COMMERCIAL BANKING SYSTEM

addresses of suppliers. The transactions will consist of deposits and withdrawals from stock, and when a quantity falls below the reordering level the computer can print out the complete order for the appropriate quantity. If the current price for each item is also held in the computer the total value of items stocked can be produced on demand. Data changes such as price increases, loss, damage, error, theft, increased or decreased demand, are fed into the computer to modify the master file as required.

Computers are used to prepare bills for utility services such as gas and electricity. The calculations form a standard routine and the large number of consumers makes the use of a computer almost essential. We will take the preparation of an electricity bill as an example, using a domestic tariff.

Example 1. The simplest tariff offered to the domestic consumer is usually of the form:

3·2p per unit for the first block of 72 units per quarter;
0·8p per unit for each additional unit per quarter.

The basic computer system could be as shown in Fig. 11.3.

A simplified flow chart of the computer procedure is shown in Fig. 11.4.

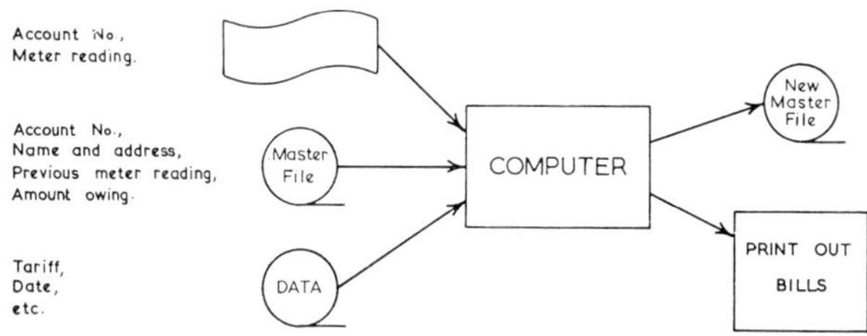

FIG. 11.3. ELECTRICITY BILLING

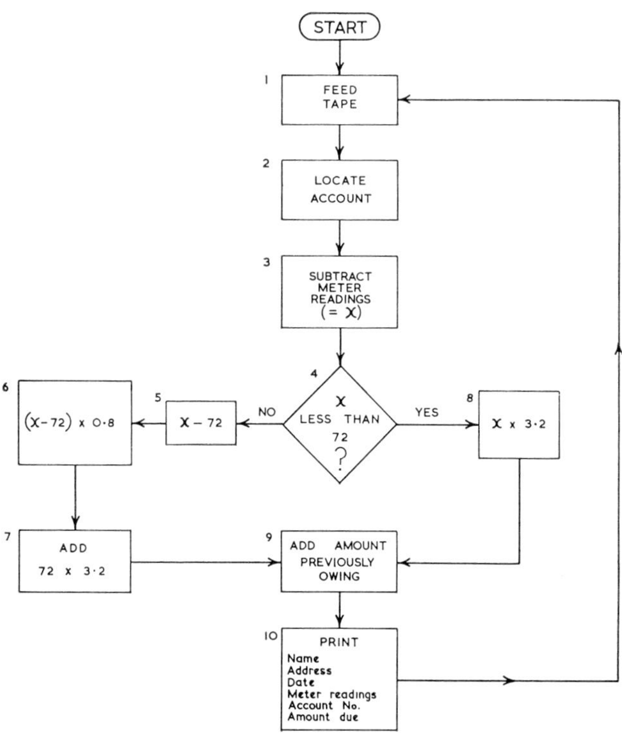

FIG. 11.4. FLOW CHART FOR ELECTRICITY BILLING

Some forms of management may be more efficient if performed by computer, as a large quantity of facts are quickly available on which to base decisions. One way of using computers in production management is by a **critical path analysis** of the processes leading up to the final product.

Example 2. Imagine a product made from pressed and cast metal parts: some to be painted, some to be drilled and bent, all to be finally assembled and tested. Let the times taken for these operations be:

Pressing	1 hour
Casting	2 hours
Painting and Drying	3 hours
Drilling	½ hour
Bending	¼ hour
Machining	1 hour
Assembling	3 hours
Testing	½ hour

It is difficult to see from this list which operations determine the overall production time. Would production time be cut if the casting operation were speeded up? To see what would happen, a critical path diagram must be drawn as in Fig. 11.5.

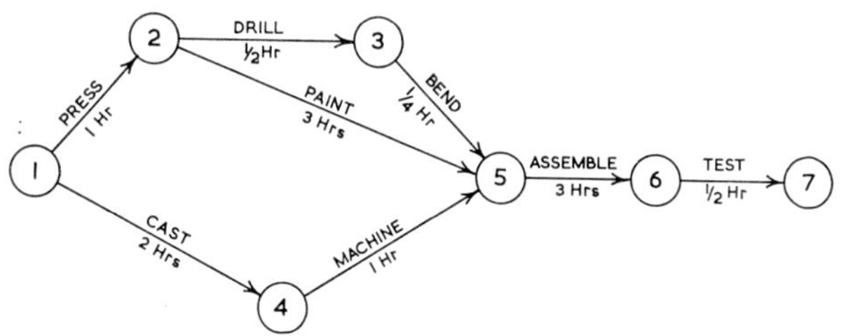

FIG. 11.5. CRITICAL PATH DIAGRAM

The longest path is obviously 1–2–5–6–7 taking 7½ hours, and this is the critical path. Increasing the speed of processes not on this path will have no effect on production time. The casting operation is therefore non-critical. If the painting and drying operations were reduced to 1 hour the critical path becomes 1–4–5–6–7 and the casting operation is now critical.

The solution to this problem did not require a computer, but imagine the critical path diagram for the production of an aeroplane, a block of flats or a nuclear power station. There will be thousands of operations incorporating delivery dates, labour availability, holidays, subcontracted items, etc. The critical path analysis is now only possible with the aid of a computer.

The 'obvious' or intuitive solution to a management problem may not always be the correct one. This is clearly illustrated by the **transportation problem.** This is an example of 'linear programming' widely used in operational research. We will consider here a very simple problem, remembering that in actual business practice the increased complexity will make the use of a computer essential.

Example 3. Suppose that engine parts are manufactured in Birmingham and London: 50,000 parts being supplied by Birmingham, and 20,000 by London. Factories at Peterborough and Coventry have a demand for 30,000 parts and 40,000 parts respectively. The best way of distributing the parts will depend upon the transport costs.

Let the costs be:

Birmingham to Peterborough	£7 per hundred
Birmingham to Coventry	£5 per hundred
London to Peterborough	£5 per hundred
London to Coventry	£4 per hundred.

The non-mathematical manager may argue that since the route from London to Coventry is the cheapest, as many parts as possible shall be sent by this route. His solution could be arranged in tabular form as:

	Peterborough	Coventry
Birmingham	30,000	20,000
London	Nil	20,000

The total transport cost is

$$(300 \times 7) + (200 \times 5) + (200 \times 4) = £3,900.$$

But this is **not** the cheapest solution.

The computer can **optimise** the distribution to give a minimum cost by first analysing the manager's trial solution. The costs for the three routes used are:

	Peterborough	Coventry
Birmingham	7	5
London		4

A fictitious cost of transport from London to Peterborough is calculated on the basis that the routes chosen give the minimum overall cost. This cost is then compared with the actual cost and if the fictitious cost is less the best solution has been found.

To calculate this fictitious cost, numbers x_1, x_2, y_1 and y_2 are entered alongside the cost table such that each cost is the sum of the x and y corresponding to its row and column, *i.e.*

7	5	y_1
	4	y_2
x_1	x_2	

Let $x_1 = 0$,

then y_1 must be 7 so that $x_1 + y_1 = 7$

x_2 must now be -2 so that $x_2 + y_1 = 5$

Finally, y_2 is 6, making $x_2 - y_2 = 4$.

The completed table is:

7	5	7
	4	6
0	-2	

On this basis the cost from London to Peterborough (the remaining blank space) should be $0 + 6 =$ £6 per hundred if the routes chosen give a total minimum cost. But the **actual cost** is only £5 per hundred, and hence some transport on this route will reduce the overall cost.

Redistributing the transport to give maximum use of this route, we have:

	Peterborough	Coventry
Birmingham	10,000	40,000
London	20,000	Nil

The cost table is now

7	5	7
5		5
0	-2	

giving the fictitious cost from London to Coventry as $5 - 2 =$ £3 per hundred. The actual cost, £4, is greater than this which indicates that the optimum solution has been found.

The revised transport cost is now £3,700 which is £200 less than the 'obvious' solution. Note that the cheapest route is not used.

On a much larger scale this type of programming may be applied to the mass distribution of consumable products such as fuel oil, where tanker costs, refinery outputs and distribution centres are taken into account in finding the optimum operating conditions. Food production and distribution also lends itself to this type of computer analysis.

Applications in Science and Technology

The obvious use of a computer in scientific work is for numerical analysis, *i.e.* the evaluation of formulae and the tabulation of the results. Some books of tables are reproduced photographically from the computer print-out, not only to save the cost of type-setting but to eliminate printing errors. (It was the existence of errors in numerical tables that first prompted Babbage to consider a mechanical computer).

There are many equations which are difficult to solve other than by successive approximations or **iterative** procedures. If the problem is very difficult it may be solved by trying a large number of random solutions. The random numbers are generated by the computer itself, and as the whole idea involves probability, these techniques are known as Monte Carlo methods.

Example 4. The basic idea of an iterative approach to a problem may be illustrated by the solution of simultaneous equations. Consider

$$10x + y = 24 \qquad \ldots\ldots\ldots\ldots \quad \mathbf{(1)}$$

$$x + 5y = 22 \qquad \ldots\ldots\ldots\ldots \quad \mathbf{(2)}$$

First let $y = 0$ and calculate x from (**1**).

Substitute this value in (**2**) and calculate a better approximation to y.

This is the first iteration.

Repeat the operation, substituting the new value for y in (**1**) and find a better value for x, etc.

(*continued overleaf*)

For the foregoing equations the successive values for x and y are:

$$(1)\ \begin{cases} y = 0 \\ x = 2{\cdot}4 \end{cases}$$

$$(2)\ \begin{cases} x = 2{\cdot}4 \\ y = 4{\cdot}32 \end{cases}$$

$$(1)\ \begin{cases} y = 4{\cdot}32 \\ x = 1{\cdot}968 \end{cases}$$

$$(2)\ \begin{cases} x = 1{\cdot}968 \\ y = 4{\cdot}006 \end{cases}$$

$$(1)\ \begin{cases} y = 4{\cdot}006 \\ x = 1{\cdot}999 \end{cases}$$

$$(2)\ \begin{cases} x = 1{\cdot}999 \\ y = 4{\cdot}000 \end{cases}$$

$$(1)\ \begin{cases} y = 4{\cdot}000 \\ x = 2{\cdot}000 \end{cases}$$

$$(2)\ \begin{cases} x = 2{\cdot}000 \\ y = 4{\cdot}000 \end{cases}$$

and we have the correct solutions $x = 2$ and $y = 4$.

In network problems the number of simultaneous equations and unknowns may exceed a hundred and a computer is essential to obtain the solutions in a reasonable time.

In engineering design both analogue and digital computers are used. In either case the output may be available as a tabulated print-out or as a visual pictorial display.

Typical design problems are:

Critical speeds in rotating machinery

Noise levels in machinery

Lubrication and oil films

Cams

Heat exchangers

Lenses

Loaded frames and structures

Aerodynamic flow (aircraft, rockets, ships, etc.)

Dynamic behaviour of propulsion systems

Voltage surges in electrical apparatus.

It was stated earlier that analogue computers may be used for the control of a machine, system or process. Digital computers are also used in control applications, their large data stores being particularly useful for systems whose behaviour is dependent upon a large number of factors. Fig. 11.6 illustrates the basic arrangement of computer control.

The process being controlled may be a machine, factory, power station, radio telescope, rocket, etc. The idea of a system may include traffic control (road, rail or air) and even economic systems. In the latter

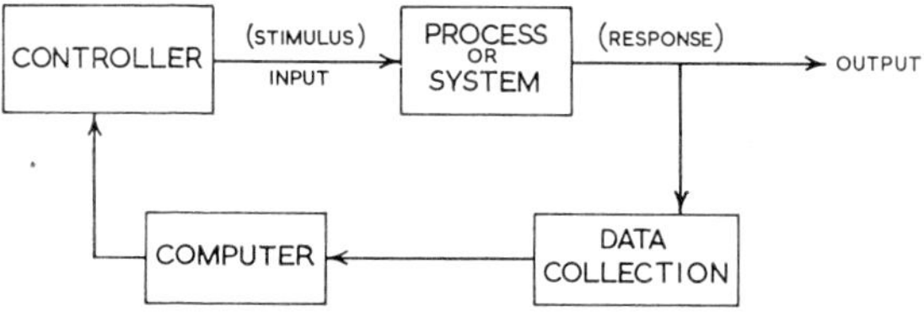

FIG. 11.6. COMPUTER PROCESS CONTROL

case an economic model must first be made from observations of financial data such as bank rate, investments, imports and exports, profit and loss, etc. The behaviour of the model is then compared with actual economic changes over a period of time, and the design of the model changed until it agrees with the observed economic pattern. The computer may then be used to predict future economic trends, to warn of impending disasters and to detect oversensitive critical factors.

This idea of **trend prediction** is also made use of in weather forecasting and seismology (earthquake prediction). In weather forecasting the data must be continually reviewed to accord with prevailing conditions. It is interesting to recall that Kelvin produced his mechanical tide predictor in 1880.

Navigation by computer (as in space flight) is yet another form of control, the input being last position, speed, rate of change of direction and similar data. The output shows the present course and position. This information may be interpreted by a human operator who manually corrects the course and speed, or the computer output may be made to 'navigate' the craft automatically.

Statistics

Many statistical calculations involve a large number of arithmetical steps. The basic arithmetic is simple but the quantity of work required makes statistical analysis very tedious. The computer is particularly well suited to this type of work having a large store to hold the data together with facilities for sorting and tabulating. By statistics we do not mean the collection of a vast quantity of unprocessed figures, but the actual **data processing** which reveals useful facts upon which future actions can be based.

One of the simplest statistical calculations is that of finding the spread or **standard deviation** of a set of numbers. We will use this as an example, although much more complicated work is also given to the computer.

If a sample of n readings, $x_1, x_2, \ldots x_n$ is obtained, the average is given by

$$\frac{x_1 + x_2 + \ldots + x_n}{n} = \frac{\Sigma x}{n}, \text{ written } \bar{x}$$

The standard deviation is defined by

$$\sqrt{\frac{\Sigma (x - \bar{x})^2}{n}}.$$

It is known that 99·9% of all expected values will lie within three standard deviations of the average.

Example 5. Let the following set of 10 readings represent a sample taken at random:

10·1, 10·4, 10·3, 10·4, 10·5, 10·4, 10·3, 10·6, 10·5, 10·3.

Is it likely that we shall obtain a value less than 10 in a large number of such readings? The answer is certainly not obvious by simply examining the table. To find out we calculate the standard deviation and the average.

x	$\lvert x - \bar{x} \rvert$	$(x - \bar{x})^2$
10·1	0·28	0·0784
10·4	0·02	0·0004
10·3	0·08	0·0064
10·4	0·02	0·0004
10·5	0·12	0·0144
10·4	0·02	0·0004
10·3	0·08	0·0064
10·6	0·22	0·0484
10·5	0·12	0·0144
10·3	0·08	0·0064
Σ = 103·8		Σ = 0·1760

$$\therefore \bar{x} = 10{\cdot}38 \qquad \therefore \frac{\Sigma(x-\bar{x})^2}{n} = 0{\cdot}01760$$

$$\therefore \text{Standard Deviation} = \sqrt{\frac{\Sigma(x-\bar{x})^2}{n}} = 0{\cdot}132$$

The minimum expected value will be 10·38 − 3(0·132) = 9·984 and we would expect 99·9% of all readings to be greater than this.

If a large sample were taken the arithmetic would be formidable and it would be worth using a computer. One advantage of the computer is that once the data is stored in the machine several statistical tests may be performed on the same set of figures without further input being required. Standard deviations can be found using calculators, but digital machines are preferable for the more difficult tests of correlation, significance, regression, etc., or where the quantity of data is large.

Miscellaneous Uses

Computers have been used to solve such a wide range of problems that it would be impossible to list them all here. Indeed, it seems that there is no branch of human activity in which computers cannot be used in some way or other.

In education computers are used to provide programmed teaching, the response of the student to a set question determining the next question.

The sequence of questions and answers depends upon the ability of the student, but the end result should be the same for all students. We must not think of this as a machine teaching a human being but rather as the programmer teaching a large number of students individually. The program contains the knowledge and experience of a good teacher together with all the decisions he would make when giving individual tuition.

Computers are used in historical research to study population movements and to catalogue documents and archives. The determination of authorship of a document is possible by analysing the literary style and comparing it with known writers of the period. In this **stylistic analysis*** some distinguishing factors must be found and expressed in numerical form (as the computer can only handle numbers). Statistical tests are then carried out to find the distributions of these factors in contemporary writers. The chance of a contemporary having written the document is then assessed by calculating the probability that the distribution of words in the unknown sample came from the same parent distribution.

Controversy exists as to the best method of expressing literary style in numerical form. The following have been used:

(1) Number of letters per word;

(2) Number of words per sentence;

(3) The relative frequency of occurrence of certain words;

(4) The vocabulary used (vocabulary spectrum).

Of these, methods (3) and (4) are the most reliable.

Extending these literary applications, it is possible to load the store with a large vocabulary of words and to program the computer to write poetry or prose. This is not entirely frivolous as it gives an insight into the structure of language and thought processes.

Musical analysis is also possible by computer and the Chorales of Bach have been studied in this way.† Computers have been programmed to compose music; this is not so difficult as may be imagined as it consists of producing a sequence of patterns in accordance with the rules of harmony and phrasing. Another application of computers as pattern generators is in the production of knitting and needlework patterns.

Computer Organization

Computers are expensive, and in the interests of cost and efficiency they must not be allowed to stand idle. If a computer is manually controlled by an operator feeding in one program at a time, much time is lost in changing over and deciding which program to run next. **Time sharing** was introduced whereby a batch of several programs could be

* Harvey, P., *Math. Gazette*, Vol. LIV, No. 390, Dec. 1970, pp 361-367.

† For further information regarding unusual and interesting computer uses the reader is referred to the excellent set of articles in *The Bulletin of the Institute of Mathematics and its Applications*, Vol. 6, No. 1, April, 1970.

loaded into the machine and executed concurrently. A supervisory or **monitor** program is also loaded into the machine to share the computer time between the various programs in the most efficient way.

The disadvantage of this system is that all programs, large or small, take the same amount of time from loading to printing, as the whole batch has to be completed before the user has access to his results. To avoid this, **on-line time sharing** was devised in which each user has his own peripheral devices (input and output). The supervisory program allocates time to each user in accordance with a master schedule, and as far as each user is aware he is the **only** user of the machine. This system requires **multiple access** to the computer to provide several input and output channels.

Off-line operation describes an arrangement whereby the user's equipment is not directly connected to the main computer but prepares paper or magnetic tape for subsequent insertion into the system. The output appears on tape and is reproduced on the user's printer away from the computer.

As the users of a particular machine may be separated from each other by distances of many miles (*e.g.* branches of a bank situated in different towns) it has become necessary to use **remote terminals** connected to the computer by **data links.** The remote terminal may consist of a teleprinter, and the data links are provided by Post Office telephone and telegraph lines or special privately-owned or leased lines.

The binary pulses passing into and out of the computer are not suitable for long distance transmission by telephone lines and must be converted to audio frequency signals by means of a **modulator.** At the other end of the line the signals must be reconverted by a **demodulator.** The modulator–demodulator units are known as **modems.** Fig. 11.7 shows a remote teleprinter unit connected to a computer.

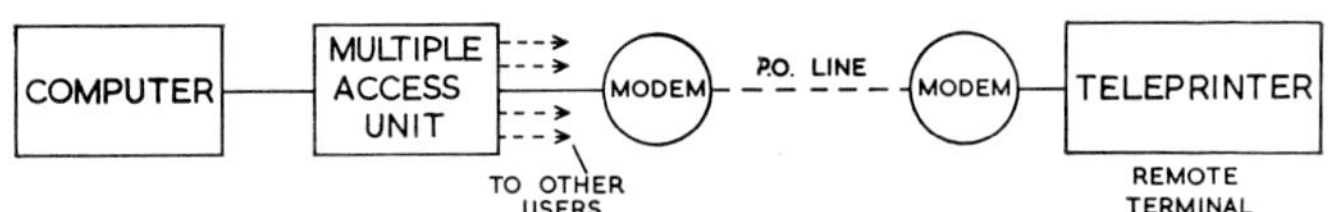

FIG. 11.7. REMOTE TERMINAL CONNECTED BY A DATA LINK

Computers themselves can now be interconnected by data links thereby increasing the power and capacity of a system and forming a network. The time is not far ahead when anyone who has a telephone, and the necessary keyboard and printer, will have access to a computer system wherever he may be.

Social Effects

In considering the social effects of computers we introduce emotions, prejudices, and fears, which really cannot be dealt with as a branch of 'computer science'. A few facts emerge which, although they do not solve the social problems, may help us to face up to the difficulties created.

Redundancy was originally feared by clerical and office workers, as the computer threatened to do the work previously allocated to them. This has proved to be generally groundless as the capacity for work which the computer has requires an army of workers to feed it with data. The real benefits of a computer in an organization are increased efficiency, increased speed, reliability of information and the reduction of tedious and repetitive tasks rather than any reduction in staff. Indeed, Parkinson's Law appears to work well here, the openings for computer operators, programmers and assistants, card and paper tape punchers more than assimilating the clerical workers.

The invasion of the privacy of the individual is another factor which has caused unrest. In fact, this is just an admission that the nation's filing system works efficiently for the first time. Our personal details had been documented before the advent of computers; but the information was scattered, and its retrieval and assembly such a long and tedious business that we all felt reasonably sure that no one would be bothered to prepare a dossier on our private affairs. Many people object to the impersonality of being referred to as a number instead of a name. But this is not new, numbers have been used to simplify the work of organizing society for a long time.

Critics of computers have highlighted the errors produced and the delay in obtaining service or commodities after a system has been 'computerized'. This, surely, cannot be a criticism of a machine, for the machine only does as it is told. The criticism should be levelled at the systems analyst, the programmer, or the people responsible for running the system. One suspects that certain people are using the computer as a cover for their own laziness, inefficiency and indifference.

People have always been reluctant to accept change; fear and ignorance playing a large part in this attitude. Perhaps the best summary of the social position has been given by C. Strachey of Oxford University, who wrote:

'The invention of the computing machine is a technological advance of greater importance than any other since the invention of printing. In the long run the effect of having a mechanical assistant to our thinking will probably have as profound an influence on our intellectual life, and hence on our whole civilization, as the introduction of more or less universal literacy. Fortunately, however, I think it will be at least two hundred years before these changes become really significant—fortunately, because like most other changes they are going to be very uncomfortable.'

APPENDICES

A

Alternative Logical Symbols

The logical symbols used in this book are those recommended in the latest British Standard, BS 3939:1969.

		BS 3939 : 1969
AND	$p . q = r$ $p \& q = r$ $p \cap q = r$	p, q → & → r
OR	$p + q = r$ $p \vee q = r$ $p \cup q = r$	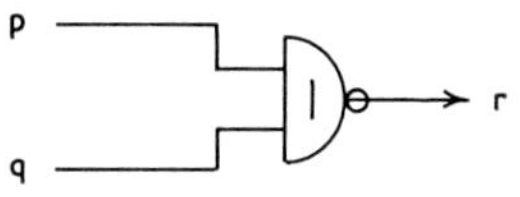 p, q → 1 → r
NOT	$\bar{p}$ $\sim p$	p → 1 ○ → $\bar{p}$
NOR	$\overline{(p + q)} = r$ $\overline{(p \vee q)} = r$ $(p \cup q)' = r$ $p \downarrow q = r$	p, q → 1 ○ → r
NOT-AND (*NAND*)	$\overline{(p . q)} = r$ $\overline{(p \& q)} = r$ $(p \cap q)' = r$ $p \mid q = r$	p, q → & ○ → r

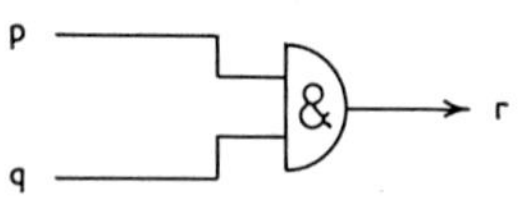

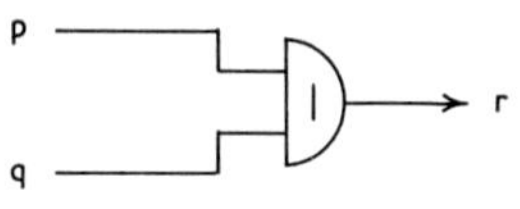

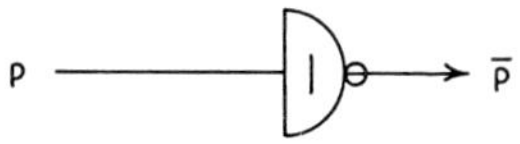

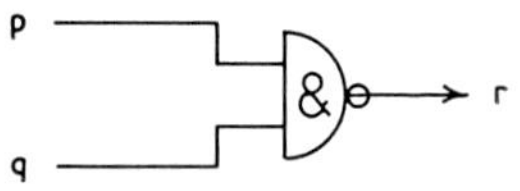

Sets and Venn Diagrams

Boolean algebra may be developed by considering 'sets' or 'classes' instead of switches (Chapter 4). These sets may be represented by Venn diagrams:

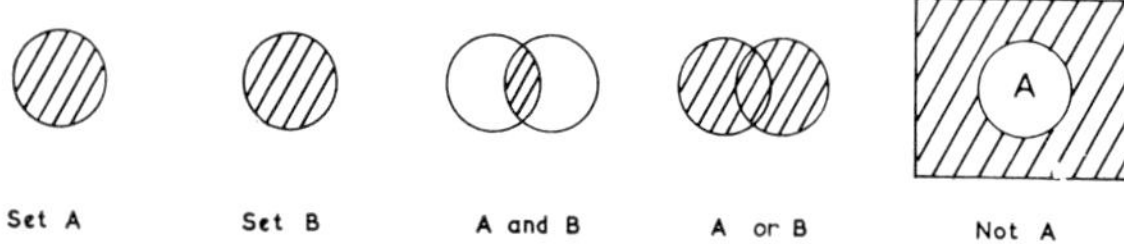

The relationships between the various sets and subsets lead to the same algebraic equations as (**1**) to (**12**) in Chapter 4.

B

ERROR-CORRECTING CODE

A 15-bit error correcting code with 11 binary digits plus four redundant digits.

If a typical word is (a b c d e f g h i j k l m n p), let the 'address' of an error digit be (q r s t).

Then

$$\begin{aligned} h + i + j + k + l + m + n + p &= q \\ d + e + f + g + l + m + n + p &= r \\ b + c + f + g + j + k + n + p &= s \\ a + c + e + g + i + k + m + p &= t \end{aligned}$$

define the 'parity' digits q, r, s and t.

The first 8 numbers of this code will be

11-bit binary number

	a	b	c	d	e	f	g	h	i	j	k	l	m	n	p
0	0	0	0	0	0	0	0	0	0	0	0	0	0	0	0
1	1	1	0	1	0	0	0	1	0	0	0	0	0	0	1
2	0	1	0	1	0	0	0	1	0	0	0	0	0	1	0
3	1	0	0	0	0	0	0	0	0	0	0	0	0	1	1
4	1	0	0	1	0	0	0	1	0	0	0	0	1	0	0
5	0	1	0	0	0	0	0	0	0	0	0	0	1	0	1
6	1	1	0	0	0	0	0	0	0	0	0	0	1	1	0
7	0	0	0	1	0	0	0	1	0	0	0	0	1	1	1
8	0	0	0	1	0	0	0	1	0	0	0	1	0	0	0

. . . etc.

Example. If 111110111011111 is fed into the computer, (q r s t) is (1 1 0 0) indicating an error in the 12th digit.

The corrected word is therefore

111110111010111

Extracting the binary number from this gives

11011010111

or 1,751 as the intended number.

C

A SHORT FORM OF THE CITY & GUILDS MNEMONIC CODE

Word Format

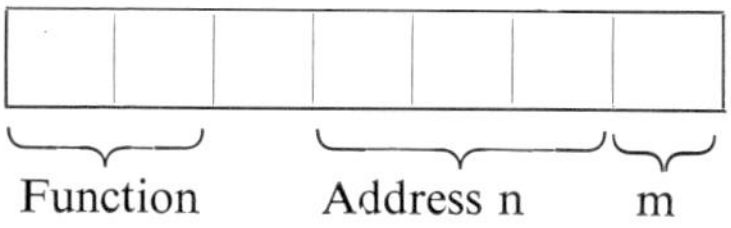

7 decimal digits.

'm' ranges from 0 to 9 and is the address of one of the 10 **index registers.** The instruction is modified by the number in the specified index register. 'n' refers to a store location in the range 0 to 999, but locations 0 to 9 are reserved as follows:

0 always contains zero;

1 is the address of the accumulator, A;

2, 3, 4, 8 and 9 are index registers;

5 is a counter register;

6 and 7 hold the number of places before and after the decimal point; they hold zero in floating point.

In what follows C is the control register, automatically increased by one at each operation.

It holds the address of the next instruction.

(continued overleaf)

The Instruction Code

FUNCTION	MNEMONIC		OPERATION	EXPLANATION
0 0	LDA	n, m	$(n+(m)) \rightarrow A$	Load into cleared acc.
0 1	ADD	n, m	$(A)+(n+(m)) \rightarrow A$	Add operand
0 2	SUB	n, m	$(A)-(n+(m)) \rightarrow A$	Subtract operand
0 3	MLT	n, m	$(A)\times(n+(m)) \rightarrow A$	Multiply by operand
0 4	DIV	n, m	$(A)\div(n+(m)) \rightarrow A$	Divide by operand
2 0	STA	n, m	$(A) \rightarrow n+(m)$	Store (A)
3 0	JUN	n, m	$n+(m) \rightarrow C$	Jump to $n+(m)$
3 1	JEQ	n, m		Jump to $n+(m)$ if $(A)=0$
3 5	JLT	n, m		Jump to $n+(m)$ if $(A)<0$
3 6	JGR	n, m		Jump to $n+(m)$ if $(A)>0$
3 9	LOP	n, m	Count	Jump if $(5)-1>0$
4 0	SQT	n, m	$\sqrt{A} \rightarrow A$	If $(A)<0$, jump to $n+(m)$
4 1	EXP	n, m	$e^{(A)} \rightarrow A$	If (A) too big, jump to $n+(m)$
4 2	LGN	n, m	$\ln(A) \rightarrow A$	If $(A)<0$, jump to $n+(m)$
4 3	SIN		$\sin(A) \rightarrow A$	(A) in radians
4 4	COS		$\cos(A) \rightarrow A$	(A) in radians
5 2	RNA	n, m	Read No. to Acc.	Jump to $n+(m)$ if in error
5 3	WNA	n, m	Print No. from Acc.	$n=$ integral digits $m=$ fractional digits Zero for floating point.
9 9	STOP		Return control to operator.	

The following input 'directives' will be required on the tape or cards:

Store n, store program sequentially from location n.

Execute n, commence execution of program at instruction in location n.

D

PUNCHED PAPER TAPE CODE

The following is a part of the International Standards Organization (I.S.O.) 7-bit code.

INTERNATIONAL ALPHABET NO. 5

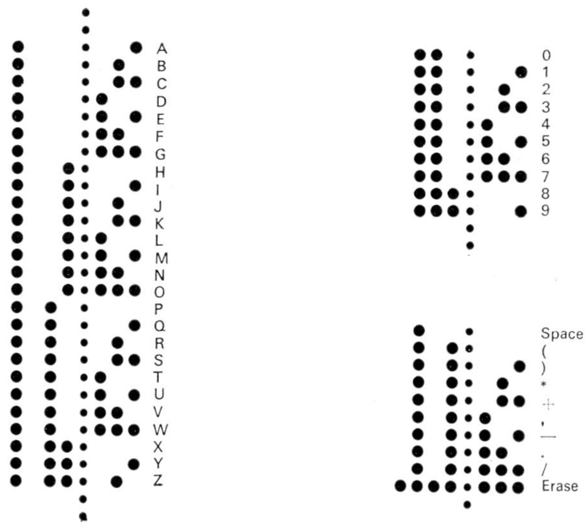

(*continued overleaf*)

For the inclusion of a parity digit the tape must have provision for 8 bits, as shown below:

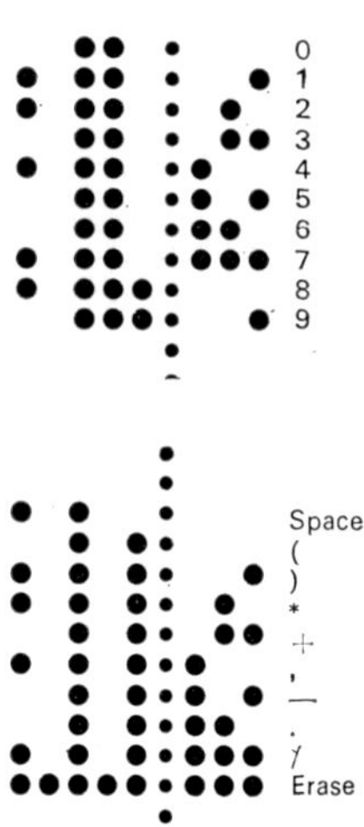

E

ACCURACY OF COMPONENTS AND PREFERRED VALUES

The accuracy of component values in a digital computer is not particularly critical as we are only interested in the presence or absence of a voltage pulse. As long as the circuits perform their triggering action satisfactorily over a reasonable variation in supply voltage no trouble will occur. In certain parts of the computer stabilized voltage supplies may be required together with high stability components. The drift in component values due to ageing or temperature rise must be taken into account when determining the tolerance of the circuit. As the quantities of resistors and capacitors in a digital computer are large it is economically desirable to use components that are not of a higher accuracy or stability than is necessary for satisfactory operation.

In analogue computers, however, the results depend directly on the values of the input and feedback components. If possible the maximum tolerance on the nominal value of these components should be limited to 1%, or even 0·1% in some cases. The components used in the operational amplifiers themselves need not be to this accuracy; their feature should be **stability** to limit the drift of the output voltage.

The range of resistors required by computer manufacturers may be 10 Ω to 10 MΩ. It is unreasonable to expect the component manufacturers to be able to supply large quantities of accurate components for every possible value in this range: some standardization must be done. The components are graded into a limited number of categories called 'preferred values'. The circuit designer calculates the theoretical value of resistor or capacitor required and then specifies the nearest preferred value. The **tolerance,** or permitted deviation from the nominal value, must also be specified.

To ensure a reasonable choice over the whole range the preferred values are determined according to a **logarithmic scale,** as in the table overleaf.

LOGARITHMIC COMPONENT VALUE SCALE

Multiples of	±10% Tolerance Range
1·0	0·90 1·10
1·2	1·08 1·32
1·5	1·35 1·65
1·8	1·62 1·98
2·2	1·98 2·42
2·7	2·43 2·97
3·3	2·97 3·63
3·9	3·51 4·29
4·7	4·23 5·17
5·6	5·04 6·16
6·8	6·12 7·48
8·2	7·38 9·02

Notice that the component manufacturer benefits by the use of such a scale as there are no gaps in the range. No component has to be rejected because of its value, only re-graded.

Similar tables of preferred values can be constructed for other tolerances:

Grade I resistors are available with ±1%, ±2%, or ±5% tolerance.

Grade II resistors are available with ±5%, ±10%, or ±20% tolerance.

The input and feedback components in an analogue computer should be high stability types of ±1%, or better. To prevent changes in value due to temperature rise they should also be of ample rating. The capacitors should be chosen from a preferred range with similar considerations in mind.

Example. The maximum percentage error in a summing amplifier using 3 input resistors and a feedback resistor, each of 1% tolerance and the same nominal value, is given by

$$\frac{-e_o}{1{\cdot}01r} = \frac{1}{0{\cdot}99r}(e_1+e_2+e_3) \qquad \text{See Fig. 10.5}$$

$$\therefore \quad -e_o = 1{\cdot}02\,(e_1+e_2+e_3)$$

and the output is 2% high.

ANSWERS TO PROBLEMS AND EXAMPLES

Chapter 1

PROBLEMS

(1) page 2 The swing of the pendulum is itself an analogue of the mean rotation of the earth. Although it is measured in 'increments' or 'swings' it is still essentially **analogue.**

(2) page 5 P. HARVEY. DEPOSIT £57361·84
ACCOUNT NO. 92073

(3) page 11 Open the book at the centre page. Is the required page number larger or smaller than this? If smaller, open the book at the middle of the first half; if larger, turn to the middle of the second half. Continue in this manner until the required page is found.
(This is known as a dichotomizing search).

EXAMPLE

(1) page 14 I.S.O. 7 BIT TAPE CODE + PARITY DIGIT

Chapter 3

EXAMPLES (page 44)

(1) (a) 10101
(b) 1011010
(c) 1111011
(d) 100·1
(e) 110·111
(f) 1100·001

(2) (a) 23
(b) 61
(c) 23·375
(d) 7·875
(e) 1109
(f) 186

(3) (a) 14; (b) 15

(4) (a) 16,777,215
(b) −8,388,608 to +8,388,607
(c) 4096 (nearly)
(d) −2049 to +2048 (nearly)

(5) $0{\cdot}000010001111_2$
$0{\cdot}0217_8$
$0{\cdot}25\%$

(6) (a) 001111010_2 122_{10}
(b) $010110{\cdot}011_2$ $22{\cdot}375_{10}$
(c) 001000010010_2 530_{10}
(d) $001{\cdot}011010_2$ $1{\cdot}40625_{10}$

(7) (a) 0000101011
(b) 0001001111
(c) 0011110001
(d) Too large for 10-bit complementary negative, which has a maximum positive range of 0 to 511.
(e) 1111100101
(f) 1111011110

(8) (a) 91
(b) 240
(c) −121
(d) −8
(e) −255

(9) (a) 1011100000_2 1340_8
(b) 101110_2 56_8
(c) 1110011000000_2 16300_8

Chapter 4

PROBLEMS

(2) page 51 (a) $r = p$
(b) $r = \bar{p}$
(c) $r = p$

(3) page 53 (a) $r = q.\bar{p}$
(b) r is always 1 and the circuit may be replaced by a permanent signal at r.

(4) page 56 $r = \overline{(p + \bar{q}).(q + \bar{p})}$ which simplifies to $\bar{p}.q + \bar{q}.p$

EXAMPLES (page 62)

(1) $r = p$

(2) $r = p.q$

(3) $r = 1$

(4) $r = p.\bar{q} + q.\bar{p}$

(page 63)

(5) $r = q.\bar{p}$

(6) $r = 0$

(7) $r = p + q.s$

(8) $r = A + B + C.(D + E)$

Chapter 5

PROBLEMS

(2) page 67 Connect the output back to the input and recirculate the number to the right

(a) 31 places

(b) 22 places.

(5) page 75 *NOR*, Output $= \overline{p + q + r}$

(6) page 77

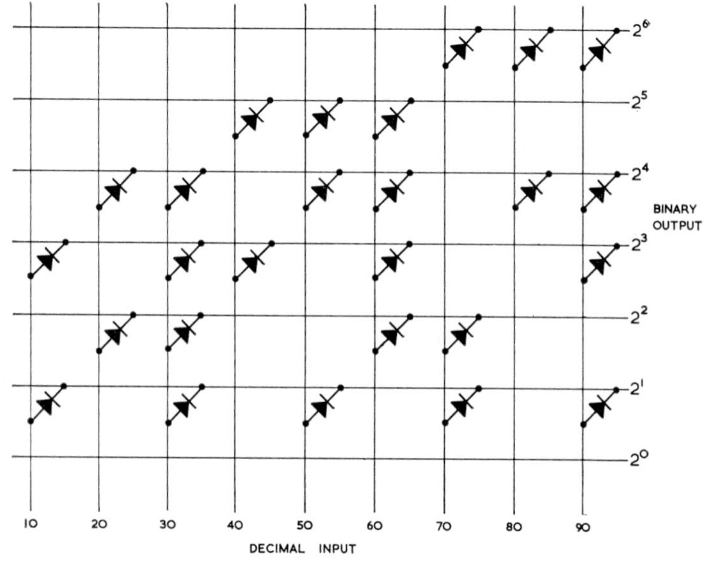

Chapter 6

PROBLEM

(1) page 87 Group 0, Track 0, Word 0; 000000000

Group 6, Track 2, Word 4; 110010100

Group 7, Track 7, Word 7; 111111111

Capacity is $8 \times 8 \times 8 = 512$ words.

EXAMPLES (page 91) (1) (a) 98,304

(b) 24

(c) 24

(d) 24

(page 92) (2) (a) 16,384

(b) 7·5 ms

(c) 16·3 bits per cm

(d) 51,200 p.p.s.

(3) 8·33 ms minimum, 20 ms maximum.

Chapter 7

PROBLEMS

(1) page 94

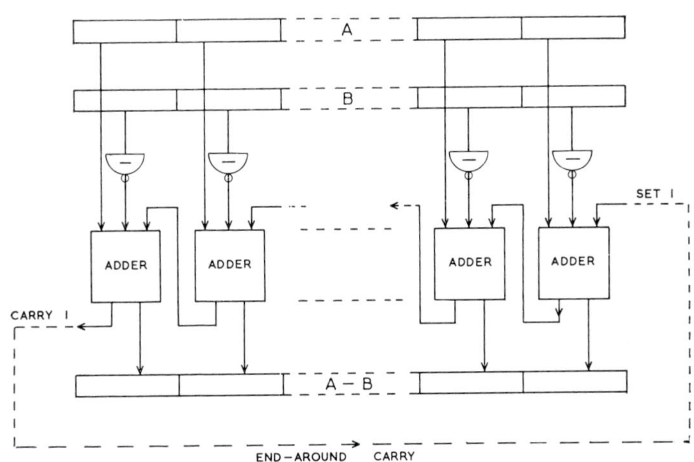

BINARY SUBTRACTOR SHOWING HOW THE 'SET' DIGIT IS OBTAINED FROM THE OUTPUT 'CARRY'

(2) page 101

MILES	FEET	INCHES	
10, 1	1000, 100, 10, 1	10, 1	←—value of card columns.

Constants required: 633600, 63360; 12000, 1200, 120, 12; 10, 1.

EXAMPLES (page 107)

(1)

YEARS	DAYS	HOURS	MINS.	
10, 1	100, 10, 1	10, 1	10, 1	←—value of card columns

Constants required: 5256000, 525600; 144000, 14400, 1440; 600, 60; 10, 1.

(2)

Decimal	7-bit Code
0	0 0 0 0 0 0 0
1	1 1 0 1 0 0 1
2	0 1 0 1 0 1 0
3	1 0 0 0 0 1 1
4	1 0 0 1 1 0 0
5	0 1 0 0 1 0 1
6	1 1 0 0 1 1 0
7	0 0 0 1 1 1 1
8	1 1 1 0 0 0 0
9	0 0 1 1 0 0 1

Chapter 9

PROBLEM

(1) page 121 The machine will print out correct squares until either the printer capacity is reached or the conversion constants are exhausted. The binary squares will be computed, however, up to the full capacity of the registers. Above this the most significant digits will be lost and the computer will perform its program on almost random numbers.

Chapter 10

PROBLEMS

(1) page 137

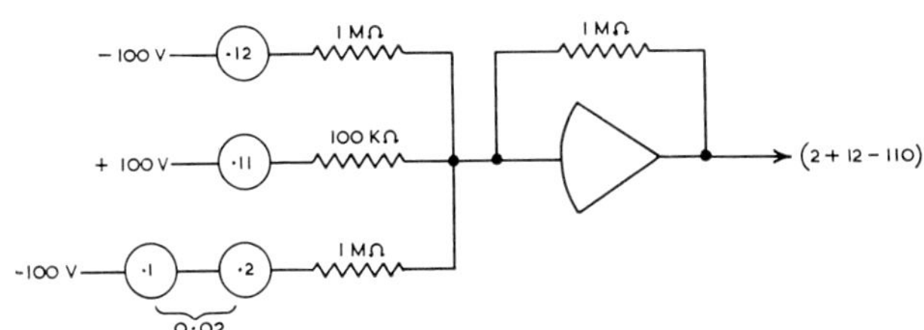

(2) page 137

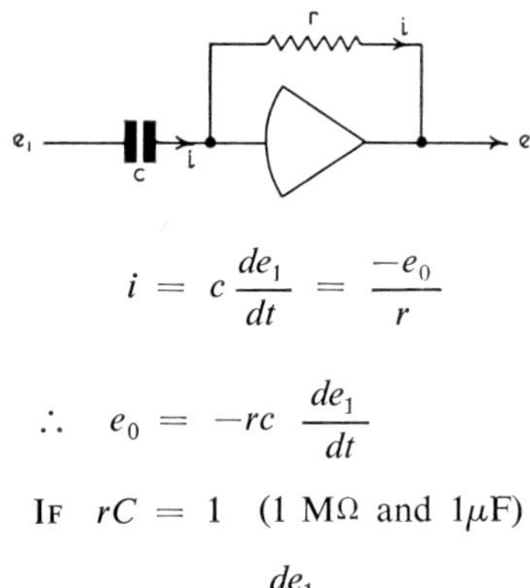

$$i = c\frac{de_1}{dt} = \frac{-e_0}{r}$$

$$\therefore \quad e_0 = -rc\frac{de_1}{dt}$$

IF $rC = 1$ (1 MΩ and 1μF)

$$e_0 = -\frac{de_1}{dt}$$

(3) page 142

$$v \sin\theta = 26 \text{ m/s}$$
$$v \cos\theta = 15 \text{ m/s}$$
$$y_{MAX} = 34{\cdot}4 \text{ m} \quad , \quad x_{MAX} = 79{\cdot}5 \text{ m}$$
$$\therefore \text{ LET } 1v \equiv 0{\cdot}5 \text{ m} \quad \text{and} \quad 1v \equiv 0{\cdot}5 \text{ m/s.}$$

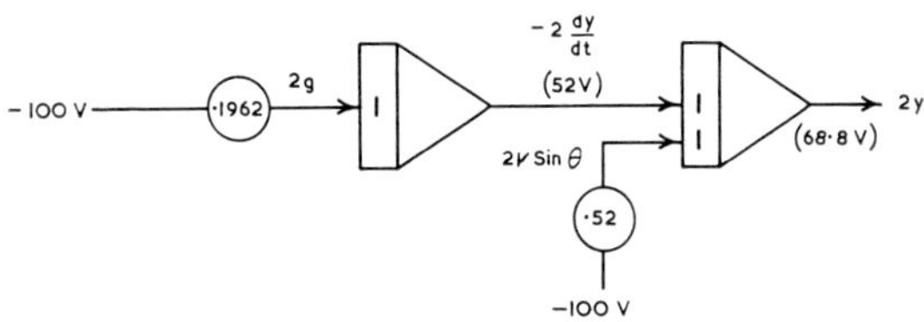

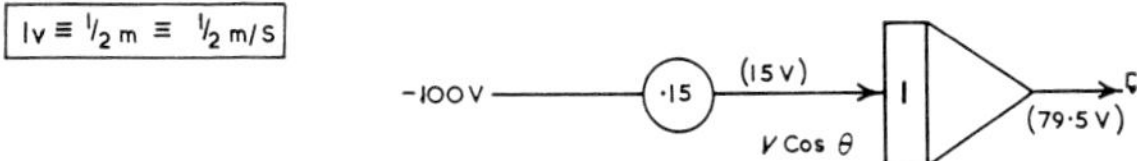

(4) page 144

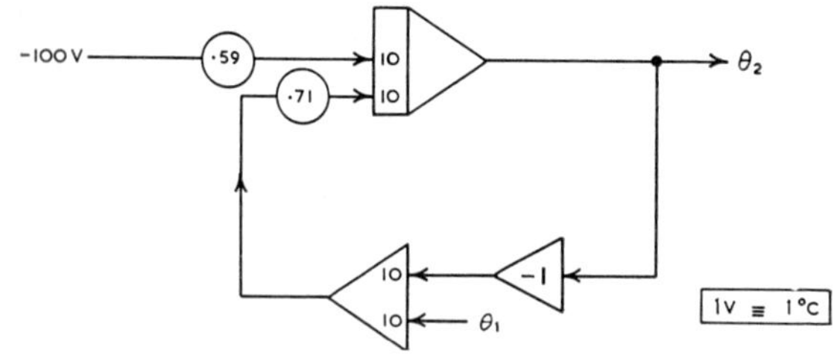

EXAMPLES (page 150) (1)

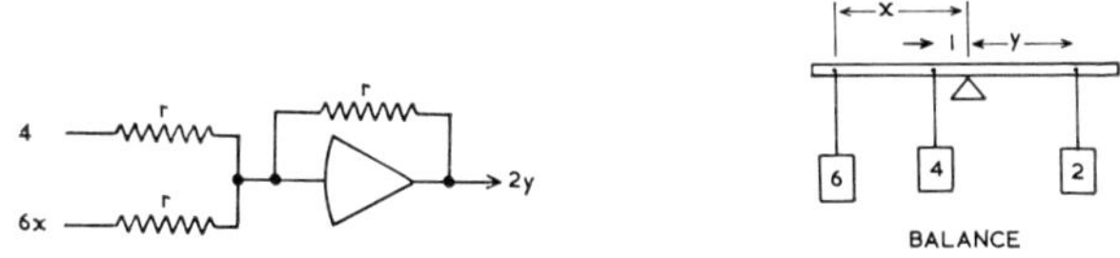

(2) (a)

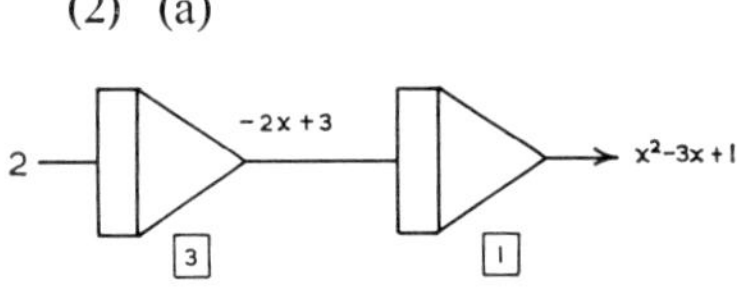

(b)

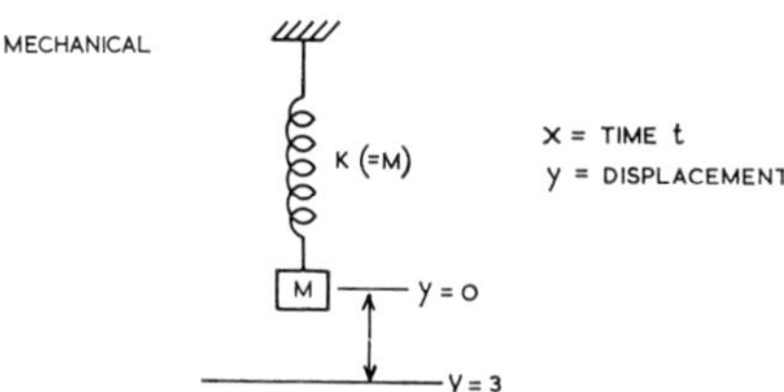

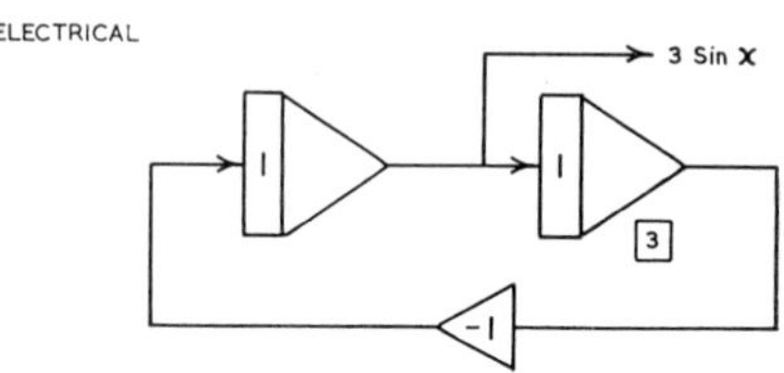

(3)

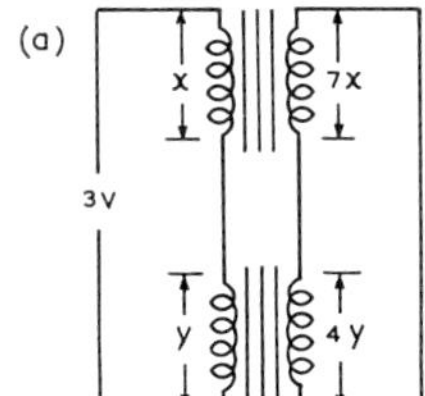
(a)
x
7x
3V
y
4y

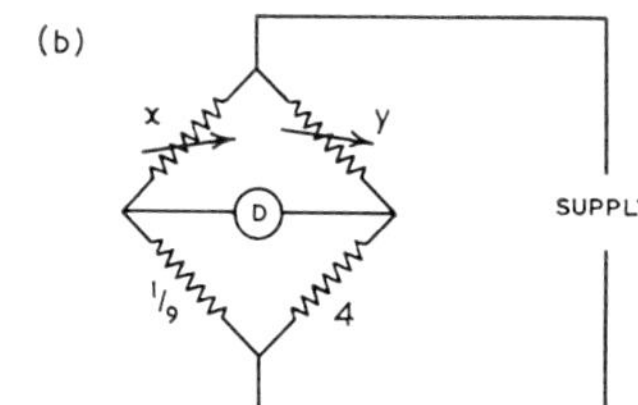
(b)
x
y
D
SUPPLY
1/9
4

INDEX